The League of Nations

FROM 1919 TO 1929

The League of Nations

FROM 1919 TO 1929

Gary B. Ostrower

Professor of History

Alfred University

Series Editor, George J. Lankevich

Avery Publishing Group

Garden City Park, New York

Cover designer: William Gonzalez
Series editor: George Lankevich
In-house editor: Elaine Will Sparber
Typesetter: Kay Rangos
Printer: Paragon Press, Honesdale, PA

The photographs on pages 5, 7, 44, 60, 64, 66, 120, 122 (top), 133, 137, 142 (top), 144, 153 (top), and 156 are used courtesy of Popperfoto, Overstone, Northampton, England.

The photographs on pages 4, 6, 9, 29, 34, 89, 90, 131 (top), 136 (top), and 138 are used courtesy of U.S. Library of Congress.

The photographs on pages 2, 13, 16, 41, 47, 65, 86, 92, 97, 98, 104, 107 (top), 107 (bottom), 119, 122 (bottom), 131 (bottom), 132, 135, 136 (bottom), 140, 141, 142 (bottom), 152, and 153 (bottom) are used courtesy of U.S. National Archives.

Library of Congress Cataloging-in-Publication Data

Ostrower, Gary B., 1939–
The League of Nations, 1919–1929 / Gary B. Ostrower.
p. cm. — (Partners for peace : v. 1)
Includes bibliographical references and index.
ISBN 0-89529-636-5
1. League of Nations—History. 2. International cooperation—History. 3. World politics—1919–1932. I. Title. II. Series.
JX1975.078 1996
341.22—dc20 94-8337
CIP

Printed in the United States of America.

10 9 8 7 6 5 4 3 2 1

Contents

To Judy,
and to Sarah and Pete,
with love

Acknowledgments

Most books are credited to an author. In fact, books are written collectively, and I am happy to acknowledge the people who helped to bring this one to the light of day. Joel Blatt and Stuart Campbell energetically challenged my interpretation of European diplomacy and critiqued my entire story. Tom Peterson injected common sense into the manuscript, while suffering through hundreds of my questions about both content and style. My editors, George Lankevich and Elaine Will Sparber, made the manuscript into a much more readable text than it was initially, while Carla Coch expertly critiqued what the rest of us did.

Others, too, gave advice that kept me from taking my own opinions too seriously. Carol Burdick, Bill Cassidy, Bill Dibrell, Vicki Eaklor, John Gilmour, and Elspeth Whitney would undoubtedly have liked to duck my questions; they never did. My secretary, Barbara Sanford, gets special thanks; she helped me not only unstintingly, but cheerfully.

I also want to thank the circulation staffs under Ann Finger at the University of Rochester and Mary Jo Lovelace at Alfred University. Thanks also to Sven Welander at the United Nations Library in Geneva, who guided me through the maze of League archives, and to Lana Meissner, who provided research space at Alfred. The scholars who gathered in Geneva under the guidance of Zara Steiner to commemorate the sixtieth birthday of the League sharpened my thinking about international organization. John Foxen, Chris Grontkowski, and Larry Greil helped me to secure funding for research. I appreciate the financial support of Alfred University and its National Endowment for the Humanities committee, and the bibliographical help of my student assistants.

And I save my most enthusiastic thanks until last—to Judy Samber, Sarah, and Pete for providing lots of love and distraction.

Foreword

Philosophers and theologians from the dawn of recorded history have been drawn to the great, perhaps unresolvable question—what is a human being? Among their many answers are a speck in primal chaos, a "reasoning animal," a creature in the image of God, a social being, a creator of art, a born hunter, and, in the words of Mark Twain, "the Only Animal that blushes. Or needs to!" Whatever answer one postulates is complicated by the undeniable tendency toward violence that seems a constant part of our nature. Whether humans are "apes or angels," warfare has been a constant companion of *homo sapiens,* and by some calculations, less than 5 percent of human history has been lived in times of peace. Yet equally a part of human nature is hope, the idealistic belief that we can somehow rise above baser instincts and achieve a better reality through cooperative effort. That dream has never lost its attraction for questing peoples even as war and its attendant evils have reached epidemic proportions. This series of volumes attempts to assess the progress of humanity toward that higher goal amidst the many horrors that have occurred during the twentieth century.

On a few occasions in the history of the globe, peace and cooperation became more than a temporary reality. During the two centuries of the *Pax Romana,* the Mediterranean Basin was freed from the scourge of war, although legions constantly battled on Rome's frontiers. Periods of great stability and ordered development were ofttimes achieved by Chinese dynasties such as the Ming, and the peace of feudal Japan was real, though imposed by the swords of the samurai. Safety was a reality for the elite members of Meso-american and African cultures, but we now understand that that condition was enjoyed by a relative few and only at the cost of much suffering at the base of the social pyramid. We may argue whether these eras represent positive advance, or merely mark the effective suppression of dissent, but they were important just the same. And in nineteenth-century Europe, after the long period of Napoleonic Wars, a conference of nations at Vienna did establish a "concert" whose melody was stability, peace, and order. For perhaps the first time, several nations attempted mutually to cooperate in a shared structure of peace, but the construct violently collapsed after less than a century. Always and everywhere, traditional enemies of peace such as poverty, imperial expansion, virulent nationalism, competitive trade, and simple fear of "the other" proved able to overwhelm the better human instincts. All too often, people avoided the "better angels" of their nature, and the world remained a battleground.

Partners for Peace: International Cooperation in the Twentieth Century is a series of volumes that examines how humanity's hope for a finer and more cooperative globe has fared in the twentieth century. The volumes chronicle the institutions, events, personalities, crises, and resolutions that have made the ageless dream of our species seem somewhat more attainable. Nations in the twentieth century have indeed taken a series of small steps toward the trust that must precede any attempt at universal peace. Powerful forces such as national sovereignty and ethnic chauvinism conspire to keep people at odds, but as wider recognition of our common interdependence has evolved, the sense of a world community has been created. In retrospect, one lesson taught by the twentieth century is that no single nation or empire is so great and powerful that it can deal unilaterally with the intractable problems of humankind. Whether the issue be war, famine, disease, trade, scientific cooperation, or ecological crisis, the nations of the world have gradually become aware that the ancient enemies of humanity can best be confronted through cosmopolitan effort. And each small advance against the traditional enemies of progress creates a more stable world community that can dare to dream of a better future.

This series traces human progress by considering national cooperation through international institutions. The first two volumes examine the checkered history of the League of Nations, and subsequent ones discuss the United Nations and the leadership provided to the world community by its successive secretaries-general. *Partners for Peace* recognizes that national insistence on sovereign autonomy made both the League and the UN vulnerable, for governments are rarely capable of putting the larger interests of humankind above their own. Yet for much of this century, the quest for cooperation beyond national boundaries has clearly inspired some world leaders. That hope has been a dominant theme of the century, even when it has been denounced as outmoded, intrusive, or foolish. In each volume of this series, a leading scholar will provide a synthetic overview of the period under consideration, along with a chronology of the vital events that have made the history of our century so turbulent. This material is hardly intended to resolve all questions, but rather is intended to provide an entry point to the history of the particular era. Substantial bibliographies are also provided so that readers can continue to study the events that created our contemporary world.

No reader will reject the assertion that politics in 1900 was dominated by societies that matured in the North Atlantic area of the globe. Impelled into modernity by revolutionary changes in literacy and mechanization, these "advanced" societies had successfully taken control of much of the Earth. These nations were envied for their capitalistic productivity, feared for their imperial ambitions, and emulated as models of human attainment by less developed societies. Yet even these nations had not overcome a tendency to savage themselves in war, and so they nurtured the hope that greater security for them all might be achieved if they could agree on rules of international conduct. Thus the nineteenth century ended with more than ritualistic discussions of such ideals as anti-imperialism, Anglo-American union, European disarmament, and schemes whereby nations would become morally accountable for their actions. Nor did it seem that these humanistic dreams were without substance. Advocates of world cooperation could point to accomplishments such as the Hague Peace Conferences of 1899 and 1907, the establishment of a Nobel Prize for Peace, agreement on a

Permanent Court of Arbitration for international disputes, and a growing belief that civilized people would be able to avert future wars, at least among themselves. As the Victorian Age came to an end, hopeful people in advanced lands believed that war was too awful to contemplate. They placed their faith in human rationality and contemplated a happy new century.

We now know that these hopes were in vain. In the summer of 1914, the conflict that would ultimately be called World War I erupted in the Balkan area of Europe and rapidly engulfed the globe. Before it ended, about 20 million people died and the facile belief in the wisdom of advanced societies would be discarded. But the dream of cooperative effort did not die. Indeed, it was held more strongly than ever by many national leaders, who called for an association of nations to work for world peace.

Dr. Gary Ostrower's volume on the creation of the League of Nations and its tumultuous first decade begins this series on *Partners for Peace: International Cooperation in the Twentieth Century.* His history starts as the "war to end war" came to its conclusion and people began once more to search for lasting peace. Thoughtful observers agreed that victory had to mean something more than the defeat of the Kaiser, and the dominant figure of Woodrow Wilson insisted that a league of nations would give deep meaning to all the bloody sacrifice. For a brief time, the president of the United States stood unchallenged as the most important individual in the world, and he used his prestige to oversee the drafting of a covenant for his association. As they made peace with Germany, the nations of the world would become members of the league and commit themselves to implement humanity's old dream of peace. Today, we understand only too well that the Treaty of Versailles neither destroyed nor accommodated Germany, and that the league Wilson advocated brought little real peace. Many thoughtful people have at some time amused themselves by speculating how the world would be different had the United States followed the vision of its president in 1920. Wilson might have convinced the world, but he had failed to convince his own nation to follow its best instincts and become part of the international community. Some politicians opposed a perceived threat to America's sovereign rights, but, as Henry Cabot Lodge made clear, the Senate's defeat of the Versailles settlement was due primarily to presidential intransigence. "We can always count on Mr. Wilson," he chortled, "he has never failed us." The final American rejection of the League and the treaty broke Wilson's heart and spirit, and perhaps also put the world on the road to a more terrible war in 1939.

But Wilson's dream endured in the form of a league that for twenty years worked for world peace. Dr. Ostrower demonstrates how difficult it was to create an internationalist viewpoint. Great empires had been destroyed during the Great War, but out of their debris emerged new nations with strong nationalistic sentiments. Were these states willing to cooperate for larger human goals? Whether nationalism is a "state of mind" or the battle cry of ethnic freedom is debatable, but there is little doubt that the League of Nations and international cooperation suffered greatly due to issues of sovereign rights. Dr. Ostrower's volume on the League's first decade deftly reminds us of the virulence of the national spirit, even as it chronicles the growing pains of the new organization. His volume suggests that the history of the twentieth century is in part a confrontation between national patriotism and the wider vision of international amity.

The League of Nations represented a major effort by humankind to construct a peaceful and orderly world community based upon reason. Dr. Ostrower's volume details a time when that cause did not appear to be mindless "tilting at windmills." The League did have its successes, and despite its failure in the U.S. Senate, it even obtained valuable assistance from Americans. By 1924, the Rockefeller Foundation had contributed over half a million dollars to League health programs, while world relief services and the drive to eliminate slavery mobilized other American citizens. The Locarno Pact, German admission to the League, and settlement of a border dispute between Greece and Bulgaria made even isolationist Americans concede the value of a world organization. When Herbert Hoover assumed the presidency in 1929, he believed that the United States should cooperate with the League to limit the narcotics trade, to end slavery, and to protect the world's cultural heritage. Some even dared to believe that this nation would yet join the League and vindicate Woodrow Wilson.

Many League accomplishments were real, and this volume helps us to understand the vitality and spirit of a decade in which hopes for world peace soared. Indeed, only three months before the stock market crashed, the Kellogg-Briand Pact was formally proclaimed and war as a means of national policy was prohibited. The statesmen who gathered each year in Geneva were too wise to put much faith in such foolishness, but they encouraged any advance toward international consciousness. In the 1920s, all things might yet be dreamed. In a second volume, we shall see how the Depression and war made the 1930s a far more terrible decade. But in this admirable start to the series, Dr. Ostrower reminds us of the promise of the League of Nations, a dream soon to violently expire.

George Lankevich
Series Editor

Preface

War fascinates contemporary audiences. Books like Barbara Tuchman's *Guns of August* and John Hackett's *The Third World War* have led the best-seller lists of our time, just as movies like *The Bridge Over the River Quai, Apocalypse Now,* and *Platoon* have thrilled huge audiences, not only in the United States but throughout the world.

Peace, however, rarely makes it to the top of any list. This is too bad, for peace is easily the more important subject of the two. Although cynics might claim that peace is simply a lull between wars, in reality it is peace—not war—that permits the flowering of culture and learning, of technology and morals. Peace is a condition for progress, and we, therefore, owe it to ourselves to pay it more heed. We need to understand the nature of peace, and this involves a careful examination of its major institutions.

This book tells the story of the League of Nations, which was one of those institutions of peace. The League was the first international organization designed to prevent war by means of a system of collective security. Covering ten years, this book surveys the League from its birth at the end of World War I to the beginning of the Great Depression. American historians call that decade the Roaring Twenties, a term connoting vitality, exuberance, progress, and prosperity. These things characterized the international scene as well as the American. There were, of course, some problems—small wars, boundary disputes, national rivalries that lingered after World War I. Nevertheless, the decade witnessed no economic crisis comparable to the Great Depression of the thirties, nor any political crises such as those that followed the appearance of fascism in Germany and Japan. The twenties reflected hope and optimism. So did the League.

In 1919, collective security was still an untested idea, a concept so new that the term "collective security" would not appear for another sixteen years. Untested or not, however, the idea had become popular, for it suggested that in the event of a threat to peace, the entire international community would unite against the aggressor. The men who created the League had one main objective—to prevent war. The League became their monument to the casualties of World War I, and its success would be measured by the degree to which it helped to keep the peace. As readers will understand when they reach the end of the book, the League failed to meet its goal. The decade of optimism prepared the way for a decade of pessimism. Then came more war.

On another level, however, the League succeeded beyond expectations. It laid a firm foundation for internationalism, a series of ideas that encouraged international cooperation in areas far beyond the narrow focus of the collective-security enthusiasts. All proponents of collective security believed in internationalism, but not all internationalists believed in collective security. The two ideas are related; they are not identical. Readers are therefore advised to keep one eye on the theme of internationalism, even though it does not explicitly emerge until the seventh chapter of this story.

The League of Nations: 1919–1929 proceeds chronologically and topically, beginning with the pre–World War I origins of the League and then surveying the League's political and administrative life from the 1919 Paris Peace Conference to the Great Crash of 1929. Because the League was a multinational organization, this volume deals with the foreign policies of many countries that joined and led the League, but it pays particular attention to the reintegration of Germany into European diplomacy (and, by extension, into the League itself) during the 1920s. Although mainly a political history, the book also discusses the League's social, humanitarian, and economic activities, which prepared the way for the specialized agencies of the United Nations. Such nonpolitical efforts constituted the most cheerful work of the League.

Setting the Scene 1

If it is true, as England's Dr. Samuel Johnson once wrote, that nothing concentrates the mind as much as the threat of an imminent hanging, then it may be equally true that nothing stimulates planning for peace as much as the fear of catastrophic war. World War I was such a war. Contemporaries labelled it the Great War. When it began in August 1914, European leaders believed it would be over by Christmas. Four years later, nearly 10 million soldiers lay dead, as did an equal number of unlucky civilians. The Russian Empire had already disappeared, and the German, Austrian, and Turkish empires would soon disintegrate. The balance-of-power "system" that had helped to preserve peace for a century ironically had not only contributed to the war's origins but also—because the military power of the two hostile sides was so perfectly proportioned—insured that the war would be a long one.

The blood and gore that covered Europe during those four years accomplished what peace activists had been unable to do in four hundred years—they discredited the international system that made war possible. Well before the armistice in 1918, European and American writers like Norman Angell and John Clarke warned that another such conflict would spell the end of Western civilization. Indeed, by 1918, a few prominent national leaders, including England's Lord Cecil (Robert Cecil) and the United States' Woodrow Wilson, echoed this fear.

However, had it not been for the horror and the carnage, plans for a league of nations would once again have been consigned to the scrap heap of lost causes. For centuries, political thinkers from many lands had devised plans to prevent war, and some had even proposed embryonic systems of international cooperation. Writers as varied as British statesman Sir Thomas More, Dutch theorist Hugo Grotius, and German philosopher Immanuel Kant had contributed ideas to this effort. And the Enlightenment of the late eighteenth century had influenced thinking about international peace by emphasizing the essential goodness of man, the inevitability of progress, and the triumph of human reason.

By the early nineteenth century, the dream of a peace association had been stimulated by the apparent unity of the American federation after 1776 and by the antiwar sentiment emerging from the French Revolution and Napoleonic conflicts. The American example seemed to prove that such an association might work. The huge loss of life in the French wars suggested to many Europeans that it must work. But the conservative statesmen who planned the peace in 1815 had too much invested in the old order to create a new Europe. Their fear of the liberalism and nationalism unleashed by the French Revolution reinforced their commitment to the older ideas of balance and equilibrium. In any case, they embraced the balance-of-power concept at the Congress of Vienna in order to restore European stability. Indeed, they turned that balance into the basis of the nineteenth-century international system.

That system, paradoxically, brought them even closer to the league idea. Continental peacemakers after Waterloo—reactionaries like Metternich of Austria, pragmatists like Castlereagh of England, opportunists like Talleyrand of France, idealists like Alexander I of Russia—devised what would soon come to be called the Concert of Europe, a plan that involved periodic conferences of the Great Powers to insure international order and cooperation. Not a formal association in any meaningful sense, these conferences took place only when the leaders of the Great Powers deemed it necessary. The Concert of Europe was, at best, an irregular system lacking universal membership, yet it increasingly made peace appear to be a cooperative venture. Eventually, eight decades of experience would prove that the cooperative ideal was no less valued among political reactionaries than it was among liberals. The Russian czar proposed conferences at The Hague, which, during 1899 and 1907, seated representatives of the smaller powers

The death and destruction that Europe endured during the four years of World War I provided the impetus for the creation of the League of Nations.

alongside those from the great states. The Hague conferences constituted a kind of global legislature that discussed subjects as varied as disarmament and the compulsory arbitration of international disputes.

Historians have noted that one characteristic of a mature industrial society is the growth of organizations to insure order amidst the swirl of urbanization and class conflict. So, too, with international society; universal organizations presumably would insure order and progress. Consequently, such organizations proliferated during the nineteenth century—first, the General Postal Union, founded in 1875; next, a telegraphic union; and then, conferences to regulate transport on the Danube, control the price of sugar, and publicize the spread of epidemic disease. Internationalism increasingly shared the stage with traditional nationalism.

Yet by the turn of the twentieth century, when many Europeans dared to believe that general war had become obsolete, these international compacts could not keep the peace. The rise of a powerful Germany helped to fragment the Concert of Europe. The new organizations promoting disarmament and arbitration proved weak and, by 1914, were overwhelmed by rivalries intensified by industrial technology, imperialism, and the arms race. The prevailing confidence in the balance-of-power system was misplaced; indeed, the balance of power in part would cause the Great War. Little wonder that new leaders—such as Woodrow Wilson of the United States, David Lloyd George of England, and Lenin of Russia—would seek not so much to repair the balance as to transcend it.

Remaking the World

Winston Churchill, Joseph Stalin, Franklin Roosevelt, and Adolph Hitler easily dominated the political landscape of World War II; the political leaders of World War I generally appeared less impressive. Only Lenin, the Russian revolutionary, and perhaps Woodrow Wilson, the American president, were of major historical stature, and historians are not all that sure about Wilson. But one thing is certain: Without Wilson, the fledgling movement to create a league of nations would have died an early death. With him, the League became a reality.

Born in Virginia in 1856, Woodrow Wilson grew up in a family that emphasized religious and academic, rather than political, values. His adult life was spent mainly at universities where the clash between political theory and political reality was rarely intense. The son of a Presbyterian minister, young Wilson developed a Calvinist sense of mission and a belief in the irreconcilability of good and evil. He carried these ideas into his public life, in which, as a single-term governor of New Jersey, he became known as one of the leading progressive reformers in the country. Progressivism, for Wilson, meant the reinvigoration of American democracy. It meant wresting control of the political system from corrupt bosses, huge trusts, and selfish political interests. It meant returning power and prosperity to the people. The golden keys to these goals were respect for the rule of law, respect for the preservation of peace, and respect for the order that made peace possible.

American President Woodrow Wilson supplied the vision and leadership that brought about the creation of the League of Nations.

But such goals did not make Wilson a pacifist. He believed that wars fought for righteous purposes were justified, sending American troops into places like Mexico and Nicaragua well before he attempted to make the entire world safe for democracy. Yet Wilson genuinely hated war. Unlike his progressive rival, Teddy Roosevelt, who was the first American to win a Nobel Peace Prize, Wilson did not believe that war ennobled the human spirit. Moreover, Wilson, along with many other American progressives, gradually came to believe that United States participation in World War I could be used not to achieve strategic or territorial goals but, rather, to create a warless world. The Great War became for them "a war to end wars."

In short, the war offered Wilson the opportunity to remake his world along the lines of a "new diplomacy." He spelled out his vision in his famous Fourteen Points Address of January 1918. The speech outlined his generous terms for a German surrender and his call for self-determination for the peoples of Europe (but not for those of what we today call the Third World), disarmament, freedom of the seas, free trade, and even freedom for the Bolsheviks to determine their own future. Wilson advocated open diplomacy "openly arrived at." Finally, in Point 14, he called for a league of nations that would provide a mechanism to keep the peace and to secure for mankind the benefits of the first thirteen points. And it is clear that Wilson's league involved two things that not all enthusiasts for a world organization embraced—equality of all nations within the organization and the use of force to prevent a nation from going to war.

Many Americans who had thought longer and harder about a league than had Wilson shared his enthusiasm. Former President William Howard Taft was president of the League to Enforce Peace, a national group advocating an association with compulsory authority. Others, such as former Secretary of State Elihu Root and Stanford University President David Starr Jordan, promoted an association with arbitration procedures rather than compulsory authority.

The League to Enforce Peace was superbly organized and financed. When this group persuaded Wilson to speak from its platform shortly before the president sent his war message to Congress, its influence soared in the struggle to shape a postwar international organization. Yet the high visibility of the League to Enforce Peace masked a great deal of disagreement among Americans about the nature of a league, especially over the degree to which a league should emphasize judicial, as opposed to economic or military, means to prevent war. Eventually, this concern surfaced in a Senate debate over American membership so destructive that even Wilson's prestige could not carry the United States into the organization.

Nor was popular support for a league found only in the United States. In Great Britain, a badly splintered pro-league movement became unified in 1918 under the leadership of Lord Grey (Edward Grey) and Viscount Robert Cecil. Until that time, British proponents had been split over whether membership should be universal or confined only to democratic states; they had also been divided over issues of compulsory authority. President Wilson's Fourteen Points Address in January of that year did not end the debate, but it did almost single-handedly transform the league idea into Britain's chief war aim. British proponents took full advantage of this when Lord Cecil, one of the few British conservatives who unreservedly supported Wilson's

Viscount Robert Cecil helped unify the badly splintered pro-league movement in Great Britain in 1918.

vision, succeeded in forming a parliamentary committee, called the Phillimore Committee, to consider a postwar organization. When the Phillimore Committee announced its support for a league in March 1918, it joined such well-known figures as the popular South African general, Jan Christiaan Smuts; the former British ambassador to the United States, Viscount James Bryce; and the Archbishop of Canterbury. Within weeks, diffuse support for a league turned into a small-scale stampede. Eventually, unification was achieved in Britain under the umbrella of the League of Nations Union, which included pacifists and socialists on the left and imperialists and anti-German patriots on the right. With such unlikely allies, the union carefully steered a middle course, which succeeded not only in attracting vast support but also in getting Prime Minister David Lloyd George to articulate a reasonably coherent league policy by the end of the war.

General Jan Christiaan Smuts of South Africa was a strong advocate of a postwar organization of nations.

While public opinion expressed itself forcefully on the issue in Britain, a league of nations was a much less pressing topic in France. French conservatives paid it little attention, preferring instead to focus on the requirements of traditional balance-of-power diplomacy. French liberals, led by Léon Bourgeois, carried the banner for a league, while the powerful socialists remained fearful that a league would mainly cloak the ambitions of international capitalism. Yet even the liberal plan for a league, formally presented in a June 1918 report to the National Assembly, contrasted sharply with the American and British approaches. The French plan called for an international military force capable of imposing powerful sanctions, while the American and British plans leaned more toward an organization emphasizing legal and juridical procedures. Nevertheless, even in 1919, the league issue failed to attract the French as it did their Anglo-Saxon allies.

Smaller states, on the other hand, developed great enthusiasm for a postwar association. Their leaders, such as Sweden's Karl Hjalmar Branting and Switzerland's Giuseppe Motta, preferred the concept of real equality of states over an international system in which influence traditionally rested on power. Furthermore, a league might insure the security of the weak to a degree never before possible. But the leaders of the smaller states were wise enough to recognize that the shape of a postwar organization would still be left to the Great Powers. They therefore played a distinctly minor role in developing the League prior to its inauguration in 1920.

The Peace Conference and the Covenant

From 1914 until mid-1918, the Great War had been a stalemate. Its destructiveness staggered the imagination of civilians and military men alike. At the Somme in 1916, the British and French suffered 57,000 casualties in the first twenty-four hours of battle. The Italians lost much of their younger generation at Caporetto. The Germans lost nearly 500,000 soldiers at Verdun; the French lost even more. For the Russians, weariness of war, deepened by uncounted millions of casualties, led to revolution in 1917. It took no genius to understand that the American declaration of war in April 1917 would profoundly affect the conflict's outcome.

During the year it took the United States to mobilize, the Germans failed to defeat the British by submarine blockade. Although the Russians surrendered in January 1918, thereby allowing the Germans to mobilize their forces on a single front, fresh Yankee doughboys and clumsy British tanks managed to tip the scales against the exhausted Germans. In point of fact, the Americans did not fight very effectively; their inexperience and logistical confusion were rivalled only by their enthusiasm. Still, when the last German offensive collapsed and all parties understood that the end was near, the confident Americans stood poised to influence the peace.

Today, peace conferences, like declarations of war and dinosaurs, have become relics of a bygone age. Such was not so in 1919. Indeed, the political maneuvering during the last few months of the Great War can be understood only if we keep the upcoming Paris Peace Conference clearly in mind. With the Allies jockeying for advantage among themselves, the Germans understandably sidled up to the Americans and their lenient Fourteen Points, hoping for, among other things, an invitation to join the soon-to-be-formed League. The Germans accepted the truce terms of November 1918, but the final peace, as hammered out at the Peace Conference, proved much less to their liking.

Woodrow Wilson was not crazy about the final terms either. The American president came away with his League of Nations, but his rivals at the Peace Conference forced him to concede much in return. In Paris, the representatives of the Great Powers clashed not only over specific issues, such as the size of German reparations payments and control over specific territories, but also over the very nature of modern diplomacy. More than any other major leader at the conference, Wilson possessed a comprehensive and idealistic vision that he used to define his diplomatic objectives. This vision included such things as genuine disarmament, self-determination for the nations emerging from the collapse of the German and Austrian empires, and a commitment to freedom of the seas. It also included the creation of the League of Nations. So central was the League to Wilson's vision of a peaceful future that he placed its constitution directly into the conference's five peace treaties—the Treaty of Versailles with Germany, the Treaty of Neuilly-sur-Seine with Bulgaria, the Treaty of Trianon with Hungary, the Treaty of St. Germain-en-Laye with Austria, and the Treaty of Sèvres with Turkey. The League would therefore become an integral part of the postwar settlement. This, Wilson believed, would serve not only to keep the peace but to redress any parts of the peace treaty needing revision or repair.

Viscount James Bryce, a former British ambassador to the United States in 1919, was also a firm supporter of a postwar league of nations.

Wilson had hoped to use American entry into the war as a means to transform the balance-of-power system into a collective-security system via the League. Others, particularly French Premier Georges Clemenceau, proved much more skeptical of the collective-security idea. Wilson, after all, represented a nation 3,000 miles from the scene of the battle, and American casualties had been comparatively light. Moreover, the Americans came away from the war with new material advantages. In 1914, the United States had been a debtor nation; in 1918, it stood as the greatest creditor nation on the globe.

France, on the other hand, had been devastated. By 1918, nearly 1,500,000 of its sons lay dead, with another 4,000,000 wounded, out of a total male population of 22,000,000. Its economy and political system were scarred in ways never appreciated by the Americans. The French had lost their age-old confidence, their élan. Less kind observers described their new outlook as paranoid of Germany and of war.

If Wilson was the embodiment of the League and of the "new diplomacy," Clemenceau was his antithesis. If Wilson placed his faith in collective security as an instrument to preserve the peace, Clemenceau remained a skeptic. Fearing yet another war with Germany, which was 35 percent larger in population than France, Clemenceau believed that old-fashioned military alliances offered more protection for his country than did noble collective-security experiments. His support for a league, therefore, proved lukewarm at best.

Clemenceau was not a militarist. He had been a leader of the Radical-Socialist Party, the anticlerical party of the typical small-property owner. He was committed to the republican ideal and symbolized the Third Republic as much as any Frenchman of his generation. But he was equally a patriot, trying to fend off even more extreme nationalists. Short, broad, sporting a bushy mustache and a gruff exterior that hid an equally gruff interior, Clemenceau was nicknamed the Tiger for good reason. He was a superb political infighter, and he marshalled all of his skills to defend the traditional interests of his country against Wilson's call for a new diplomacy.

Of course, many other statesmen joined the debate in Paris. Paul Hymans of Belgium, a wise and gentle diplomat who eventually became the president of the very first League Assembly, served as the unofficial spokesman for the smaller powers. He was an ardent internationalist, and he was ably assisted by other smaller-power representatives, including Eduard Beneš of Czechoslovakia and Eleutherios Venizelos of Greece. They all sought to protect the interests of the lesser states, but they were outgunned in influence by the representatives of the larger states, who met separately as, first, the Council of Ten (the Big Ten), then the Council of Five (the United States, Great Britain, France, Italy, and Japan), and finally the Council of Four, as the Japanese representative, Baron Nobuaki Makino, stopped attending the meetings except when they were concerned with questions relating directly to his own country. Indeed, Baron Makino had much less interest in the league idea than in simply securing Japan's territorial expansion in the Pacific and, with his Chinese colleague, in committing the conference to a position of racial equality (the conference refused after the United States insisted that racial equality was strictly a "domestic matter"). Otherwise, Baron Makino played strictly a marginal role, occasionally dozing during arcane discussions about European matters. The Italian representative was Vittorio Orlando, a soft-spoken and gentle man who had the task of persuading the Allies to honor the territorial promises they had made in 1915 to lure Italy into the war. Neither Baron Makino nor Orlando had an easy time, and each threatened, at different moments, to leave the conference if the other delegates ignored his demands. Orlando did leave, only to hurry back at his government's command.

The conference included one other delegate of major stature—Great Britain's Prime Minister David Lloyd George. A liberal who had split his party by forging a coalition government in 1916, Lloyd George was as bright and dynamic as he was untrustworthy. He shared Wilson's belief in self-determination, but he rejected it for peoples outside of Europe who might threaten the British Empire. He also shared Wilson's desire to bring Germany back into the mainstream of European diplomacy. However, Lloyd George felt little passion one way or the other about a league, and he lacked completely Wilson's sympathy for open diplomacy and freedom of the seas. Where Wilson took his principles seriously, even at the cost of his own popularity, Lloyd George never met a popular majority he would not join. There was little room for courage in the prime minister's political vocabulary. Thus, when the British public, in the "khaki election" of 1918, endorsed revenge, Lloyd George promised to squeeze Germany until "the pips squeaked." Englishmen rejected the "new diplomacy," and Lloyd George trudged to Paris as their agent.

There were countries that should have been represented in Paris but were not. Germany, Austria, and Hungary, vanquished in 1918, had no real voice at the conference. Neither did Russia, for the Allies had not only excluded the Bolsheviks from Paris but had sent troops into Russia in July 1918 to overthrow the revolutionary government. As the vanquished in war, Berlin, Vienna, and Moscow all had more sympathy for the principles of the "new diplomacy" than did the victorious Allies. Their absence from Paris reduced support for Wilsonianism when it was most needed.

Curiously, the American public also lacked enthusiasm for the "new diplomacy." In contrast to the British leaders, who received the "khaki" endorsement, and the French government, which in December 1918 received an

(From left to right) Great Britain's Prime Minister David Lloyd George, Italian representative Vittorio Orlando, French Premier Georges Clemenceau, and American President Woodrow Wilson—known as the Big Four—were the main architects of the peace after World War I.

overwhelming vote of confidence, Wilson got a stinging rebuke from the American public in the congressional elections of November 1918. Wilson symbolized the war and progressive reform; with the armistice at hand, however, the American public voted for change. The election was not quite a vote of no confidence, but it sounded an inauspicious note upon which to launch Wilson's journey to Paris. Moreover, it meant that the U.S. Senate and its important Foreign Relations Committee would now be chaired by opponents of both the League and Wilson.

Such setbacks hardly concerned the American president as he launched his noble crusade. Ignoring the counsel of his closest advisers and the hopes of his European counterparts, he set sail for Paris in early 1919 because he believed that only his presence could prevent the resurrection of the old diplomacy and the scuttling of the League. He may well have been right, but by personally attending the conference, he affixed his prestige to the treaty in ways that ultimately served neither his country nor the cause of peace.

The American president hoped to turn his attendance at the conference to political advantage, in part by capitalizing on his European popularity. Having experienced the terror of war, millions of Europeans believed that Wilson was the one man who could banish war forever. He was more celebrated on the Continent than at home. Huge throngs of Europeans greeted Wilson as they had greeted the victorious caesars of ancient times. Banners proclaimed him the savior of the West; "Welcome to the God of Peace" was typical. Flowers and parades heralded his celebrity status. Always in the habit of taking himself too seriously, Wilson naturally exaggerated the political meaning behind this applause. Like other tragic figures, he believed what he wanted to believe and heard only the advice he wished to hear. Economist John Maynard Keynes, one of the most perceptive observers at the Paris Peace Conference, said caustically that Wilson's temperament was theological, not intellectual. Harold Nicolson, a British diplomat who kept a fascinating diary at the conference, lamented Wilson's rigidity and obsessive ignorance. Both descriptions contained a large measure of truth.

When, therefore, President Wilson became involved in the nitty-gritty negotiations with the representatives of the other powers, the high hopes raised by his reception quickly faded. Having called for open diplomacy, he agreed to meet behind closed doors. Having championed self-determination, he made territorial compromises regarding Eastern Europe that guaranteed an escalation of postwar anger. Having once called for a peace without victory, he endorsed military and territorial clauses that the Germans and Austrians viewed as bitterly humiliating. Why? It was not that Wilson was a hypocrite. He just firmly believed that a league of nations—*his* version of a league of nations—would rectify any injustices that might later threaten the peace. Let everything revolve around the League, said Wilson. "Once that is a *fait accompli*, nearly all serious difficulties will disappear."

In short, Wilson's faith in the future paralleled his faith in his Presbyterian God. Security, he believed, would rest on the pillars of his league. He therefore spent most of his time in Paris drafting the League's constitution. He called it a covenant, something characteristically biblical and legal. An examination of the Covenant—and of its origins in Great Britain, France, and the United States—will help to clarify both its purpose and its failure.

The Western Allies and the Covenant

It is often said that success has many fathers, while failure is an orphan. This certainly is not true of the League, for while it was not a success, it did have many fathers. They included the following.

Great Britain

The original British draft of the Covenant came from the Phillimore Committee. This draft was neither an official proposal of the British government nor a serious challenge to the principle of national sovereignty. Calling for more of a political than judicial league, it extended the ideas of arbitration and inquiry, which would be supervised by the Allied powers, and provided for both economic and military sanctions against any government that ignored these procedures.

The British Cabinet did not enthusiastically accept the report of the Phillimore Committee. The government, a fragile coalition of wartime parties, contained both socialists and conservatives who feared including a sanctions mechanism that would compel nations to accept a league decision. In addition, various factions within the British government had their own plans for a league. The Foreign Office proposed a league that unlike the Phillimore Committee's version would have two councils, roughly foreshadowing the actual Council and Assembly. This league would sponsor activities in the social and humanitarian spheres in addition to peacekeeping efforts. South Africa's General Jan Smuts also offered a plan. As a representative of a smaller state, Smuts unsurprisingly injected a demand for smaller-power representation, not found in the earlier British plans. Still others, like Lord Cecil, saw a league as a means to forge transatlantic cooperation, with the United States replacing the weakened states of Europe as a British ally. This latter league, which resembled Smuts's vision, would promote stability, while at the same time consolidating British imperial interests from South Africa to the Middle East.

Most British Cabinet and Foreign Office officials viewed the proposed league as a Great Power conference system. In so doing, they deemphasized sanctions as a means to prevent war. Yet because they wanted to mollify President Wilson, they did not entirely reject the sanctions provisions of the Phillimore Report. Prime Minister David Lloyd George had no strong feelings about sanctions, but he did understand that he could not secure Wilson's support for British interests at the Peace Conference if he abandoned the League. He also realized that the British public wanted a league with or without strong sanctions.

These developments help to clarify the British government's approach to the League. Lloyd George and other key members of the government recognized that the League had become a central issue in both British domestic politics and Anglo-American diplomacy. With some notable exceptions, especially Lord Cecil and Lloyd George, British leaders favored a league without sanctions, one that would not infringe on the traditional prerogatives of national sovereignty in areas such as arms limitation, tariffs, and imperial control. They wanted a league that would recreate—rather than challenge—a balance of power, albeit a balance anchored by an Anglo-

American alliance. This was far from a supergovernment. It represented a limited vision, a *conservative* vision, of world order. Not until they travelled to Versailles would the British come to understand just how different this was from Wilson's plan, for Wilson had refused to reveal any details of his thinking for fear of stirring up political opposition. That Lord Cecil, the chief British representative on League affairs in Paris, stood closer to Wilson than to his own government helps to explain why this limited British league plan failed to see the light of day.

France

Unlike the extensive debates in both England and the United States, wartime comment on the League in France was surprisingly sparse. This undoubtedly reflected not just the immediacy of the war for France but also the character of its wartime leader. Premier Georges Clemenceau was more intent on crushing the Germans than on designing the peace. Indeed, prior to the armistice, he had never publicly discussed his postwar plans beyond his simple November 1917 promise "to win." Clemenceau was an old-time politician. He subordinated his ideals to his interests, fully recognizing that his government might need to compromise or "sacrifice" issues such as the League in order to secure other more important objectives.

French planning for the League exhibited a curious paradox. The French, even more than the British, remained skeptical of the value of a league. Premier Clemenceau and most other important French leaders, including President Raymond Poincaré, were reluctant to trust French security to an untested plan of international cooperation. To the extent that the French would support a league, they hoped it would mainly prolong the wartime alliance.

In trying to shape the Covenant, the French threw their weight onto the side of a strong league. Where Lloyd George feared sanctions, Clemenceau thought a league without sanctions would be worth little more than a prayer. Consequently, the French contributed a draft that emphasized the mobilization of international military force to prevent aggression. Coordinated by Léon Bourgeois, a former premier and France's leading proponent of a league, the French draft not only demanded the submission of disputes to arbitration and inquiry but allowed the league to require—not just recommend—a settlement. To accomplish this, the French proposed that the league have a permanent military staff, something that was not found in any other nation's draft. These military provisions reflected the French belief—or hope—that sanctions would prevent any future aggression by Germany.

Nevertheless, the skeptical French refused to place too much stock in any league. When it came to insuring French security, Clemenceau demanded a British-American guarantee of French borders quite apart from the proposed league mechanism. For obvious reasons, this guarantee did not reassure the smaller nations of Europe about the effectiveness of a future league. After all, they thought, if France, one of the Great Powers, refused to place its security in the hands of a league, why should a less powerful state do so?

The United States

Woodrow Wilson addressed the issue of retaining confidence in the League by saying that its Covenant would contain a sacred promise, a guarantee of mutual support, to keep the peace. It would constitute a moral obligation so powerful that the people of the world would permit no government to ignore it.

Wilson's own plan had been pieced together by Colonel Edward House, his confidant and adviser. House was one of the more puzzling characters of the wartime period. A vain and manipulative man who had superb political instincts, House, oddly, understood Wilson better than Wilson understood himself. He was a self-conscious Texan who unashamedly promoted himself by using the honorary title of "colonel" (he served not a single day in military service), and he knew as little about Europe as did most other Texans. Nevertheless, he rarely let his lack of knowledge stand in the way of his (and the president's) goals, and he was, admittedly, a fast learner.

Although Wilson and House would have a parting of the ways during the Peace Conference, the Texan exerted considerable influence (some historians say enormous and malign influence) on Wilson's foreign policy going back to the days before the war. When the president and his adviser left Washington for Paris in January 1919, they were largely agreed about the shape of the new international organization that would eventually become the League of Nations. Drawing from the efforts of the League to Enforce

Colonel Edward House (left), shown here with French Premier Georges Clemenceau (center) and Mrs. House (right), was Woodrow Wilson's confidant and adviser. He is credited with piecing together the American president's proposal for the structure of the League.

Peace, House created a working proposal that straddled the British emphasis on arbitration and the French emphasis on sanctions. At its heart was the famous Article 10, which contained a guarantee to preserve the peace; both conference and arbitration procedures as well as economic and military sanctions could be employed if a government violated it.

In one important way, this Wilson-House plan departed from the British draft—it called for a league that would be a permanent association of nations to prevent war, rather than one that would come together just during times of crisis. Wilson also proved more willing to entertain a role for the smaller powers. The president refused to discuss his draft publicly for fear that his political opponents would try to scuttle the plan. In truth, his draft contained important elements that were not widely understood or accepted by the American public. Most Americans felt more comfortable with judicial and arbitration mechanisms for settling disputes. In contrast, Wilson loaded his draft with provisions calling for the use of force and international guarantees. The victory of the opposition Republican Party in the November 1918 congressional election should have tipped off the president to the necessity of compromise. Instead, he dug in his heels and thereby complicated the rest of his political life.

The Smaller Powers

Planning for the League of Nations was in large measure left to the Great Powers, not to the more numerous smaller states. This is not to say that the governments of these smaller states ignored the subject, for some were represented on the Peace Conference's League of Nations Commission. They just understood—as smaller states often do—that limited military and economic power translates into limited political power.

Nevertheless, Wilson's popularity carried into many of these states and even into the former members of the Central Powers. This reinforced the American president's influence, which paid substantial dividends at the Peace Conference. The smaller states tended to support Wilson's plan. They did so for two overriding reasons—a league might protect them against the traditional "might makes right" attitude of the Great Powers; and a league, with its formal procedures and votes, would provide them with a degree of equality on the international stage that they had rarely experienced. This promise of equality seemed real when Wilson, echoing Smuts, called for a League council that included representatives of the smaller powers, not one drawn exclusively from the Great Powers. However, it bears mentioning that the representatives of these smaller powers were only marginally involved in hammering out the final draft of the Covenant. Great power, after all, still had its privileges.

The Covenant

The Covenant that emerged from the Peace Conference contained twenty-six articles. (For the Covenant as it stood when it emerged from the Peace Conference, see page 19. For the Covenant as it stood when fully amended, see *The League of Nations: 1929–1946*.) Like all such documents, it reflect-

Locating the League

A little-known historical oddity is that the League of Nations, like its successor, the United Nations, spent its first days in London. Not until the League was ten months old did it move to its permanent home in Geneva, Switzerland.

The choice of Geneva was built directly into Article 7 of the Covenant. That article also gave the League Council the right to decide "at any time" that the seat of the League should be elsewhere, a provision included in case the League should decide that Switzerland had become an inappropriate place to hold meetings. Actually, many officials, even *before* the Treaty of Versailles had been signed, hoped that the League would wind up in a city other than Geneva. Some internationalists, including the French and the newly appointed secretary-general of the League, favored Brussels; a few others proposed Washington or London. Most, however, did want the League in neutral Switzerland, which meant the city of Geneva. The commissioners who authored the Covenant felt that Geneva was less tied to the memories of war. And Swiss lobbying for Geneva did not hurt the city's cause.

Selecting Geneva was one thing. Locating there was another. A building had to be acquired and furnished, a bureaucracy created and staffed. In the meantime, London would serve as the temporary home. From the fall of 1919, when real organizational efforts began, until November 1920, the Secretariat was lodged in Curzon House, on London's Sunderland Street. Curzon House contained cramped quarters never designed for the League's diverse and sprawling activities. However, in spite of their discomfort, many League officials in 1920 were willing to put up with Curzon House because they considered London to be among the world's great cities and, like diehard United Nations officials in New York today, hardly relished resettling in more remote Geneva. They considered Geneva not only more remote but downright provincial and boring. Indeed, Geneva's historic association with the Protestant reformer John Calvin—who had turned the community into a puritanical commonwealth during the 1500s—saddled Geneva with a grim and austere reputation that lasted until the twentieth century.

Boring or not, the decision had been made. Now the practical problems surfaced. Geneva had only one available building big enough to house the League. That building was the Hôtel National, empty in 1919 while undergoing renovation. With its stately exterior and 200-room interior, it possessed both the size and the dignity for the Secretariat's purposes. When it became clear that the Swiss government as well as the Geneva city government would facilitate the hotel's transfer from private hands to League ownership, and when the owners of the hotel reduced their price from 6.5 to 5.5 million francs, Secretary-General Sir Eric Drummond, acting on behalf of the Council, agreed to purchase the property. And although most League officials understood that the hotel would be only a temporary home, they admired its lovely grounds, about a half-hour walk from the center of town and near beautiful Lake Geneva. The quiet of those grounds, though, was nonexistent during 1920. Carpenters, electricians, plumbers, and painters worked around the clock to finish the renovations before the members of the new international organization moved into the building. There is no record of cost overruns, but the work did run over schedule, forcing Secretariat officials to contend with sawdust and the not-so-sweet sounds of construction during the first weeks of their occupancy.

The new Secretariat was a strange building. Reminding American observers of the old State Department building, which still stands next to the White House in Washington, its Beaux Arts architectural style could most charitably be called eclectic. It combined classic columns on the ground level with a dozen arched windows on the top floor, all below a mansard roof, providing an effect that seemed both cluttered and proud. It looked less like an international office—or even a hotel—than a palace for nineteenth-century royalty.

In practical terms, perhaps the most important shortcoming of the building was its lack of a hall to accommodate the full Assembly. To the rescue came the city of Geneva, which provided a modest building, called—appropriately enough—the Salle de la Reformation (Reformation Hall). Frank Walters, the League's semi-official historian, called it "a bare and badly lit hall of unimpressive proportions" containing no conference areas, no committee rooms, no delegates' lounge area, and no office space. Understandably, it initially impressed no one. In the wake of World War I, however, it did not need to impress anyone. Function, not design, would prove to be more important to the League's success, and the Salle de la Reformation functioned well enough. It hosted Assembly meetings throughout the 1920s. If Walters was correct, the Salle was so quirky that, for all its shortcomings, many delegates came to love it; at least, many of them opposed the move to larger quarters in the 1930s.

Once the League had established itself, officials began thinking seriously about building a new headquarters, one that would house the entire operation. Although the Covenant allowed cities other than Geneva to be considered, and some officials introduced a resolution to move the League to German-speaking Vienna after Germany entered the League in 1927, most delegates resolved to construct a new building not very far from the old. The League, therefore, began negotiations with Geneva to purchase a site overlooking the lake in a park that had been given to the city years earlier. The site, which today houses the European headquarters of the United Nations, is quietly majestic. A contest to design the building drew over 100 sets of plans, only to see an architectural jury deadlock over a final selection. The result extended the process by more than a year, bruised many egos, and left the decision to a committee that, like most committees, compromised as it combined the designs of five different architects. The building that resulted from this curious process was monumental though undistinguished. Aided by a $5 million gift from John D. Rockefeller that also included monies for a library, the League broke ground for the structure in 1929. The building was completed in 1936, just about the time that Benito Mussolini's attack on Ethiopia destroyed the morale and the effectiveness of the world's first collective-security organization.

The Palais des Nations, which today is the European headquarters of the United Nations, here nears completion in the mid-1930s.

ed compromise, though not enough compromise to distort Wilson's dream. The first seven articles of the Covenant provided the nuts and bolts of the new organization. They defined its membership, officially excluding Germany and the other Central Powers; guaranteed the right of withdrawal; outlined the composition and authority of the Assembly, in which all members had equal representation; and described the Council, which had permanent seats for the Great Powers and nonpermanent seats for four smaller states. A critical right-to-veto provision was included in Article 5, which required all important Assembly or Council decisions to be unanimous. Article 6 established the Secretariat, the permanent office structure of the new organization; and Article 7 headquartered the League in Geneva, a somewhat remote location in postwar Europe. (For a further discussion of the League in Geneva, see "Locating the League," on page 15.) Articles 8 and 9 pledged League members to reduce arms consistent with the demands of national, not merely domestic, security.

The heart of the Covenant—the capstone of the League ideal—came in Article 10, which obligated each League member to respect the territorial integrity and political independence of other states. Each member would promise to protect all other members against any nation violating this provision. This constituted the first legal statement of genuine collective security in world history. In short, Article 10 outlawed aggressive war.

Subsequent articles spelled out the mechanisms to achieve the goal of Article 10. Article 11 authorized any member to call for League consideration of an attack or a threatened attack; and articles 12 through 15 outlined the arbitration, judicial, and political procedures to settle a dispute peacefully. Article 16 was the sanctions section of the Covenant. It provided for coordinated economic and/or military measures against an aggressor state if the nonforce provisions of articles 11 to 15 failed, and it pledged League members to cooperate when employing sanctions. It also gave the Council and Assembly the power to expel an aggressor state from the organization, subject, of course, to the veto provisions of Article 5.

The next six articles were designed to coordinate the Covenant with existing treaties and to exempt existing regional understandings like the Monroe Doctrine from its terms. By exempting the Monroe Doctrine, the commissioners in Paris effectively recognized an American sphere of influence in the New World. This was done for one simple reason—Wilson had warned the conference that the U.S. Senate would never approve the Covenant without such a consideration. The result was a scramble for political concessions by other countries. One example was Clemenceau's demand for an Anglo-American promise to guarantee French security outside of the League framework. Tokyo's demand for special rights in China's Shantung province was another.

With a single exception, the remainder of the Covenant was noncontroversial. It included provisions to make the League an umbrella organization for other international agencies, authority to extend League efforts into the social and humanitarian fields, and a method to amend the Covenant. Ironically, this remaining section of the Covenant—especially articles 23 and 24, which projected the League into areas as diverse as labor, health, communications and transit, and economics and finance—laid the foundation for some of the League's longest-lasting accomplishments. The development of twentieth-century internationalism owed much to these articles. Activity in such areas continued long after the League's collective-security efforts came to a sad end during the late 1930s.

The controversial exception was Article 22, which established the colonial-mandate system. This article gave the victorious Allies authority—under League auspices—to administer the former German and Turkish colonies. The Covenant justified such action as deriving from the principle that "the well-being and development of [colonial] peoples form a sacred trust of civilization. . . ." Stripped of its noble language, Article 22 created an international spoils (of war) system.

The completed Covenant emerged from committee in early May 1919. It was, of course, a series of compromises incorporated directly into the peace treaty, which was itself a compromise. The problem with compromises, however, is that most people do not like them. The Germans were no exception. They resented their exclusion from the treaty-drafting process and from membership in the new organization. Nor did they like the rest of the treaty. Among other things, it saddled them with formal guilt for the war and with disarmament provisions that placed them in an inferior military position on the Continent. The treaty gave Poland and France some formerly German land containing rich natural resources and industrial cities. It stripped Germany of its prewar colonies and entitled the Allies to collect reparations totalling billions of marks (the exact amount would not be decided until 1923). It made no difference to Berlin that the treaty was much less harsh than were many other peace treaties, including the one that their Kaiser had forced the Russians to sign just a year earlier. The Germans complained bitterly even before they saw the final terms. To make matters worse, a starving Germany would continue to suffer an Allied blockade of its ports until the German national assembly ratified the treaty.

The compromise that became the treaty displeased not only the Germans. The British complained because they wanted a much less compulsory league. The Italians resented the refusal of the Peace Conference to grant them colonies and authority over Fiume. The Japanese felt humiliated after the conference rejected their demand for racial equality. The Chinese were angry over having to transfer all former German interests in Shantung province to Japan. And the French protested because the treaty permitted Germany to retain the Rhineland in return for English and American military guarantees that never materialized.

Even the Americans disliked the final product in spite of Wilson's generally successful efforts to tailor the treaty to the interests—and prejudices—of the U.S. Senate. It is entirely possible that the Covenant would have been ignored by the Europeans had it not been included in the treaty; but it is also possible that the treaty, which was rejected by the United States, would have been accepted by Washington had it not contained the Covenant. In any case, once Woodrow Wilson linked the two so closely, the idealism that gave birth to the League was seriously tarnished even before the League held its first meeting. And this, in turn, critically affected the entire history of this first collective-security organization and the attempt to establish a firm basis for peace.

The Covenant of the League of Nations

THE HIGH CONTRACTING PARTIES,

In order to promote international co-operation and to achieve international peace and security
by the acceptance of obligations not to resort to war,
by the prescription of open, just and honourable relations between nations,
by the firm establishment of the understandings of international law as the actual rule of conduct among Governments, and
by the maintenance of justice and a scrupulous respect for all treaty obligations in the dealings of organised peoples with one another,
Agree to this Covenant of the League of Nations.

ARTICLE 1.
MEMBERSHIP AND WITHDRAWAL

1. The original Members of the League of Nations shall be those of the Signatories which are named in the Annex to this Covenant and also such of those other States named in the Annex as shall accede without reservation to this Covenant. Such accessions shall be effected by a declaration deposited with the Secretariat within two months of the coming into force of the Covenant. Notice thereof shall be sent to all other Members of the League.

2. Any fully self-governing State, Dominion or Colony not named in the Annex may become a Member of the League if its admission is agreed to by two-thirds of the Assembly, provided that it shall give effective guarantees of its sincere intention to observe its international obligations, and shall accept such regulations as may be prescribed by the League in regard to its military, naval and air forces and armaments.

3. Any Member of the League may, after two years' notice of its intention so to do, withdraw from the League, provided that all its international obligations and all its obligations under this Covenant shall have been fulfilled at the time of its withdrawal.

ARTICLE 2.
EXECUTIVE ORGANS

The action of the League under this Covenant shall be effected through the instrumentality of an Assembly and of a Council, with a permanent Secretariat.

ARTICLE 3.
ASSEMBLY

1. The Assembly shall consist of representatives of the Members of the League.

2. The Assembly shall meet at stated intervals and from time to time, as occasion may require, at the Seat of the League or at such other place as may be decided upon.

3. The Assembly may deal at its meetings with any matter within the sphere of action of the League or affecting the peace of the world.

4. At meetings of the Assembly each Member of the League shall have one vote and may have not more than three Representatives.

ARTICLE 4.
COUNCIL

1. The Council shall consist of representatives of the Principal Allied and Associated Powers [United States of America, British Empire, France, Italy and Japan], together with Representatives of four other Members of the League. These four Members of the League shall be selected by the Assembly from time to time in its discretion. Until the appointment of the Representatives of the four Members of the League first selected by the Assembly, Representatives of Belgium, Brazil, Greece and Spain shall be Members of the Council.

2. With the approval of the majority of the Assembly, the Council may name additional Members of the League, whose Representatives shall always be Members of the Council; the Council with like approval may increase the number of Members of the League to be selected by the Assembly for representation on the Council.

3. The Council shall meet from time to time as occasion may require, and at least once a year, at the Seat of the League, or at such other place as may be decided upon.

4. The Council may deal at its meetings with any matter within the sphere of action of the League or affecting the peace of the world.

5. Any Member of the League not represented on the Council shall be invited to send a Representative to sit as a Member at any meeting of the Council during the consideration of matters specially affecting the interests of that Member of the League.

6. At meetings of the Council, each Member of the League represented on the Council shall have one vote, and may have not more than one Representative.

ARTICLE 5.
VOTING AND PROCEDURE

1. Except where otherwise expressly provided in this Covenant or by the terms of the present Treaty, decisions at any meeting of the Assembly or of the Council shall require the agreement of all the Members of the League represented at the meeting.

2. All matters of procedure at meetings of the Assembly or of the Council, including the appointment of Committees to investigate particular matters, shall be regulated by the Assembly or by the Council and may be decided by a majority of the Members of the League represented at the meeting.

3. The first meeting of the Assembly and the first meeting of the Council shall be summoned by the President of the United States of America.

ARTICLE 6.
SECRETARIAT AND EXPENSES

1. The permanent Secretariat shall be established at the Seat of the League. The Secretariat shall comprise a Secretary-General and such secretaries and staff as may be required.

2. The first Secretary-General shall be the person named in the Annex; thereafter the Secretary-General shall be appointed by the Council with the approval of the majority of the Assembly.

3. The secretaries and the staff of the Secretariat shall be appointed by the Secretary-General with the approval of the Council.

4. The Secretary-General shall act in that capacity at all meetings of the Assembly and of the Council.

ARTICLE 7.
SEAT, QUALIFICATIONS OF OFFICIALS, IMMUNITIES

1. The Seat of the League is established at Geneva.

2. The Council may at any time decide that the Seat of the League shall be established elsewhere.

3. All positions under or in connection with the League, including the Secretariat, shall be open equally to men and women.

4. Representatives of the Members of the League and officials of the League when engaged on the business of the League shall enjoy diplomatic privileges and immunities.

5. The buildings and other property occupied by the League or its officials or by Representatives attending its meetings shall be inviolable.

ARTICLE 8.

REDUCTION OF ARMAMENTS

1. The Members of the League recognize that the maintenance of peace requires the reduction of national armaments to the lowest point consistent with national safety and the enforcement by common action of international obligations.
2. The Council, taking account of the geographical situation and circumstances of each State, shall formulate plans for such reduction for the consideration and action of the several Governments.
3. Such plans shall be subject to reconsideration and revision at least every 10 years.
4. After these plans shall have been adopted by the several Governments, the limits of armaments therein fixed shall not be exceeded without the concurrence of the Council.
5. The Members of the League agree that the manufacture by private enterprise of munitions and implements of war is open to grave objections. The Council shall advise how the evil effects attendant upon such manufacture can be prevented, due regard being had to the necessities of those Members of the League which are not able to manufacture the munitions and implements of war necessary for their safety.
6. The Members of the League undertake to interchange full and frank information as to the scale of their armaments, their military, naval and air programmes and the condition of such of their industries as are adaptable to warlike purposes.

ARTICLE 9.

PERMANENT MILITARY, NAVAL AND AIR COMMISSION

A Permanent Commission shall be constituted to advise the Council on the execution of the provisions of Articles 1 and 8 and on military, naval and air questions generally.

ARTICLE 10.

GUARANTEES AGAINST AGGRESSION

The Members of the League undertake to respect and preserve as against external aggression the territorial integrity and existing political independence of all Members of the League. In case of any such aggression or in case of any threat or danger of such aggression the Council shall advise upon the means by which this obligation shall be fulfilled.

ARTICLE 11.

ACTION IN CASE OF WAR OR THREAT OF WAR

1. Any war or threat of war, whether immediately affecting any of the Members of the League or not, is hereby declared a matter of concern to the whole League, and the League shall take any action that may be deemed wise and effectual to safeguard the peace of nations. In case any such emergency should arise the Secretary-General shall on the request of any Member of the League forthwith summon a meeting of the Council.
2. It is also declared to be the friendly right of each Member of the League to bring to the attention of the Assembly or of the Council any circumstance whatever affecting international relations which threatens to disturb international peace or the good understanding between nations upon which peace depends.

ARTICLE 12.

DISPUTES TO BE SUBMITTED FOR SETTLEMENT

1. The Members of the League agree that, if there should arise between them any dispute likely to lead to a rupture, they will submit the matter either to arbitration or to inquiry by the Council, and they agree in no case to resort to war until three months after the award by the arbitrators or the report by the Council.
2. In any case under this Article the award of the arbitrators shall be made within a reasonable time, and the report of the Council shall be made within six months after the submission of the dispute.

ARTICLE 13.

ARBITRATION OR JUDICIAL SETTLEMENT

1. The Members of the League agree that, whenever any dispute shall arise between them which they recognize to be suitable for submission to arbitration and which cannot be satisfactorily settled by diplomacy, they will submit the whole subject-matter to arbitration.

2. Disputes as to the interpretation of a treaty, as to any question of international law, as to the existence of any fact which, if established, would constitute a breach of any international obligation, or as to the extent and nature of the reparation to be made for any such breach, are declared to be among those which are generally suitable for submission to arbitration.

3. The Members of the League agree that they will carry out in full good faith any award that may be rendered, and that they will not resort to war against a Member of the League which complies therewith. In the event of any failure to carry out such an award, the Council shall propose what steps should be taken to give effect thereto.

ARTICLE 14.

PERMANENT COURT OF INTERNATIONAL JUSTICE

The Council shall formulate and submit to the Members of the League for adoption plans for the establishment of a Permanent Court of International Justice. The Court shall be competent to hear and determine any dispute of an international character which the parties thereto submit to it. The Court may also give an advisory opinion upon any dispute or question referred to it by the Council or by the Assembly.

ARTICLE 15.

DISPUTES NOT SUBMITTED TO ARBITRATION OR JUDICIAL SETTLEMENT

1. If there should arise between Members of the League any dispute likely to lead to a rupture, which is not submitted to arbitration in accordance with Article 13, the Members of the League agree that they will submit the matter to the Council. Any party to the dispute may effect such submission by giving notice of the existence of the dispute to the Secretary-General, who will make all necessary arrangements for a full investigation and consideration thereof.

2. For this purpose the parties to the dispute will communicate to the Secretary-General, as promptly as possible, statements of their case with all the relevant facts and papers, and the Council may forthwith direct the publication thereof.

3. The Council shall endeavour to effect a settlement of the dispute, and, if such efforts are successful, a statement shall be made public giving such facts and explanations regarding the dispute and the terms of settlement thereof as the Council may deem appropriate.

4. If the dispute is not thus settled, the Council either unanimously or by a majority vote shall make and publish a report containing a statement of the facts of the dispute and the recommendations which are deemed just and proper in regard thereto.

5. Any member of the League represented on the Council may make public a statement of the facts of the dispute and of its conclusions regarding the same.

6. If a report by the Council is unanimously agreed to by the Members thereof other than the Representatives of one or more of the parties to the dispute, the Members of the League agree that they will not go to war with any party to the dispute which complies with the recommendations of the report.

7. If the Council fails to reach a report which is unanimously agreed to by the Members thereof, other than the Representatives of one or more of the parties to the dispute, the Members of the League reserve to themselves the right to take such action as they shall consider necessary for the maintenance of right and justice.

8. If the dispute between the parties is claimed by one of them, and is found by the Council, to arise out of a matter which by international law is solely within the domestic jurisdiction of that party, the Council shall so report, and shall make no recommendation as to its settlement.

9. The Council may in any case under this Article refer the dispute to the Assembly. The dispute shall be so referred at the request of either party to the dispute, provided that such request be made within 14 days after the submission of the dispute to the Council.

10. In any case referred to the Assembly, all the provisions of this Article and of Article 12 relating to the action and powers of the Council shall apply to the action and powers of the Assembly, provided that a report made by the Assembly, if concurred in by the Representatives of those Members of the League represented on the Council and of a majority of the other Members of the League, exclusive in each case of the Representatives of the parties to the dispute, shall have the same force as a report by the Council concurred in by all the members thereof other than the Representatives of one or more of the parties to the dispute.

ARTICLE 16.

SANCTIONS OF PACIFIC SETTLEMENT

1. Should any Member of the League resort to war in disregard of its covenants under Articles 12, 13, or 15, it shall *ipso facto* be deemed to have committed an act of war against all other Members of the League, which hereby undertake immediately to subject it to the severance of all trade or financial relations, the prohibition of all intercourse between their nationals and the nationals of the covenant-breaking State, and the prevention of all financial, commercial or personal intercourse between the nationals of the covenant-breaking State and the nationals of any other State, whether a Member of the League or not.

2. It shall be the duty of the Council in such case to recommend to the several Governments concerned what effective military, naval or air force the Members of the League shall severally contribute to the armed forces to be used to protect the covenants of the League.

3. The Members of the League agree, further, that they will mutually support one another in the financial and economic measures which are taken under this Article, in order to minimize the loss and inconvenience resulting from the above measures, and that they will mutually support one another in resisting any special measures aimed at one of their number by the covenant-breaking State, and that they will take the necessary steps to afford passage through their territory to the forces of any of the Members of the League which are co-operating to protect the covenants of the League.

4. Any Member of the League which has violated any covenant of the League may be declared to be no longer a Member of the League by a vote of the Council concurred in by the Representatives of all the other Members of the League represented thereon.

ARTICLE 17.

DISPUTES INVOLVING NON-MEMBERS

1. In the event of a dispute between a Member of the League and a State which is not a Member of the League, or between States not Members of the League, the State or States not Members of the League shall be invited to accept the obligations of membership in the League for the purposes of such dispute, upon such conditions as the Council may deem just. If such invitation is accepted, the provisions of Articles 12 to 16, inclusive, shall be applied with such modifications as may be deemed necessary by the Council.

2. Upon such invitation being given, the Council shall immediately institute an inquiry into the circumstances of the dispute and recommend such action as may seem best and most effectual in the circumstances.

3. If a State so invited shall refuse to accept the obligations of membership in the League for the purposes of such dispute, and shall resort to war against a Member of the League, the provisions of Article 16 shall be applicable as against the State taking such action.

4. If both parties to the dispute when so invited refuse to accept the obligations of Membership in the League for the purposes of such dispute, the Council may take such measures and make such recommendations as will prevent hostilities and will result in the settlement of the dispute.

ARTICLE 18.

REGISTRATION AND PUBLICATION OF TREATIES

Every treaty or international engagement entered into hereafter by any Member of the League shall be forthwith registered with the Secretariat and shall as soon as possible be published by it. No such treaty or international engagement shall be binding until so registered.

ARTICLE 19.

REVIEW OF TREATIES

The Assembly may from time to time advise the reconsideration by Members of the League of treaties which have become inapplicable, and the consideration of international conditions whose continuance might endanger the peace of the world.

ARTICLE 20.

ABROGATION OF INCONSISTENT OBLIGATIONS

1. The Members of the League severally agree that this Covenant is accepted as abrogating all obligations or understandings *inter se* which are inconsistent with the terms thereof, and solemnly undertake that they will not hereafter enter into any engagements inconsistent with the terms thereof.

2. In case any Member of the League shall, before becoming a Member of the League, have undertaken any obligations inconsistent with the terms of this Covenant, it shall be the duty of such Member to take immediate steps to procure its release from such obligations.

ARTICLE 21.

ENGAGEMENTS THAT REMAIN VALID

Nothing in this Covenant shall be deemed to affect the validity of international engagements, such as treaties of arbitration or regional understandings like the Monroe Doctrine, for securing the maintenance of peace.

ARTICLE 22.

MANDATORY SYSTEM

1. To those colonies and territories which as a consequence of the late war have ceased to be under the sovereignty of the States which formerly governed them and which are inhabited by peoples not yet able to stand by themselves under the strenuous conditions of the modern world, there should be applied the principle that the well-being and development of such peoples form a sacred trust of civilization and that securities for the performance of this trust should be embodied in this Covenant.

2. The best method of giving practical effect to this principle is that the tutelage of such peoples should be entrusted to advanced nations who by reason of their resources, their experience or their geographical position can best undertake this responsibility, and who are willing to accept it, and that this tutelage should be exercised by them as Mandatories on behalf of the League.

3. The character of the mandate must differ according to the stage of the development of the people, the geographical situation of the territory, its economic conditions and other similar circumstances.

4. Certain communities formerly belonging to the Turkish Empire have reached a stage of development where their existence as independent nations can be provisionally recognised subject to the rendering of administrative advice and assistance by a Mandatory until such time as they are able to stand alone. The wishes of these communities must be a principal consideration in the selection of the Mandatory.

5. Other peoples, especially those of Central Africa, are at such a stage that the Mandatory must be responsible for the administration of the territory under conditions which will guarantee freedom of conscience and religion, subject only to the maintenance of public order and morals, the prohibition of abuses such as the slave trade, the arms traffic and the liquor traffic, and the prevention of the establishment of fortifications or military and naval bases and of military training of the natives for other than police purposes and the defense of territory, and will also secure equal opportunities for the trade and commerce of other Members of the League.

6. There are territories, such as Southwest Africa and certain of the South Pacific islands, which, owing to the sparseness of their population, or their small size, or their remoteness from the centres of civilization, or their geographical contiguity to the territory of the Mandatory, and other circumstances, can be best administered under the laws of the Mandatory as integral portions of its territory, subject to the safeguards above mentioned in the interests of the indigenous population.

7. In every case of mandate, the Mandatory shall render to the Council an annual report in reference to the territory committed to its charge.

8. The degree of authority, control or administration to be exercised by the Mandatory shall, if not previously agreed upon by the Members of the League, be explicitly defined in each case by the Council.

9. A permanent Commission shall be constituted to receive and examine the annual reports of the Mandatories and to advise the Council on all matters relating to the observance of the mandates.

ARTICLE 23.
SOCIAL AND OTHER ACTIVITIES

Subject to and in accordance with the provisions of international conventions existing or hereafter to be agreed upon, the Members of the League:

(a) will endeavour to secure and maintain fair and humane conditions of labour for men, women and children, both in their own countries and in all countries to which their commercial and industrial relations extend, and for that purpose will establish and maintain the necessary international organisations;

(b) undertake to secure just treatment of the native inhabitants of territories under their control;

(c) will entrust the League with the general supervision over the execution of agreements with regard to traffic in women and children, and the traffic in opium and other dangerous drugs;

(d) will entrust the League with the general supervision of the trade in arms and ammunition with the countries in which the control of this traffic is necessary in the common interest;

(e) will make provision to secure and maintain freedom of communications and of transit and equitable treatment for the commerce of all Members of the League. In this connection, the special necessities of the regions devastated during the war of 1914–1918 shall be borne in mind;

(f) will endeavour to take steps in matters of international concern for the prevention and control of disease.

ARTICLE 24.
INTERNATIONAL BUREAUS

1. There shall be placed under the direction of the League all international bureaus already established by general treaties if the parties to such treaties consent. All such international bureaus and all commissions for the regulation of matters of international interest hereafter constituted shall be placed under the direction of the League.

2. In all matters of international interest which are regulated by general conventions but which are not placed under the control of international bureaus or commissions, the Secretariat of the League shall, subject to the consent of the Council and if desired by the parties, collect and distribute all relevant information and shall render any other assistance which may be necessary or desirable.

3. The Council may include as part of the expenses of the Secretariat the expenses of any bureau or commission which is placed under the direction of the League.

ARTICLE 25.
PROMOTION OF RED CROSS AND HEALTH

The Members of the League agree to encourage and promote the establishment and co-operation of duly authorised voluntary national Red Cross organisations having as purposes the improvement of health, the prevention of disease and the mitigation of suffering throughout the world.

ARTICLE 26.
AMENDMENTS

1. Amendments to this Covenant will take effect when ratified by the Members of the League whose Representatives compose the Council and by a majority of the Members of the League whose Representatives compose the Assembly.

2. No such amendment shall bind any Member of the League which signifies its dissent therefrom, but in that case it shall cease to be a Member of the League.

Infancy 2

The Covenant authorized the president of the United States to call the first meeting of the League Council. The Council would meet in Paris, for in early 1920, the League had yet to move to its Geneva headquarters. In Washington, Woodrow Wilson proudly issued his invitation, and on January 16, 1920, the League formally began its life when former French premier and ardent internationalist Léon Bourgeois opened the initial Council meeting.

Bourgeois spoke grandly of "the birth of the new world." It was not to be an easy delivery. The complexion of the political world in 1920 belied the rosy expectations of those who had recently met in Paris. Ideological differences and old-fashioned nationalism reinforced each other. Fighting in Eastern Europe continued between Russians and Poles. England, France, the United States, and Japan were still involved in a military intervention against the Bolsheviks in Russia. Hungary had experienced an abortive communist revolution under Béla Kun. In Germany, revolutionary ferment and a general distaste for the "diktat" of Versailles existed side by side.

American Rejection of the League

Most importantly, the birth of the League was complicated by the refusal of the United States to join the organization. Here was the grand irony of the immediate postwar period. Not only did the country that led the movement for the League reject membership in it, but President Wilson, the most important League proponent, unintentionally undermined its American support. United States membership required the consent of two-thirds of the Senate. True, a handful of senatorial "irreconcilables" cleverly devised a strategy to first delay, then kill, American ratification of the Covenant. And it is equally true that Wilson suffered a crippling stroke as he campaigned in favor of membership. Nevertheless, an increasingly self-righteous and stubborn president made any real compromise on American entry unlikely. Members of his own party who favored membership with "mild reservations" were compelled to stand fast by an ailing president who required absolute loyalty to an *unamended* Covenant. Unfortunately, standing fast meant going down with the ship.

To complicate matters, relations between London and Washington deteriorated during the Senate debate over ratification. Wilson coldly spurned the efforts of Lord Grey, Britain's former foreign minister, who proposed a compromise on the Senate reservations in order to pave the way for

American membership. Grey, along with many other British officials, originally hoped that the League might become an instrument for long-term Anglo-American cooperation. But with the failure of Lord Grey's diplomacy, officials in London became fearful that British membership in the League would not only create friction with Washington but lead to unwelcome British entanglements on the Continent without American support.

Nor were the French better off. Clemenceau's initial reservations about the League had turned into real enthusiasm following the agreement with Wilson and Lloyd George to defend French security. But when Washington backed away from the League, it also backed away from its promise to guarantee French borders. Since the British would not defend the French borders with Germany once the Americans bailed out of their commitment, the French suddenly found themselves in a much more vulnerable position.

Until the fall of 1920, European leaders—and especially League officials—naively refused to believe that the American defection was permanent. But the United States' presidential election in November 1920 ended their optimism. By the following spring, the recently appointed American ambassador to Britain, a bigoted newspaper editor named George Harvey, curtly announced that the new Harding administration would have nothing to do with the League "directly or indirectly, openly or furtively." He spoke with the same contempt that thousands of American isolationists had been directing toward Europe. Although the isolationists did not speak for the American public, which generally supported membership in the League with some reservations, Harvey did speak for the administration. Only gradually did American and European internationalists understand that the debate over American League membership had ended. Because the Allied leaders at Versailles had written the Covenant with United States membership in mind, the abstention struck, in the words of Frank P. Walters, the League's quasi-official historian, "a blow whose effects can hardly be overestimated."

The Secretariat

Even before the U.S. Senate debated ratification of the Covenant, the Peace Conference appointed the League's first secretary-general, the only official actually named in the Covenant. Originally, conference officials had expected the League's chief to be called the chancellor. He was to have wide-ranging powers, including the authority to convene sessions of the Council and Assembly on his own initiative. British officials, already worried about the League's compulsory powers, sought to have Greece's pro-British premier, Eleutherios Venizelos, appointed to the position. But when Venizelos, an ardent internationalist and highly respected diplomat, turned down the offer, and when other possible candidates—including Lord Cecil, President Wilson, and Czech President Tomáš Masaryk—refused to seriously consider taking the position, British and French officials scaled down their conception of the office to more modest proportions. Rather than investing it with political authority, they redefined it as a strictly administrative post and renamed it "secretary-general."

Sir Eric Drummond served the League of Nations as its first secretary-general from the organization's inception in 1919 until July 1, 1933.

The search for a secretary-general then began. British officials offered the job to Sir Maurice Hankey, secretary to the British Cabinet. After two months of indecision, Hankey declined the offer because he considered it a step downward. Lord Cecil, on behalf of the British government, then approached Sir Eric Drummond, an officious, safe, yet bright and ambitious British civil servant. Born into a Scottish aristocratic family in 1876, Drummond had attended the proper schools and had joined the Foreign Office at the age of twenty-four. He had spent most of his nineteen years with the Foreign Office serving as a private secretary to higher officers, including Prime Minister Herbert Asquith and Foreign Secretary Arthur Balfour. He had not distinguished himself for courage or imagination, but he had proven to be a master of detail and a patient man during an impatient wartime period. Although not physically impressive, he had a correct appearance, which undoubtedly pleased foreign officials. Only forty-two years old when offered the post of secretary-general, Drummond relished the opportunity to run his own operation. However, it is significant that he never surrendered his Foreign Office title or pension. As secretary-general from 1919 to 1933, he carefully nourished a reputation as a "non-political" international civil servant. It was not fully deserved. Drummond occasionally crafted his work to serve the interests of Great Britain. For instance, he quietly exchanged information with the Foreign Office. He was not partisan, but he was certainly political.

The French acquiesced in the appointment of a British diplomat as secretary-general on the basis of a friendly quid pro quo. Both governments agreed that a Frenchman, Albert Thomas, would head the new International Labour Organisation (ILO), a separate organization created at the Peace Conference to address work and labor issues. An Englishman, Arthur Henderson, became Thomas's chief deputy at the ILO, while Jean Monnet, a brilliant, young French technocrat, would serve as Drummond's chief deputy at the League. Each deputy was to eventually succeed his chief, thereby preserving both British and French influence in each organization.

Drummond's authority in Geneva grew steadily. The first secretary-general had tact, common sense, and the wisdom to let principle yield to intelligent compromise. It is true that many members of the League, both in and out of the Secretariat, saw him as distant and aloof. It is also true that he lacked the temperament Dag Hammarskjöld would later employ to vitalize the United Nations. Nevertheless, Drummond's conservative vision and organizational skills suited the infant organization during its formative years. Indeed, the new League faced formidable handicaps—French skepticism; British fear of compulsory powers; and American, German, and Russian nonmembership. The League could not afford simple idealism. Drummond, combining a genuine commitment to international cooperation with a practical understanding of the diplomatic universe, proved to be an important asset. Certain of his attitudes, such as his anticommunism and strong commitment to Catholicism, may have hindered his relations with some governments. But his main biographer, James Barros, convincingly argued that neither of these attitudes interfered with his efforts to make the League a genuinely universal institution. That Drummond failed was less a product of his background than of forces over which he had no control.

Drummond apportioned the key League posts in such a way as to satisfy all the major powers. Because the United States had not yet turned its back on the League in 1919, Drummond appointed a young Wilsonian, Raymond Fosdick, as under secretary-general along with Monnet. He appointed Frenchman Pierre Comert to direct the Press and Information Section, Norwegian Erik Colban to head the Minorities Section, and Italian Bernardo Attolico to run the Communications Section. He placed the Economics and Financial Section under British economist Sir Arthur Salter, and the Mandates Section under a Swiss lawyer, William E. Rappard, who replaced American George Beer, who resigned because of illness. (Rappard served until 1924 and then became a member of the League's Permanent Mandates Commission until 1928.)

There were a few other appointments of importance. Drummond named French writer and diplomat Paul Mantoux to head the Political Affairs Section, which mainly defined frontier questions. The Disarmament Section, originally called the Armaments Section, was headed by Salvador de Madariaga after 1922. The Legal Section went to a Dutchman, Joost van Hamel, and the Social Affairs Section (later renamed the Social Questions and Opium Traffic Section) went to the only woman in the Secretariat, Dame Rachel Eleanor Crowdy of Great Britain. Although the League was, in theory, committed to equality between the sexes, Drummond, in fact, had tried to sidetrack Crowdy's appointment and never conferred the title of director upon her (she was called a chief, not a director). Drummond appointed a few officials from the Great Powers as his deputies, including Italian lawyer Dionisio Anzilotti and Japanese educator Inazo Nitobe. Significantly, he appointed no Latin Americans and few citizens from the smaller powers.

Supposedly nonpolitical, these appointments were actually a reflection of Drummond's political objectives. Drummond viewed Secretariat officials as liaisons with their home governments. For example, following the Senate's rejection of the Covenant, Drummond tried to keep Fosdick from resigning in order to preserve contact with the United States. He also gave special consideration to Arthur Sweetser, an American in the League's Press and Information Section who wound up serving as the main link between Geneva and Washington throughout the interwar period. Perhaps to facilitate communication and command within the Secretariat, under secretaries and section chiefs generally appointed subordinates from their own country. The idea that the Secretariat was purely an international civil service was mostly myth, Drummond acknowledged in a 1950 interview, yet the pretense that the Secretariat was apolitical did keep it *less* political than it otherwise might have been. Drummond and other League officials might have appeared hypocritical by proclaiming time and again that they acted in a nonpolitical fashion, but their apparent hypocrisy paid important dividends. In fact, Barros reported, Drummond's attempts to appear impartial were so successful that British officials occasionally criticized him for elevating League interests over British interests. Nevertheless, London often refused to give the League the kind of support that Drummond sought. The British government, like the American, remained exceedingly wary of getting involved in Continental political affairs. Indeed, some Foreign Office personnel even contemplated withdrawal from the League following the

American rejection of the Covenant, although membership proved too popular in Britain for that option to be considered seriously.

Retreat From Collective Security

Drummond used his power of appointment to build support for the League among the Great Powers, but it was from some of the smaller powers that the organization encountered early resistance. While critics of the League, particularly those on the political left and in Germany, charged that the new organization amounted to little more than an alliance of the wartime Allies, many smaller states enthusiastically signed the Covenant in 1919 because they viewed the League as an organization that could protect them from the ambitions of their larger neighbors. They also hoped that the League would provide them with a reasonable degree of equality in an international arena where smaller powers usually sat on the sidelines. Asian and Latin American officials cheered the Assembly's nearly universal character; and even the Council, which reflected the power of the large states, included representatives of the smaller countries.

Nevertheless, the Covenant institutionalized a paradox that especially worried the smaller powers. In order to prevent war, Article 16 called for sanctions—force—to be employed against an aggressor state. Theoretically, no single state would challenge the power of all the other League members combined. But what if a strong aggressor did just that? Would not such a challenge threaten nearby weaker states? Article 16 did not leave room for the traditional category of wartime neutrality. Once the League invoked Article 16, *all* states would become belligerents, including those small countries ill-equipped to defend themselves against attack.

Washington's refusal to ratify the treaty triggered a controversy over this issue. As long as the smaller states could count on the military protection of *all* the Great Powers, the collective-security provisions of Article 16 did not appear very threatening. But with the United States sitting on the sidelines, weaker states participating in sanctions under Article 16 might suffer retaliation by more powerful aggressors. Consequently, a number of smaller states, led unsurprisingly by Canada, sought to modify their Article 16 responsibilities almost as soon as Warren Harding became the new American president.

The Canadians, subjects of the British Empire since 1763, had been ambivalent about the League ever since the beginning of the Peace Conference. On one hand, they welcomed League membership as a means to step onto the world stage independent of Great Britain. On the other hand, they viewed the League as potentially infringing on Canadian sovereignty. They also worried about American rejection of the League, for geography made Ottawa highly sensitive to the nuances of American diplomacy. After the United States absented itself from the League, Canadians feared being asked to join in sanctions without the virtually automatic protection of the U.S. Navy.

Consequently, the Canadian representative to the League Assembly introduced a resolution to delete Article 10 from the Covenant. Few Canadians advocated complete withdrawal from the League; Ottawa's main objective was to eliminate the collective-security guarantee, for the Canadians understood that the threat of League action against an aggressor looked much less impressive without the Americans. Although it tabled the resolution in 1921, the Assembly debated Canada's amendment in 1922 and, by 1923, "clarified" rather than "eliminated" Article 10. The 1923 Assembly reinterpreted the Canadian amendment to mean that the Council would take each state's "geographical situation and special conditions" into account when considering collective action and permit each state to determine itself to "what degree" it would employ its military force to preserve the independence and integrity of others.

But the Canadian amendment undermined the Wilsonian foundation for a collective-security system—the belief that all states should share equal interest in and responsibility for preventing aggressive war. The amendment implied that national interest could override international interest. Because no state would compromise its national sovereignty, the amendment now stated what most governments believed. In a technical sense, the Canadian amendment failed because Persia, alone among the League members, cast a negative vote; Article 5 required a unanimous vote to pass important resolutions. Nevertheless, the point had been made—only a foolish government would base its security exclusively on Article 10. Nor did the campaign to weaken the Covenant end here. A Scandinavian amendment was introduced to permit a state to "postpone" its participation in sanctions. This paralleled a resolution permitting the Assembly to allow "each Member of the League to decide for itself whether a breach of the Covenant has been committed. . . ." Would this backsliding have occurred if the United States had joined the League? Had the Americans joined without any reservations, it would have been unlikely. However, one of the Senate reservations proposed by Wilson's political opponents would have eliminated Article 10 altogether.

On the Outside Looking In

Whether looking at the Covenant from the perspective of the large states or the smaller, all historians agree that the League's early sessions reflected real uncertainty about the organization's future. To build confidence in the League, Drummond understood that failure—or, more importantly, the appearance of failure—would be terribly damaging. Consequently, he risked little at first. He refrained from involving the League in any of the more important conflicts—Turkey versus Greece, Poland versus Russia, or the reparations tangle involving Britain, France, and Germany. But this inaction was not only a product of Drummond's caution. It also reflected the unwillingness of governments to surrender their authority to the new League. Indeed, the former Allies, the very powers that gave life to the League, continued to conduct most of their affairs outside the framework of the new organization.

To address the major issues stemming from the recent war, the former Allies used the Allied Supreme Council, which dated from the war, and the

Conference of Ambassadors, which the five major Allies had created to oversee the 1919 peace treaties. Additionally, the Peace Conference had set up specialized groups to handle postwar developments; for instance, the Rhineland High Commission oversaw implementation of the Treaty of Versailles in a demilitarized area of Germany, the Inter-Allied Reparations Commission handled German debt payments, and the Inter-Allied Military Control Commission oversaw German and Hungarian disarmament as mandated by the peace treaties. Occasionally, one of these bodies referred questions to the League for resolution, as did the Reparations Commission when the Genoa Conference deadlocked over payments in 1922. But for the most part, the Allies refused to allow the untested League to tinker with their vital interests. The League, therefore, often stood on the outside looking in.

French Premier Raymond Poincaré (left) and British Prime Minister David Lloyd George share a light moment away from the Reparations Commission in the spring of 1922.

Ironically, this Allied unwillingness to refer major disputes to the League may have helped to strengthen the organization by shielding it from failure. For example, the conflict between Greece and Turkey remained an open sore for years. It tarnished the British when their Foreign Office tried unsuccessfully to resolve the conflict, and there is no reason to think that the League would have had any more success than did London. Noninvolvement meant nonfailure, even though cynical commentators might see inaction as advertising League impotence. In another instance, the League managed to duck failure even when a dispute was directly referred to the Council. The Russians, only recently excluded from the League and beginning to flex their revolutionary muscles, attacked Enzeli, a port in northern Persia, on May 18, 1920. When Persia appealed to the League under Article 11, the Council refused jurisdiction by claiming that the Enzeli dispute was already being negotiated by the two parties. This was technically correct. The Council's real reason for avoiding the question, however, was Drummond's belief that Moscow would not accept the jurisdiction of a league that it viewed as hostile. The Council acted wisely if not boldly.

Drummond also understood that the inertia built into the traditional system of diplomacy served to limit the League's usefulness. For centuries, governments had conducted their affairs in familiar ways and took things like national sovereignty and the right to fight for granted. But old habits, in diplomacy as in love, remain intact long after they outlive their usefulness. To the extent that the League challenged some of these habits, it had to do so carefully.

In short, officials like Drummond and Cecil were cautious realists. They had no desire to involve the League in disputes in which it had only a tiny chance to succeed. They did not, however, always have the opportunity to avoid problems. The Covenant mandated League involvement in some controversial places, such as the Saar, a coal-rich area that the Treaty of Versailles had severed from Germany and placed under League administration, and Danzig, a German port that the Peace Conference had converted into an internationalized city in order to give newly independent and landlocked Poland access to the sea. In the case of the Saar, the Peace Conference had ceded Europe's third-largest coal fields to France as compensation for Germany's destruction of French coal mines in 1918. League-appointed commissions were to determine the borders and administer the territory until a 1935 election would allow the 800,000 residents to accept French control, return to German rule, or endorse the continuation of League authority. Given the deep distrust—even hatred—between France and Germany, this was not a simple feat. (For a discussion of the League's involvement with the Saar, see "League Administration—The Saar," on page 36.)

In Danzig, where German-Polish distrust rivalled the German-French suspicions in the Saar, Article 102 of the Treaty of Versailles had created a "free city"; a League guarantee would protect the city's unique constitutional status. Here, the League had less direct administrative authority than in the Saar but more headaches because of the complex legal status of Danzig. Of critical importance was that the Treaty of Versailles had mandated a constitution for the Free City and a High Commissioner directly responsible to the Council. The Peace Conference had assigned Poland the

League Administration— The Saar

Tucked between France and Germany, about seventy-five miles southeast of Frankfurt, is the Saar Basin, a German-speaking territory smaller than Rhode Island that contained fewer than 800,000 people in 1920. Size, however, is not everything in politics, for the Saar had coal—*lots* of coal. In an age when coal heated more homes and ran more factories than did oil, the Saar's importance was self-evident.

League involvement with the Saar stemmed from the German occupation of northern France during World War I. Near the end of the war, the retreating Germans had destroyed France's major coal fields. Following the armistice, French Premier Georges Clemenceau had demanded the coal-rich Saar as compensation for French losses. Although the other Allied governments had willingly ceded to France such disputed German territories as the provinces of Alsace and Lorraine, they balked at an outright transfer of the more German-speaking Saar Basin. Instead, the Allies engineered a compromise that became Article 49 of the Treaty of Versailles. The article created a League trusteeship over the Saar to last for fifteen years, after which a plebiscite would let the inhabitants of the territory choose from among three options—restoration of German rule, incorporation into France, or continuation of League administration.

From 1919 until 1935, the League wrestled with its responsibilities as trustee. Trouble began almost immediately, when the French proposed a wholly separate agreement between the Allies and the Germans regarding the Saar's status. Sir Eric Drummond, speaking for the Secretariat, believed that a separate pact might weaken the League's authority in the district and successfully mobilized opposition to the plan. But when League Council members appointed a five-member Saar Basin Governing Commission in February 1920, Drummond was unsuccessful at urging the Council to appoint a chairman from a neutral nation as a way to minimize the expected German resistance to its authority. Instead, the Council appointed a Frenchman, Victor Rault, because the Allies, so soon after the war, were in no mood to conciliate the Germans. Perhaps Drummond might have insisted on a neutral appointment if he had not recently acquiesced in the Council's appointment of an Englishman as High Commissioner to Danzig. As it stood, he could hardly deny Paris what he had refused to deny London.

The Council did more than just appoint the Saar Basin Governing Commission, however. It also drafted the rules and procedures by which the commission was to administer the territory and gave the commission full power to appoint and dismiss officials and to create administrative and parliamentary bodies. The Council also gave the commission authority to modify taxes and to amend laws. Although Council rules required the Governing Commission to cooperate with local Saar representatives, the commission was clearly the senior partner.

The Council gave the Governing Commission additional powers as well. It authorized the commission to ask Paris for troops, which the commission quickly did. The Council theoretically made the five-member commission into a supercabinet for the territory. Real administrative authority, however, remained largely local. Although the commissioners imported about seventy officials to run the various agencies of the Saar, the bureaucracy retained its prewar German complexion. Given the importance of restoring stability, practical considerations dictated that the existing bureaucracy remain intact.

Administering the Saar gave ulcers to even the best-intentioned commissioners. No sooner did the Governing Commission establish its authority than the local population challenged its work. When the commission appointed a few foreigners to administrative posts in 1920, most of the local employees went on strike for roughly a week. When the commission called in French troops in response to the strike, the Saar inhabitants repeatedly petitioned the Council with claims that the troops amounted to nothing less than a military occupation force. Allied officials viewed the League administration as enlightened and fair, but the Saar residents thought otherwise. Echoing the views of most Germans, they mocked the League as a creature of the Allies and the commission as a front for Allied exploitation. Only after Germany joined the League in 1926 did the stream of protests to Geneva abate.

In fact, the Germans protested too much. Hostile to the French, oblivious that their armies had destroyed French mines and factories, unwilling to admit the extent of their defeat, and resentful of the postwar settlement, the Germans were unable to fairly assess League administration of the Saar. In reality, the League exercised its authority in a remarkably evenhanded manner. While the local Saarlanders believed that Victor Rault had a decidedly pro-French bias, Frenchmen called him too lenient and complained that he elevated the interests of the League over the interests of France. Every official appointed by the Governing Commission had to swear loyalty to the League and remain answerable to the Council. The Council received regular reports from the commission, and on occasion, such as during a long 1923 strike ostensibly over low wages (but really a protest against French occupation of the Ruhr region), the Council even summoned commissioners back to Geneva to review local grievances.

Throughout its trusteeship, the League remained very sensitive to the welfare of the local population. The Council established a regular procedure for receiving petitions of protest and considered scores of them during its fifteen years. On March 24, 1922, a Council decree established a locally-elected Landsrat (Advisory Council); elections were held in 1922, 1924, 1928, and 1932. All Governing Commission decisions went to this Advisory Council for review, although Saarlanders correctly noted that Advisory Council judgments were not binding. In addition, the League Council created a Technical Committee, composed of local experts in administration and finance. And at the Council session of March 12, 1927, the League ordered the French garrison to withdraw from the Saar and replaced it with the 800-member international Railway Defense Force, which was later transformed into a local police force. By the fall of 1927, German membership on the Council gave Saarlanders renewed confidence in the League. Although a few local protest petitions still made their way to Geneva, German government protests on behalf of the Saar ended, along with Berlin's willingness to finance opposition to the League.

Yet even with Germany's entry, the Saar remained a hotbed of German nationalism, and the League inevitably suffered from its effects. Nevertheless, the League Council and its Governing Commission deserve credit for their usually unrewarded efforts. The Saar prospered under the commission. The commission balanced the budget, restored the educational system to excellence, and protected the civil rights of unpopular groups. Even during periods of economic recession, the Saar did not experience any breakdown of public order. The Governing Commission may have placed a lower priority on encouraging Saar self-government than on maintaining League authority, but the existence of the Advisory Council and the scheduled plebiscite were constant reminders that the League neither would nor could ignore local sentiment.

The final chapter of the League's administration of the Saar was written in 1935, when the long-awaited plebiscite returned the district to German rule. The League lowered its flag after a contentious fifteen years, but its record in the Saar helped to pave the way for the system of United Nations trusteeships after World War II.

responsibility for Danzig's military defense, even though it prohibited arms and fortifications in the city. The Allies also gave Warsaw the right to conduct Danzig's foreign affairs, although the Treaty of Versailles required that every agreement and treaty also be approved by Danzig's mostly German representatives. When, therefore, the Poles viewed their own military requirements in conflict with the disarmament of Danzig, or when the High Commissioner feared that Danzig's "free" status might be compromised by Polish treaty negotiations, it was the League Council—not local authorities—that had to wrestle with the ensuing problems. Added to this box of troubles were the numerous complaints by the Free City's minority Poles about their treatment by the majority Germans and the innumerable quarrels over League-supervised elections. Danzig turned the League into a glorified municipal government.

To escape from this burden, the Council adopted procedures in June 1925 to solve most of the minor issues at the local level. These new procedures gave the Council some breathing room, but Danzig would remain a nagging concern of the League, particularly since the majority German population resented the League as much as the Poles did for interfering in local matters. Resentment notwithstanding, League administrative efforts in the Saar and Danzig were quite effective during the 1920s. Unfortunately, these efforts often went unappreciated by the local residents and were forgotten when the Saar and Danzig returned to German rule during the Hitler years. By then, however, the League had entered its decade of decline.

A Troubled Poland

The legacy of the First World War included Germany's loss of control over areas such as the Saar and Danzig. It also included a host of disputes stemming from the creation of a reconstituted Poland. A proud land sandwiched between Russia and Germany, Poland was populated not only by the majority Poles but also by ethnic minorities including Germans, Russians, Jews, Hungarians, Lithuanians, and Czechs. Predictably, just as the Poles used Woodrow Wilson's concept of self-determination as a weapon to gain their country's independence, Poland's minorities used the concept against Poland itself. The minorities called for help from their ethnic brothers in neighboring states. The Poles' elation over independence, therefore, soon turned into a fear of more war, and by 1920, Warsaw found itself in hostilities with Russia, Germany, Czechoslovakia, and Lithuania. The last two, like Poland, had become independent as a result of the world war.

The most serious conflict pitted Poland against the revolutionary regime in Russia. The two governments fought over Poland's eastern frontier at the same time that civil war raged in Russia. The situation was highly complicated, for the French had earlier promised Russia, their ally in 1914, control over all of Poland, yet the Peace Conference had awarded Poland an ample eastern boundary (the Curzon Line) that reflected Allied hostility to the new Bolshevik government. In any case, the battlefield proved more important than diplomatic line-drawing. In July 1920, the Russians occupied the city of Vilna (known today as Vilnius) and turned it over to their

Lithuanian allies. Lithuania claimed title to the area even though the city had a majority of Jews and Poles. Because the map drawn by the Peace Conference included Vilna as Polish, the Poles appealed for help from the new League, knowing full well that the French, now a Polish ally, would prove sympathetic should the Council consider the issue. They were right. The League accepted jurisdiction and appointed a commission, which asked the Lithuanians to withdraw from Vilna in return for Polish recognition of Lithuanian independence. It was a commendable proposal, even though it technically violated Woodrow Wilson's principle of self-determination. Had it been implemented, it would have brought credit to all sides. Unfortunately, a maverick Polish general, Lucian Zeligowski, took matters into his own hands and launched an unauthorized attack on Vilna. The Polish government publicly disclaimed responsibility but flatly refused to repudiate Zeligowski, which amused neither the Russians nor the Lithuanians.

Consequently, the Lithuanians returned the quarrel to the Council. Fearing a Polish attack, Lithuania cited the need for League action under articles 11 and 17 even before the new round of fighting. Caught in the middle of this deteriorating situation, Drummond sensibly proposed that a plebiscite based on Wilson's principle of self-determination decide Vilna's future. But sensible solutions carry little weight when nationalism runs rampant. The Lithuanians were as reluctant to hold the plebiscite as the Poles were to withdraw their troops in favor of an international police force, which was also proposed by Drummond. An impasse followed. Although the Conference of Ambassadors awarded Vilna to Poland a few years later without consulting the League Council, the controversy continued to bedevil the League until Poland and Lithuania ended their state of war in 1928.

Other Major and Minor Disputes

A happier outcome for the League resulted from a dispute between Finland and Sweden over the Aaland Islands. An archipelago of about 25,000 people, the Aaland Islands were geographically near Finland, although their population was Swedish in language, culture, and heritage. When the collapse of the Russian Empire in 1917 led to self-determination for the Finns and several of their neighbors, the Islanders declared their association with Sweden. But the Finns had other ideas. When Sweden proposed a plebiscite to settle the issue, the new Finnish government replied by dispatching two companies of troops to the Islands. Sweden quickly severed diplomatic relations with Finland, while Britain brought the dispute to the League on June 19, 1920.

Unlike the Polish-Lithuanian dispute, the Aaland Islands question had little connection with the Great Powers. Moreover, neither Finland nor Sweden had much appetite for war. Despite initial Finnish attempts to define the matter as a domestic question and thereby avoid League involvement, both countries proved willing to consider the recommendations of a League Commission of Inquiry appointed to investigate the issue. The commission carefully tailored a compromise, recommending that the Islands formally remain subject to Finnish authority but with ironclad guarantees to protect local autonomy, including the Swedish language and cultural traditions. In the summer of 1921, the League sponsored a resolution to protect the neutrality of the Islands. A nonfortification agreement followed in October, signed by most of the important European states. However, Russia, a neighbor of Finland but a nonmember of the League, was not invited to the signing ceremony; European fears of revolution had led the Allies to elevate ideology over national interest, and no one at that time could have suspected that the snub would contribute to a Soviet attack on Finland in 1939. Nevertheless, during the early 1920s, the Aaland Islands settlement gave a needed shot in the arm to League morale and prestige.

Early observers of the League might have noticed that when the stakes were small and did not involve any Great Powers, as in the Aaland Islands dispute, the League had a reasonable chance to settle a conflict. But when Great Power interests clashed in the newly independent countries, as in the Polish-Lithuanian controversy, a settlement became more problematic. Drummond understood this. Other League enthusiasts, more willing to believe what they wanted to believe, did not.

Yet even League activity involving Germany, among the greatest challenges to Geneva during the interwar years, occasionally succeeded before Hitler's accession to power. The competing Polish and German claims to Upper Silesia following the 1918 armistice provide a good example. Straddling the border of both countries, Upper Silesia had three things that guaranteed problems—a large Polish minority in a formerly German area, a mishmash of Polish and German settlements that defied the drawing of clear borders, and great industrial wealth owned mostly by the Poles. Both countries understandably wanted control of the territory during a period when mutual hatreds remained fresh. To resolve this problem, the Peace Conference authorized a plebiscite in the disputed area. The belief that popular democracy via plebiscite was a cure-all for such problems was one of the more enduring illusions of the postwar period.

Matters were further complicated because the Upper Silesian affair threatened to divide the Allies. The British increasingly considered the restoration of Germany vital to the political and economic revival of Europe. Lloyd George, therefore, became sympathetic to German control of Silesia as a means of shoring up the German economy and securing German support for British goals in Europe. On the other hand, the French feared Berlin and saw Poland, their new ally, as a counterweight to a revived Germany. Consequently, French support for Poland in the Silesian controversy came naturally.

No wonder the Allies awaited the plebiscite nervously. When finally held, on March 20, 1921, it favored the incorporation of Upper Silesia into Germany. Predictably, the Poles cried fraud. In addition, the British and French quarrelled, threatening to destroy the Allied coalition. Unfortunately, neither the Allied Supreme Council nor the Conference of Ambassadors could resolve the problem, so Upper Silesia was dropped into the lap of the League.

The League reacted efficiently. The Council appointed a committee of respected international experts to study the issue and then convened an Upper Silesia Conference to review the committee's recommendations. Working quickly, the conference resolved that Poland should incorporate the southeast section (which, while small in area, contained Upper Silesia's valuable mineral and industrial resources), while Germany should control most of the contested territory. All parties, including the Council, accepted the recommendations. Drummond praised the outcome, knowing full well that it would not satisfy everyone. "It eliminated a factor which has been disturbing both the economic and the political life of Europe far too long," he wrote to British diplomat Philip Kerr on November 21. The settlement did not outlast Hitler, but it did illustrate the usefulness of the League after World War I, when national rivalries could easily have prevented the Europeans from resolving such potentially dangerous problems.

There were many disputes less important than Upper Silesia that European leaders referred to the League following the Peace Conference. A Polish-Czechoslovakian wrangle over control of Teschen in early 1920 prompted Czech Foreign Minister Eduard Beneš to appeal for League help. Drummond had encouraged Beneš, believing that the League had clear authority to consider the dispute. Eventually, however, British objections to League consideration of the matter led the League to refer the problem to the Belgian king. Both Poland and Czechoslovakia agreed to this procedure, but the king could not settle the issue either. Finally, on July 28, 1920, the Conference of Ambassadors proposed a partition that both sides accepted. It lasted until Poland gobbled up the disputed area following the dismemberment of Czechoslovakia at Munich.

Memel, a port on the Baltic Sea that, like Vilna, sat uneasily between Poland and Lithuania, constituted still another headache for the young League. Immediately after the war, the Poles administered the city, but the Peace Conference determined that this formerly German city should go to Lithuania. When hostilities delayed the transfer of authority, however,

Memel, a port on the Baltic Sea, was the site of a League success in 1924.

Lithuania forcibly snatched Memel from Poland. In early 1923, Poland appealed to the League, which appointed an impartial commission to recommend a solution. A year later, the Council accepted the commission's recommendations and approved Lithuanian control of Memel with guarantees for Polish use of the port and for the city's German minority. The League had again succeeded in reducing tension in an area of marginal importance to the Great Powers. The Memel settlement also lasted until Hitler rose to power.

Quarrels between Hungary and Rumania; Finland and Russia; Yugoslavia and—at various times—Austria, Albania, and Greece; and France and England (this last one over a nationality issue in Morocco) also found their way to the Council during the early years. Other controversies, such as a March 1921 French military occupation of three cities in Germany's Ruhr region, did not. Most of these disputes were as inconsequential as the Council attempts to settle them.

The League's record, then, was uneven when it came to resolving or preventing conflict during the years following the Peace Conference. In some cases, the League managed to avoid involvement, as with the Russian-Persian skirmishes over Enzeli, while in other instances, as with the Saar and Danzig, the Covenant mandated League responsibility. All these cases emerged from the political turmoil at the end of World War I. The disintegration of the old German, Austrian, Russian, and Ottoman empires created opportunity for the new states that emerged in 1918 and 1919. But the absence from the League of Germany, Austria, Hungary, revolutionary Russia, and Turkey increased the likelihood that opportunity would be accompanied by instability and that, when addressing disputes between the new states and the nonmembers, the League might be ineffective. Many of the disputes, including those over Memel and Vilna, arose between new states with uncertain boundaries, and most were complicated by the crazy-quilt pattern of minority populations in Eastern Europe. Virtually all of the disputes involved the Great Powers at least indirectly, since the smaller states remained clients of the larger.

The League's difficulty in resolving these disputes inevitably advertised the lack of unity among the Great Powers. As early as the Paris Peace Conference, British officials, although elected in 1918 on promises of revenge against Germany, recognized the importance of reintegrating Germany into the European political and economic mainstream. Many of them even called for German membership in the League. French officials, meanwhile, continued to fear Germany and, therefore, supported France's new-but-weak allies when they clashed with Berlin. That the League succeeded at all in resolving some of the early disputes can be explained by three factors—the general fear of disorder in postwar Europe, Drummond's caution and willingness to work with the foreign offices of the major powers, and the degree to which the disputes did not threaten the vital interests of the Allies. Where the major powers believed their vital interests were at risk, such as when French and Belgian troops militarily occupied the Ruhr region of Germany in 1923 in retaliation for Germany's failure to make timely reparations payments, the League generally stayed clear. When it did not stay clear, it risked failure. As we shall soon see, the Corfu Crisis of 1923 proved the point.

Violations | 3

The years between 1919 and 1923 witnessed a mixture of exhaustion and elation. To the gratification of its champions, the League through these years looked increasingly hearty. Although Drummond, along with the Belgians and the French, had recommended Brussels as the permanent site for the League, the Americans, the Swiss, and Albert Thomas of the ILO had successfully lobbied for the more neutral Geneva. In November 1920, internationalists cheered as the League finally moved to Geneva from its temporary quarters in London. League salaries were paid on time, and the staff expanded. The annual budget of $4 million was balanced. The League produced an impressive volume of paper consisting mainly of reports and transcripts in the organization's two official languages, French and English. Europe's leading statesmen regularly travelled to the Swiss city to attend quarterly meetings of the Council. Although critics charged that these leaders gave the League more prestige than it deserved, internationalists saw their presence as testimony of their commitment to the Covenant.

To say that the League looked hearty, though, is not to say that it had become the center of international politics. The Washington Conference on the Limitation of Armaments, which met from November 1921 to March 1922, highlighted one of the League's glaring weaknesses—the organization was not universal. In an important sense, the Washington Conference stood as a rival to the League in the area of disarmament. The Covenant's Article 8 mandated action to speed disarmament, but little was accomplished during the League's formative months. That inaction, combined with Washington's uneasy recognition that the League might be here to stay, led President Harding to call a conference to limit the size of navies. A shipbuilding rivalry among the United States, Great Britain, and Japan had been threatening to unbalance postwar budgets, and so representatives from all the major naval powers, including France and Italy, agreed to attend. Among other things, the Washington Conference managed to place strict limits on the construction of capital ships (battleships and aircraft carriers), and it secured the status quo in the western Pacific. It represented the most successful approach to arms limitation during the entire interwar period, and it stood wholly outside the League.

Other critical diplomatic developments during the period also had little or no relationship to Geneva. These included the 1922 Genoa Conference on economic cooperation; the Rapallo Treaty of 1922, which led to military cooperation between Germany and the Soviet Union; the Lausanne Agreement of 1923 to settle a dispute over reparations; and the Ruhr

French troops occupy the Ruhr region of Germany as ordered by Premier Raymond Poincaré on January 11, 1923, after Germany failed to make a required coal delivery.

crisis of 1923, in which France marched troops into the heartland of German industry. The Ruhr crisis was particularly important, for it nearly bankrupted Germany, threatened to unbalance the French economy, and ended what historian Stephen Schuker called the "era of French predominance" in Europe.

The Ruhr crisis erupted on January 9, after France charged Germany with failure to meet the schedule of reparations payments. French Premier Raymond Poincaré ordered French and Belgian troops into the industrial Ruhr region of Germany, hoping not only to punish the Germans but also to confiscate their coal and steel as compensation for Berlin's failure to make the scheduled payments. What ensued, though, took all the parties by surprise. From January 19 to September 26, German workers engaged in a display of passive resistance, striking in factories and mines, and plunging the German economy into chaos. The French were too powerless to force the Germans back to work and also too powerless to admit failure. When Poincaré refused to remove French troops from the Ruhr, the

German currency experienced a dizzying inflation, which wiped out much of the German middle class and even threatened to disrupt the entire European economy. The British, more anxious to keep Germany economically healthy than were the stubborn French, called for an end to the occupation and effectively suspended the British-French wartime alliance. With Paris now confident of the support only of Belgium and the members of the Little Entente (Czechoslovakia, Rumania, and Yugoslavia), French officials would never again orchestrate European diplomacy as well as they had before this crisis.

The Ruhr crisis did not do much for the League's reputation either. Throughout the crisis, the most serious since the armistice, the League remained on the sidelines. Germany, as a nonmember, could not bring the dispute to the Council; France kept away from Geneva for fear that the League might expose the shaky legal foundation of the occupation; and France's allies refused to embarrass Paris by bringing the issue to the attention of the Council, especially since they knew that a French veto might thwart League intervention anyhow.

So the League played a secondary role in European developments through 1923. And even when it did exert its authority, it was not very effective; for instance, its skillful administration of the Saar did little to improve French-German relations. The League played still less of a role in reintegrating the Bolsheviks into Europe. While there were periodic efforts to bring Germany into the League during this period, League officials entirely ignored the Soviets. It seems clear that aside from matters the Peace Conference had mandated to the new organization, disputes involving the Great Powers were too risky for the League to resolve. The troubling Corfu incident between Italy and Greece during the autumn of 1923 illustrates why the League remained ineffective in such circumstances.

The Corfu Crisis

The origins of the Corfu incident can be traced to 1913, when an independent Albania emerged after one of the periodic Balkan crises. Situated on the east coast of the Adriatic Sea, just north of Greece and south of territory that after World War I had become Yugoslavia, Albania still had poorly defined borders in 1921. Following the armistice, both Yugoslavia (which was disbanded amid civil strife in 1992) and Greece appealed to the League and the Conference of Ambassadors to clarify the frontiers. They appealed to the League under its authority to address issues that might disturb international peace, and to the Conference of Ambassadors as the Allied body that was overseeing the peace settlement. The Albanians, meanwhile, asked the Italians for support, since Italy had extensive interests in Albania.

The League Council first considered the matter in 1921. It resolved to defer to the deliberations of the Conference of Ambassadors, establishing a precedent in which the League would remain uninvolved in controversies before that body. Eventually, the Conference defined the borders in a manner more satisfactory to the Albanians than to the other countries. It then sent a commission to Albania to mark the boundaries. The commission was led by an Italian, General Enrico Tellini, whom the Greeks did not trust. On August 27, 1923, unidentified assassins gunned down the general, along with three of his aides and an Albanian translator, on the Greek side of the Albanian-Greek border. The Greeks blamed the Albanians. The Albanians blamed the Greeks. It is possible that General Tellini may not even have been the intended victim. Instead, he may have been murdered because of a mix-up in the commission's motorcade when his car overtook a Greek vehicle that had broken down. It is also possible that the Italian dictator, Benito Mussolini, had ordered the killing as an excuse to launch military operations against Greece. According to James Barros, the leading historian of this subject, authorities in Athens were shocked by the crime and made serious efforts to discover the identity of the assassins. Greece, a weak and unstable country recently defeated in war by the Turks, was not looking for trouble with Rome.

Even if—as is probable—Mussolini had not ordered the killing, he most likely did see political opportunity in Tellini's sad fate. Mussolini was himself a product of the war. Before World War I, he had been an opponent of Italian colonialism, imprisoned for opposing military action in Libya, and he also had been the fiery editor of Italy's major socialist newspaper. But within a year after the 1914 assassination of Austrian Archduke Francis Ferdinand, the incident that had touched off World War I, he had experienced a metamorphosis, turning into a nationalist and demanding Italian intervention in the war. Between 1919 and 1922, Mussolini tapped the resentment that many Italians felt in the wake of World War I. Although Italy had come out of the war with some small gains at Austria's expense, it had failed to achieve its main territorial objectives in the Balkans. It had also suffered military humiliation, and the government remained economically and politically unstable in the aftermath of the armistice.

In the midst of this economic and political uncertainty, Mussolini practiced the politics of anger. He was a classic demagogue. Although not handsome by ordinary standards, he nevertheless had a commanding presence. Built like a fireplug, with a shaved head and an arrogant scowl, he assumed an aggressive posture in public by ostentatiously jutting his jaw while throwing back his shoulders. Having repudiated his early socialism by the end of the war, he was instead glorifying the state and violent action. He spoke admiringly of Roman imperial conquest, national glory, and Italian destiny. In October 1922, his fascist legions marched on Rome and seized the government with the blessing of King Victor Emmanuel.

Mussolini's nationalism deeply influenced his thinking on foreign policy. He had little respect for the Conference of Ambassadors and even less for the League of Nations. He viewed both as institutions seeking to preserve a status quo favorable to England and France but not to Italy. His approach to these international organizations assumed critical importance during the Corfu affair, the most serious affront to the League during the 1920s. More than any other event during the decade, Corfu exposed the weaknesses of the Covenant and illuminated the degree to which the League had not seriously altered the nature of the international system. Historians quarrel over whether the episode constituted a severe defeat for the League or only a moderate defeat. No historian has ever called it a victory.

Some historians still wonder if Italian dictator Benito Mussolini ordered the killing of Italian General Enrico Tellini on Greek soil in August 1923 to create an excuse to launch military operations against Greece.

When word of Tellini's assassination reached Rome on August 27, 1923, Mussolini reacted forcefully. He had already been considering an occupation of Corfu, a Greek island in the Adriatic Sea near the Albanian-Greek border, and approved its seizure within hours of receiving the Tellini news. Three days later, the Italians executed their plan, the first time that a major power challenged the peace-keeping machinery constructed in 1919. To mollify his foreign critics, Mussolini requested unconditional British and French support, then issued an ultimatum to the Greek government that included a demand for the arrest and execution of the murderers within five days and payment of a huge 50-million-lire indemnity. Many observers agreed that Greece should compensate the Italians, for the assassination had occurred on Greek soil. The problem, however, was that not only were Mussolini's demands extreme, but he insisted on a Greek response within twenty-four hours. When the Greeks failed to respond, he ordered an unnecessary and brutal bombardment of Corfu, which killed scores of civilians, before his troops occupied the island. The Greeks then appealed to both the Council of the League and the Conference of Ambassadors.

If Greece had appealed solely to Geneva, it is probable that the League would have tackled the dispute with more dispatch. But by appealing to both bodies, Greece gave the Council an opportunity to pass the buck. Athens' appeal to the Conference of Ambassadors did make sense, for it was this body that had originally authorized Tellini's border mission. But because the League Council and the Conference of Ambassadors had been asked to handle the dispute, the critical issue became not the merits of the Albanian and Greek claims but rather the degree to which leading Council members were willing to address the dispute impartially—or even to address it at all.

During the Corfu affair, the League suffered from a badly divided Council. The smaller states generally favored a strong League defense of the Covenant, which meant a defense of Greece against the aggressive Mussolini. The League, said Greek delegate Nicolas Politis, was being subjected to a "rude test" and must show that "it is still worthy of the trust which had been placed in it." Delegates from the smaller states, led by Sweden's Karl Hjalmar Branting, demanded "energetic steps" in light of the breach of the Covenant. But Italy, reflecting Mussolini's contempt for the League, initially denied that Geneva had any jurisdiction at all. No violation of the Covenant had occurred, claimed Rome's representative to the Council, Antonio Salandra, who even tried to keep the deliberations secret in order to mute their effect on public opinion. Still more ominously, Mussolini raised the stakes by threatening to withdraw from the League if the Council rejected Italy's case. Corfu thus escalated from a local problem into an international crisis.

The cabinet in Paris understood this immediately. According to historian Joel Blatt, French diplomacy during the crisis reflected the interplay of foreign and domestic pressures, revealing four major concerns. First, Blatt claimed, the French government, led during these months by Poincaré and his conservative coalition, viewed the League as a mechanism to supplement French military ties with Eastern European countries in order to provide security against a revived Germany. In other words, Paris viewed the League as a convenient tool, not as an organization to replace the old balance-of-power system. Second, according to Blatt, Poincaré feared that League opposition to Mussolini might establish precedents undermining France's unpopular occupation of the Ruhr. Third, Poincaré soft-pedaled the Greek appeal to the League in order to maintain Mussolini's support for France's Ruhr policy. And finally, the French feared that a League rebuff of Mussolini might lead to his downfall, thereby contributing to instability in the Mediterranean. Blatt showed conclusively that French leaders did *not* relish the possible emergence of a radical or socialist government in Rome because they feared it would threaten French interests. In sum, they gave precious little support to the Covenant in 1923.

The British government was less fearful of offending Italy and therefore more willing to support the League. The Foreign Office under Lord Curzon (George Curzon) believed that the British public stood solidly behind the Covenant; to abandon the League might bring the government down, which all the major British politicians understood. But the League continued to mean different things to different British officials. James Barros analyzed why conservative British diplomats like Curzon and Prime Minister Stanley Baldwin—Barros called them "traditionalists"—saw the League as merely one among many instruments to supplement the older methods of diplomacy. To these men, he said, the League was little more than a large council of nations serving London's national interest and in no way challenging British sovereignty. On the other side were League enthusiasts such as Lord Cecil—"collectivists," according to Barros—whose Wilsonian view placed the League at the center of world politics. What appeared puzzling, however, was that Lord Curzon, a "traditionalist," initially approved a League policy toward Corfu that paralleled the views of Lord Cecil, who favored a very active role for Geneva. The result placed the British and French governments at odds.

Within days of the occupation, the Greek government asked the League Council to invoke articles 12 and 15, which required disputes to be submitted to judicial inquiry, arbitration, or the Council. Lord Curzon insisted that Britain back up Greece or else "the institution may as well shut its doors." Threats from Italy to "reconsider" its membership in the League did not deter the Foreign Office from supporting Geneva. By September 5, London's course was clear—Britain and its Dominions would defend the Covenant.

Ironically, the Greeks unintentionally complicated things. Having originally appealed only to the League, on September 2 Athens also appealed to the Conference of Ambassadors. Nicolas Politis, representing Greece at the Council, quickly recognized that the appeal to the Conference weakened his position, but the damage had already been done. Both the Italians and the French realized that the Conference could be used to sidetrack the League. They argued, therefore, that the Conference was the more appropriate body to handle the question because General Tellini had been a Conference agent. When the British initially rebuffed the Italians, Mussolini approached the more friendly French government about going the Conference route. He got what he wanted. On September 4, French Premier Poincaré worked out a plan that permitted the Council to outline the "facts" of the dispute and then turn the issue over to the Conference. Poincaré's strategy allowed the Council to save face while surrendering its real authority. "It is quite certain," Poincaré later wrote, "that the League had jurisdiction in the Corfu Affair," but he could not admit this publicly. The cynical French, fearful of disrupting a relationship with Italy that someday might pay handsome dividends against Germany, believed that the Conference of Ambassadors' secret deliberations, rather than the public sessions at Geneva, would best protect French security.

Within four days, the British reversed their course and adopted the French strategy. Conservatives in the Foreign Office had not outmaneuvered the League enthusiasts; rather, both Lord Cecil and Lord Curzon had come to believe that Italy's use of the Covenant's veto might paralyze the League. Cecil feared that the veto would allow a permanent member of the Council to block "everything which comes up." A continuation of the crisis would therefore damage not only the League but, by extension, the entire postwar settlement.

If Lord Cecil, the League's foremost British champion, now wanted to avoid a direct challenge to Italy in Geneva, the "traditionalists" must have been delighted. Many British conservatives already believed that economic sanctions would never work, while British naval experts worried that military sanctions might lead to war. Moreover, the Foreign Office did not want to alienate the French while other important issues—like reparations and the Ruhr occupation—were being independently negotiated. Therefore, when the French shifted attention to the Conference of Ambassadors, both Cecil and the Foreign Office came to see the Conference as a way to get Mussolini out of Corfu *and* to save the League's face.

France and Britain thus joined forces to have the Council forward to the Conference of Ambassadors a set of proposals to resolve the crisis. Despite Italy's formal rejection of these proposals, they nonetheless became the basis for a satisfactory formula—Greece would pay an indemnity to Rome and, in return, Italy would withdraw from Corfu. The Council also called for a commission to investigate the murder of Tellini. The commission worked quickly but incompetently. Although it never pinpointed responsibility for the assassination, it did include enough innuendo for the Conference of Ambassadors to blame the victim—Greece—when it came time to hammer out a final settlement.

Plenty of haggling occurred between September 12, when the Conference took real control of the question, and September 27, when Mussolini's troops finally left Corfu. The Italian dictator demanded a higher indemnity, a more sweeping repudiation of League authority, and a more direct admission of Greek responsibility than was warranted. He got all three. Then he dragged his diplomatic feet, delaying Italy's departure from Corfu for two weeks. But once he promised to evacuate the island in order to avoid League condemnation, Mussolini allowed both Great Britain and France to duck the critical question of League jurisdiction. The League should never have relinquished its authority to the Conference of Ambassadors. By doing so, the Allies subordinated League principles to satisfy their short-term interests.

This setback to the League stung most smaller states at Geneva, some influential members of the Secretariat, and the more principled members of the British Foreign Office. True, the crisis had passed and the Conference had preserved the peace, but all at the expense of the League. While the British government praised the Council for placing "the permanent interests of peace" over "the immediate interests of the League itself," the Covenant had been wounded. Among the first to realize this was Drummond, who wrote to his colleagues, "I am afraid that unless something further is done to restore the general confidence in the sanctity of the obligations of the Covenant, a severe blow will be struck at the future usefulness of the League." Italy had ignored the Covenant "with impunity" and had increased its own prestige in the process. In order to address the injury to the League, Drummond, relying on Japan and the smaller states, asked the Council to authorize a juridical inquiry into questions raised by the Corfu affair. Could the Council take jurisdiction of a dispute when one party claimed that Article 15 did not apply? Might the Covenant address the use of force even if the force had not been intended as an act of war? Did a state necessarily bear responsibility if a crime was committed on its territory? The jurists who answered these questions in early 1924 destroyed the arguments that Italy had used to defy Council jurisdiction in 1923, but by then it was too late.

The Corfu crisis strengthened Mussolini, the first of the dictators to challenge the status quo. The Italian strongman had not only humiliated Greece and received an outrageous indemnity, but he had increased his own prestige at home and abroad. More importantly, the Corfu crisis had exposed the League's weakness and thereby contributed to making it even weaker. Drummond, along with the smaller powers, understood this. Except for Italy, the Great Powers on the Council preferred to think about other things. They were enjoying what historian Sally Marks called the "illusion of peace" by failing to confront a simple truth: Unless the members of the Council were willing to invoke sanctions, there could be no guarantee of peace. Unless collective security were truly collective, there would be no security at all.

The Greco-Bulgarian Dispute

Had the Corfu crisis been the only League effort during the twenties to protect the Covenant's collective-security principles, internationalists might have become disillusioned with Geneva long before they finally did in the thirties. Fortunately for the League, other episodes had happier endings. Just as Corfu represented the League's greatest pre-1930 disappointment, a border quarrel between Greece and Bulgaria stood as its most notable pre-1930 success. Coming just two years after Corfu, the Greco-Bulgarian dispute further illuminated the character of collective security in the League's first decade.

The northern border of Greece ran approximately 500 miles, most of it along Bulgaria and what was Yugoslavia. In the middle of that frontier line was a semidesolate region near the village of Demir-Kapu patrolled by both Greek and Bulgarian soldiers. The soldiers commonly fraternized, playing cards or soccer while fighting the boredom of their assignment. But on October 19, 1925, one of those card games may have turned sour. We know few details of the incident, but we do know that two Greek soldiers died in an exchange of gunfire. One was a sentry; the other, an officer apparently carrying a white flag while approaching the Bulgarians to arrange a cease-fire. The fighting soon became more generalized, and the Bulgarians drove the Greeks from a border station on the Greek side within a few hours. The Greek and Bulgarian versions of the skirmish differed sharply, with the Bulgarians claiming that the first Greek casualties fell on Bulgarian territory and the Greeks claiming the opposite. The real cause remains obscure to this day.

Whatever the facts, a series of false or distorted messages helped to transform a simple border clash into what James Barros dryly called a "serious situation." Garbled messages received in Athens were misinterpreted to suggest that the Bulgarians had attacked in battalion strength. The Greeks responded by ordering two army corps to prepare an advance into Bulgaria. As with Corfu, a local incident became a problem for Europe. Within two days, the Bulgarian Foreign Ministry notified all European governments of its efforts to contain the dispute. Unfortunately, the Greek foreign minister had resigned just hours before word of the clash arrived, leaving the Foreign Ministry in Athens drifting when it most needed decisive leadership.

Hurried conferences among officials of the two governments filled the next few hours, but events somehow overtook them. On October 22, even Greek diplomats were unaware that Greek troops had advanced into southern Bulgaria on a 30-kilometer front. Whether the confusion stemmed from incompetence, bureaucratic rivalry between the Greek ministries of war and foreign affairs, or the military's desire to settle old scores, the Greek generals stiffened their terms for a truce, while the diplomats continued to talk. Perhaps the only thing that kept the hostilities from spreading was Bulgaria's military weakness. The Treaty of Neuilly, signed in 1919 after Bulgaria's defeat in World War I, had largely disarmed that nation. Nor did Bulgaria have allies. Unable to resist militarily, the government in Sofia did what most weaker parties do—it tried diplomacy. On October 22, Bulgaria therefore appealed to the League under articles 10 and 11.

Even before the appeal arrived, League officials conveyed their concern to Greek officials in Geneva. Secretary-General Drummond, Deputy Secretary-General Joseph Avenol, and Director of the Political Affairs Section Paul Mantoux stressed the danger to the Covenant and to Greece, which, they recalled, had received League sympathy during the Corfu crisis. But the concern of both the League officials and the representatives of the Great Powers was also related to other recent developments in European diplomacy. Less than a month before the border incident, five major European powers had signed the Locarno Pact, the most important agreement of the mid-twenties. Locarno had restored Germany to the European diplomatic fold and at least appeared to pave the way for a genuine resolution of Franco-German differences. In other words, Locarno had persuaded many Europeans that the festering sores of the First World War might heal. Euphoric over Locarno, the last thing European diplomats wanted at this time was a Balkan crisis that might undo their work. For this reason, Greece's advance into Bulgaria disturbed British Foreign Secretary Austen Chamberlain, as well as French Foreign Minister Aristide Briand. Briand informed the British on October 23 that the matter required "immediate and energetic action." He wanted the League to handle the crisis, perhaps in part because he was serving as president of the Council. Indeed, according to Barros, Briand had decided to convene a Council session to discuss the matter even before the Bulgarian appeal arrived.

This, then, was the background to Briand's announcement that the Council would consider the dispute on October 26 under Article 11, which allowed any League member to bring a threatening situation to the Council's attention. He also warned both Athens and Sofia that Article 12 required them to refrain from acts of war and to withdraw their troops to behind their respective borders. Since even Mussolini endorsed this approach, Locarno appeared to have created the basis for a surprisingly united front. The importance that Britain placed on a League solution was further emphasized when the British Cabinet, on October 23, authorized Chamberlain to attend the Council meeting. At the same time, Sir Eric Drummond independently asked him to attend, unaware that the foreign secretary was already making travel arrangements. Even before the Council convened, the British spoke in terms that made unmistakable their intention to settle the conflict quickly. And to underscore this intention, London's ambassador in Sofia emphasized in no uncertain terms that if the Greeks ignored the League, the British fleet would back up the organization "in order to bring [the Greeks] to their senses." The French expressed similar sentiments.

The seriousness with which the Council members discussed sanctions highlighted a major difference between the Greco-Bulgarian dispute and the Corfu incident. According to Barros, on the evening of October 27, the Council met informally, without the representatives of either Bulgaria or Greece. The Council had earlier heard both the official Bulgarian and Greek versions of events. Now the Great Powers got down to business. First, Italy's Vittorio Scialoja quickly raised the question of Article 16, the sanctions article. Next, Drummond offered a plan of action, recommending initially the withdrawal of diplomatic representatives from any state that violated the Covenant. Briand apparently demanded stronger action, insisting, "It was essential for the Council to act once and act strongly." Sanctions, however, presented some difficult choices, and the members of the Council deferred any decision for the time being. Nonetheless, it was clear that Article 16 was being taken seriously, and a naval demonstration, if not more drastic action, was becoming a real possibility. (For an in-depth discussion on "The Internal League Debate on Sanctions," see page 55.)

But one thing did not happen. Independent mediation of the dispute was not allowed to interfere with the League's attempt to restore peace. Drummond vividly recalled the Enzeli incident in 1920, when the League had welcomed independent efforts in order to avoid its own responsibilities. He also remembered how the Conference of Ambassadors in 1923 had elbowed the League out of position to settle the Corfu crisis. With both Enzeli and Corfu, the League had feared failure. Now, in 1925, with statesmen like Chamberlain and Briand shoring up League confidence, no one in Geneva encouraged outside efforts. It is true that the Rumanian and

Turkish governments separately offered to help resolve the dispute—the Rumanians by mediation, and the Turks by organizing a commission of inquiry—but Bulgarian officials rejected their intervention. The question remained securely in the lap of the League.

And there it was settled. On October 28, less than a day after the debate over sanctions, the Greek representative, Alexandro Carapanos, promised the Council that all Greek military units would evacuate Bulgarian territory and that Greece would facilitate the movement of neutral observers to the disputed area. Carapanos made it clear that the Greek government would not defy the League. The Council then established a Commission of Inquiry, headed by Britain's ambassador to Madrid, Sir Horace Rumbold. The commission would investigate the causes of the dispute and make recommendations to prevent a similar incident in the future.

During the next few weeks, the Rumbold Commission traversed the Balkans in order to investigate the matter. It met with Yugoslav officials as well as officials from Greece and Bulgaria. It then carefully drafted its key recommendation, a Greek indemnity to be paid to Sofia. When word of the recommendation reached Athens around December 1, the Greek government began an informal campaign to head off the indemnity. Among other things, Athens sought to deduct the indemnity from the World War I reparations owed to Greece by Bulgaria. League officials wisely kept the two issues separate. Paul Mantoux, director of the Political Affairs Section, recognized that wartime reparations were quite different from an indemnity paid by a League member that had violated the Covenant. Drummond agreed, but the issue remained alive for longer than anyone wanted. The Greeks even shifted their defense, demanding Bulgarian compensation for the first Greek casualties and for the cost of moving Greek troops to the frontier in response to those shootings. Officials in Athens also tried to soften the report's conclusions concerning responsibility. For instance, in order to make the report more palatable to the public, the Greeks recommended that the garbled messages that led to the escalation of hostilities be prominently mentioned. The Council's final report conceded that Athens had not launched a premeditated attack.

But Greece could not duck the central conclusion that it had violated Article 10 of the Covenant. This was an international crime, and it justified the indemnity that the Council ordered Greece to pay within two months. A few more requests for delay by the Greeks punctuated the process, but by March 1926, the Greeks completed paying the indemnity—a modest £45,000—and the issue faded into the fog of Balkan history.

Comparing the Crises

It is tempting to compare the League's success with the Greco-Bulgarian dispute to its failure with Corfu. In both crises, Greece played a major role, first as the victim in 1923, then as the aggressor in 1925. In both crises, the circumstances of the initial clash were murky. Historians still do not know who fired the first shots, though they know all too well who fired the last. In both crises, appeals to the League quickly followed the outbreak of

The Internal League Debate on Sanctions, 1925

Article 16 of the Covenant stated that a League member using force in disregard of articles 12, 13, and 15 would be deemed to be committing aggression against *every* member of the organization. In such a case, all members would invoke economic sanctions by severing commercial and financial contacts with the violator. In addition, Article 16 gave the Council the right to recommend that military force be used to protect the Covenant. Thus, Article 16 was potentially a double-barrelled weapon in the service of peace.

The first serious opportunity to invoke Article 16 occurred during the Greco-Bulgarian dispute of 1925. Despite the confusion surrounding the initial clash near Demir-Kapu, there was no question that Greek troops systematically and quickly occupied Bulgarian territory. This appeared to violate the Covenant, especially Article 10, which guaranteed the "territorial integrity" of all members. Furthermore, unlike earlier instances in which countries occupied the territory of others, the Great Powers on the Council were unanimous that Greece should not get away with its aggression. This unanimity was a product of many developments, especially of the unity that emerged from Locarno, Greek military weakness, and French Foreign Minister Aristide Briand's belief that a strong League meant a secure France. There had been little agreement during the Corfu crisis, but when unanimity appeared in 1925, League officials, for the first time, probed the meaning of Article 16.

Sir Arthur Salter, the English economist who headed the Secretariat's Economic and Financial Section, was among the more creative League officials during the 1920s. During World War I, he had coordinated England's maritime activities brilliantly. He combined an understanding of war and of politics, and more than many League enthusiasts, he recognized the inevitability of using force in international affairs. Aware that incidents like the Greco-Bulgarian dispute would eventually occur elsewhere, he analyzed, in 1925, considerations relevant to invoking Article 16 after what the Covenant termed a "resort to war."

But was there a "resort to war" in this case? Greek troops were occupying Bulgarian territory, but the Bulgarians were *not* resisting. Might this mean that although the Greeks were violating international law, there was no war? Suppose the Council authorized a naval demonstration and withdrew diplomatic representatives from Athens, as Secretary-General Drummond had suggested. Might this free League members from other obligations under Article 16? And on the tricky issue of economic sanctions, could the League forego commercial pressure altogether in favor of less costly and speedier military measures under Article 16? For Salter, such a course ran counter to the whole thrust of the Covenant, which in his estimation made military measures a last resort. In fact, Salter favored economic measures precisely because they would require *all* states to sacrifice, whereas military sanctions would likely fall on the shoulders of only a few states. Salter believed that economic sanctions, not military force, symbolized the truly collective character of the League.

Salter's analysis did not focus exclusively on Article 16 but also looked at articles 10 and 11. Article 10, for instance, did not merely guarantee the territorial integrity and the independence of League members but also required the Council to "advise upon the means by which this obligation shall be fulfilled." Did this mean that a naval demonstration could be authorized under Article 10? Salter refused to rule out this option, yet he cautioned that because Article 10 was the most contested section of the Covenant, it should be approached very cautiously. Article 10, he recalled, had contributed to the U.S. Senate's rejection of the Covenant, and he remembered that most

League members had sympathized with Canadian efforts to weaken it three years later.

Salter's analysis illuminated the political dilemmas created by the use of sanctions. He preferred realistic solutions to legalistic arguments, but he never freed himself entirely from legalisms. Certainly he saw Article 11 as more germane to the use of force than was Article 10, for Article 11 authorized the League to take "any action that may be deemed wise and effectual to safeguard the peace of nations." Yet even here, Salter argued, while economic sanctions or a naval demonstration might be covered under the term "any action," neither should be employed without reference to Article 16 when the League responded to a "resort to war." In short, Salter wanted to avoid entirely the use of force in response to a *minor* breach of the peace. He also wanted clear-cut legal authorization to use force, and when colleagues suggested that the League might use force without reference to any specific article whatsoever—allowing League authority to increase by means of "precedent" and "case law," as created by the World Court—Salter saw red. He derided the plan as "distinctively British and non-continental" and reminiscent of a new Concert of Europe dominated by the Great Powers. "The rights of the small powers depend on the sanctity of the written word," he wrote in defense of a strict reading of the Covenant.

What all this boiled down to was his recommendation, on September 8, 1925, that Britain, France, and Italy send ships to Greece under articles 10 and 11. Salter would not sidestep Article 16, but he wanted a naval demonstration *before* invoking (if it proved necessary) its economic or military sanctions. He was unafraid of the Covenant's force provisions, but he did worry that League measures might provoke an unnecessary quarrel with Washington and recommended keeping the Americans informed of Council plans.

Certainly no one wanted a problem with Washington, since that could easily short-circuit the success of League sanctions. Joost van Hamel, the Dutch director of the Secretariat's Legal Section, responded in detail to Salter, and Drummond commented on the proposals of both men. All three agreed that any League action must be based on specific authority granted by the Covenant, that the action must be genuinely collective, and, as Drummond put it, that "the use of the economic weapon in preference to any other is one of the essential bases of the Covenant." But van Hamel took issue with some parts of Salter's argument. He drew an important distinction between voluntary action and obligatory action, claiming that obligatory action could be based only on Article 16, while voluntary action could also rest on other articles. Moreover, he refused to devalue the importance of Article 10, as had Salter. Most interesting, however, was that although he was a lawyer, van Hamel was even less willing than was Salter to concern himself with legal technicalities. Where Salter worried about the definition of a "resort to war," van Hamel did not. Where Salter feared that Article 10 might be relevant only when an invading army formally took territory, van Hamel did not. Van Hamel argued that if the League could act only if territory was taken, the invader, in effect, could decide whether the League would act at all. This was no small matter, and the League eventually adopted van Hamel's position when the postwar settlement unravelled in the 1930s.

In one other area, too, van Hamel took issue with Salter. Where Salter refused to divorce the use of force from Article 16, van Hamel argued that because economic sanctions might be difficult to organize in certain situations, it made sense to use modest military force *before* using the economic arm. Theoretically, the economic sanctions of Article 16 were of primary importance; in reality, according to van Hamel, they should be secondary to limited military measures.

So the lawyer proved less legalistic than the economist, and the diplomat—Secretary-General Drummond—agreed with the lawyer. But on the key point that economic sanctions must precede military options, Drummond and Salter agreed. They relied on the Covenant, while van Hamel relied on logic. Fortunately for all of them, the simple *threat* of Article 16 allowed the Council to resolve the Greco-Bulgarian dispute without actually having to resort to either economic or military sanctions. During the next decade, however, neither the Japanese militarists nor Hitler nor Mussolini would be intimidated by League threats at all. These aggressors would ignore Article 16; and when the League finally had no choice but to invoke sanctions, they would prove to be so ineffective that the Covenant would be fatally discredited.

fighting. And in both crises, the injury to the Covenant was clear. Beyond this, the differences between the two are more important than are the similarities.

The bombardment and occupation of Corfu resulted from a premeditated action by a major power. Italy may not have had the prestige of France or Britain, but it still coveted—and was accorded—Great Power status. Its withdrawal from Geneva, only three years after the refusal of the United States to ratify the Covenant, would have been a severe blow to the fledgling organization. Mussolini, of course, did threaten to withdraw. Yet even while remaining a member of the League Council, he was able to threaten the collective-security responsibilities of the League by vetoing any attempt to invoke articles 10 through 16 against his country. Moreover, since the French government relied on Italian support against a resurgent Germany and saw Mussolini as a bulwark against Mediterranean instability, at least one of the two major Council members was sympathetic to the Italian position. Consequently, the Council had little heart for a confrontation with the Italian dictator.

The Greco-Bulgarian clash was very different. Not only were the stakes minor, but neither Greece nor Bulgaria occupied key positions in the European security system. Bulgaria had been virtually disarmed after the Peace Conference and was serving the interest of no other power. Greece was not only weak (though not as weak as Bulgaria), but it was also unaligned. With the direct interests of Britain, France, and Italy untouched and unthreatened, all the member states could stand painlessly on principle. By threatening to utilize the powerful, but as yet untried, sanctions of Article 16, they forced the Greeks to understand that the consequences of militarily confronting Bulgaria posed more of a risk than did the consequences of dampening nationalistic opinion at home. After all, the Greeks knew what everyone else knew—the British fleet alone, never mind in combination with the fleets of other Council members, could devastate Greece's coastal cities. So the Greeks conceded, comforting themselves with the thought that they might someday use the Covenant against neighbors like Yugoslavia in much the way that Bulgaria had used it against Greece.

In short, the League's success depended on the unanimity of the Great Powers. Yet as James Barros reminded us, so long as these powers stood united, the international system hardly needed a League; the League was no more, no less, than the willingness of the Great Powers to cooperate. When divided, as Britain and France were over the use of the Covenant in the Corfu affair, Geneva had the strength of cotton candy. When united, as during the Greco-Bulgarian dispute, the League looked as if it really could fulfill the hopes of its founders. The Greek withdrawal in 1925 contributed to the myth of collective security, which even some Great Powers at that time failed to recognize as a myth. Only the crises of the next decade, beginning with Japan's occupation of Manchuria in 1931 and ending with Italy's attack on Ethiopia in 1935, would convince internationalists that they could no longer afford to believe in myths.

Germany and Locarno 4

With the wisdom of hindsight, we know today that the mid-twenties were the golden age of the League. A series of agreements concluded in September 1925 at the Swiss resort town of Locarno led to a surge of optimism over the prospects for peace. Although Locarno became the centerpiece for the diplomacy of the twenties, other events reinforced its impact, including the resolution of the Greco-Bulgarian dispute in October 1925, the first meeting of the Preparatory Disarmament Conference in December 1925, and League-sponsored social and technical cooperation that surpassed earlier expectations.

The optimism of the mid-twenties rested on broader developments as well. The increasing popularity of the automobile and of air travel, along with the wonder of radio, helped to diminish the sense of separation and isolation common to Europeans of earlier periods. More importantly, the prosperity of the mid-1920s contributed to a growing sense of confidence among the middle classes. In this postwar environment, it made less and less sense to permit the past to imprison the present. All of this led to a serious reconsideration of Germany's position in relation to the former Allies and to their monument, the League. In light of what we now know about the thirties, the statesmen of the twenties may seem naive in their commitment to an ideal of collective security. Nevertheless, the ideal seemed more attainable after mid-decade than before, and internationalists around the world took it seriously. One point especially elicited agreement, at least in principle—the closer the League could come to the Wilsonian ideal of universality, the more effective it would be. Yet Wilson himself had failed to live up to this ideal because he rejected League membership for autocratic states. In Paris, he claimed to look forward to *eventual* membership for the former Central Powers, but he offered no timetable. What he could not know was that his own government would reject membership. In an important sense, the American abstention placed even more importance on German membership than anyone had anticipated in 1919.

Because nations, like individuals, thrive on self-deception, the Germans had initially expected much more in Versailles than they eventually received. The Allied refusal to grant them League membership turned their optimism upside-down, contributing to their fear that the victors would extend injustice into the new decade. The Germans regarded nonmembership as a form of second-class citizenship. Berlin was even more rankled after December 1920, when the first Assembly of the League offered membership to Austria and Bulgaria, two wartime allies of Germany. Two years later, the Assembly approved Hungary's application for membership. Of the former Central Powers, only Germany and Turkey remained outsiders. The Turks showed no interest in Geneva. The Germans never lost theirs.

Swiss League representative Giuseppe Motta spoke approvingly of German membership after Austria was admitted on December 15, 1920.

So long as the French would not consider Germany for membership, there could be no change in this situation. As early as the 1920 Assembly, French Premier Raymond Poincaré warned that German membership would be followed by French withdrawal. When Swiss representative Giuseppe Motta spoke approvingly of German membership after the Assembly admitted Austria, the French representative followed with a bitter statement about German misdeeds and the need to enforce the demilitarization clauses of the Treaty of Versailles. Seen from Berlin, the French looked vengeful. Seen from Paris, though, the French seemed prudent. The bitter Ruhr occupation in 1923 did not make the French more tolerant; the subject of German membership never once came up that year.

But from 1924 to 1926, the situation changed, albeit in a herky-jerky fashion. Negotiations over a series of agreements—including the Draft Treaty of Mutual Assistance, the Geneva Protocol for the Pacific Settlement of International Disputes, and the Locarno treaties—led to a dramatic improvement in the political tone of Europe. New leaders in a number of European nations clearly believed that to continue the hostilities of the early twenties would eventually spell disaster for the Continent. Along with League supporters like England's Lord Cecil, they sought to balance security with disarmament. They succeeded modestly, opening the door for Germany to join the League in 1926. It was all part of the story of Locarno.

To understand the road to Locarno, it is important to realize that the Covenant did not prohibit war. It just limited the circumstances under which one country could attack another, mainly by the investigation and arbitration procedures spelled out in articles 11 through 15. The Covenant also mandated partial disarmament among League members, testifying to the belief that arms were a cause of war rather than merely a reflection of existing rivalries. Whatever the intentions of the Covenant's authors, most nations just did not feel secure during the League's early days. To make matters worse, the United States' abstention and the weakening of Article 16 by the smaller states further eroded confidence in the League. All this led the French to develop an independent network of military alliances, the Little Entente, to provide protection against a revived Germany. The British, too, placed less and less faith in the League as a bulwark for peace. But while neither nation took its security for granted, the French made it a central concern. Because geography left the British more secure, London was also less paranoid.

The Draft Treaty of Mutual Assistance

This, then, was the background to League involvement with disarmament. Certainly Geneva had not ignored the subject; during the League's first two years, more time had been spent discussing disarmament than any other matter. In addition, a number of groups—including the Secretariat's Disarmament Section; the Assembly's highly publicized Temporary Mixed Commission on Armaments, composed of both civilian and military experts who focused on nontechnical issues; and the Council's Permanent Advisory Commission on Armaments, composed strictly of military people and much less interested in reducing arms than were the others—were formed to make recommendations in this area. Understanding that governments would view disarmament skeptically as long as they felt insecure, League officials, led by Lord Cecil of Great Britain (who actually represented South Africa during this period), proposed a scheme in July 1922 that would protect a state against aggression only if that state agreed to a League-sponsored disarmament proposal. Unlike later propositions, this one placed the League itself at the center of the plan. Called the Draft Treaty of Mutual Assistance, it gave the Council extensive authority, including the right to determine if aggression had occurred and against whom. It also permitted the Council to invoke sanctions and to specify which states should participate in applying them. Where the Covenant authorized the Council to "recommend" the use of military sanctions, the Draft Treaty permitted the Council to "decide" which forces should be placed at the League's disposal.

Oddly, the French, originally so cool toward the League, found the plan terribly attractive, while the British, under a new Labour Party government after January 1924 that was led by Prime Minister James Ramsay MacDonald, a socialist, quietly strangled the plan despite publicly praising it. French support for the Draft Treaty was easy to explain, since there was no longer an Anglo-American commitment to defend France against a resurgent Germany. Paris had postwar military alliances with only three relatively weak Eastern European states and so increasingly looked to the League to guarantee its security. Moreover, the weakening of Article 10 during the previous two years had made the French acutely aware that the Covenant did not, in itself, guarantee anything. Hence, the French willingness to support a new arrangement that would beef up the security obligations of the Great Powers became logical.

But British opposition to the Draft Treaty was a bit more perplexing and revolved around the character of the new prime minister. For 200 years, English prime ministers had come from the upper classes. Educated at the "best" schools, committed to a strong navy and the balance of power, and (usually) comfortable with an imperial system dating back to the sixteenth century, they were suspicious of anything that might compromise British sovereignty. James Ramsay MacDonald, however, broke this mold. Born into a family of working-class Scots, MacDonald had become a socialist early in life and had helped to organize the new Labour Party. He was not a bomb-thrower. He rejected the Marxist commitment to revolution in favor of gradual change within the democratic system. In fact, he came very close to being a pacifist and was even vilified during the First World War for opposing that conflict. But unlike many of his fellow socialists, he was a tactful man, willing to compromise when fundamental principles were not at risk. When passions subsided following the First World War, he returned to his respected place in British politics and eventually helped the Labour Party become the official opposition party.

MacDonald viewed the League ambivalently. On one level, he saw it as a hopeful institution, reflecting the obsolescence of the old balance-of-power system. On another level, he distrusted it as a coalition of victors, a union of capitalist states that would pursue its own imperial objectives. As did many

Americans, he favored a league that would emphasize arbitration and judicial procedures, rather than the force provisions of articles 10 and 16. In short, MacDonald and his Labour Party colleagues called themselves internationalists despite rejecting the concept of collective security. Because the Draft Treaty strengthened the collective-security apparatus of the Covenant, MacDonald had little sympathy for it.

So the British government disliked the very thing about the Draft Treaty that the French government liked—the machinery to strengthen the Council's ability to quickly identify an aggressor and invoke sanctions. To MacDonald, the treaty made war *more* likely, not *less*, and many British conservatives agreed with him. Without British support, the Draft Treaty went nowhere. Presented to the Assembly in September 1923, it died the following summer. Almost all the Continental countries supported it, but rejection by London and the Dominion capitals in July 1924 consigned the treaty to the dustbin of lost causes.

The Geneva Protocol

By mid-1924, the British were in a pickle. Wary of Continental commitments, they nevertheless feared alienating their French allies. The result was that MacDonald joined his French counterpart, Premier Edouard Herriot, in advocating a substitute for the failed Draft Treaty. Herriot, the leader of France's Radical-Socialist Party, represented mainly the urban middle class standing to the right of the Socialist Party. He had only recently defeated Poincaré and the French conservatives on a platform that had linked French security to renewed cooperation with Britain and unvarnished support for the Covenant. MacDonald and Herriot had a lot in common, including their left-wing idealism and their doubts that peace could be maintained by an old-fashioned alliance system. Neither man trusted Germany, yet both would soon consider steps to integrate Germany into the postwar European system.

In the fall of 1924, with internationalists in both countries unhappy about the demise of the Draft Treaty, leaders in Paris and London encouraged the Assembly's Political Committee to draft another agreement, the Geneva Protocol for the Pacific Settlement of International Disputes. Called the Geneva Protocol for short, it was meant to strengthen the enforcement provisions of the Covenant and place the League at the very center of the peace movement. The Protocol would be an amendment to the Covenant, providing an alternative method to enhance the Council's authority when peace was threatened. Where the Draft Treaty would have allowed the Council alone to identify an aggressor and decide on sanctions, the Protocol would refer only disputes of a political character there; it would refer all disputes of a judicial character to the Permanent Court of International Justice (PCIJ), also known as the World Court. The World Court would then make recommendations, and the recommendations would be binding for all of the parties involved in the dispute. If the dispute was fundamentally political rather than judicial, it would be sent to the League Council. If the

Council did not issue a unanimous recommendation, none of the parties could resort to war, even if it waited the ninety-day cooling-off period stipulated by the Covenant. Instead, the Council could order compulsory arbitration, with all the parties required to accept that decision.

The Geneva Protocol was fine in theory. It gave the League a means to consider both political and judicial disputes, and Court or Council judgments would be binding upon all parties in conflict. But what would happen if a government refused to accept a Court or Council recommendation or an arbitrator's decision? Here the Protocol introduced the use of force—the Council could define the recalcitrant party as an aggressor and order reprisal action in the form of military sanctions. This was the real heart of the Protocol. It closed the loophole in the Covenant's Article 12 that allowed for legal war if arbitration, judicial settlement, and Council investigation had failed.

But although the Protocol strengthened the Covenant's antiwar character, it paralleled the Draft Treaty's retreat from truly universal sanctions. While all member states would, according to the Protocol, pledge their loyalty to the Covenant, their actual military participation in sanctions would remain dependent on their geographical position and readiness. Therefore, not only could individual states refuse to contribute forces, but they could retain control over their own troops and ships even if they did contribute to a common defense. This was far from a genuine League of Nations command in which troops from all member countries would serve under one League flag. The men who drafted the Protocol had learned well from the Scandinavian and Canadian attempts to water down Article 10.

The Protocol also resembled the Draft Treaty in that it connected peace with disarmament. The Protocol was not to come into effect until a general disarmament conference had adopted a plan to reduce armaments. In this fashion, MacDonald and Herriot hoped to fulfill the original aims of those who had linked security and disarmament when drafting the Covenant.

Curiously, despite its good intentions, the Protocol got no farther than the Draft Treaty. As with the Draft Treaty, the Continental countries endorsed it, while Great Britain and the Dominions feared that it would infringe on their sovereignty. It may seem odd that the British turned against the Protocol after MacDonald had helped to draft it, but this was no more odd than Woodrow Wilson's government turning against the Covenant. In any case, by the time Britain turned thumbs down on the Protocol, MacDonald had been replaced by Stanley Baldwin and his conservative government, though it is unclear whether the Labour government would have approved the Protocol had MacDonald remained in power. Many Labourites, including MacDonald, remained suspicious that the League was an alliance of Great Powers rather than a world community dedicated to peace and equality. Finally, the British press and public were still nervous about accepting international military commitments. Because the British navy would necessarily have played *the* major role in applying League sanctions, Parliament displayed little enthusiasm for the Protocol. This would have been true even if MacDonald had remained in office.

Locarno

Historians occasionally ignore the role of individuals in history in order to emphasize the importance of impersonal forces such as economic developments or that abstraction called national interest. However, such an approach would do a real injustice to the mid-twenties. In 1925, European diplomacy became intimately connected with four men who rescued the fading ideal of cooperation at a time when the failure of the Draft Treaty and the Protocol might have left France, Britain, and Germany in a semipermanent state of suspicion and isolation.

Even before the Protocol became a dead letter, the new French foreign minister, Aristide Briand, championed its objectives in one of the most memorable speeches ever delivered at the League of Nations. Briand had publicly said very little about the League before he addressed the Assembly, but he soon became its most outspoken champion. Indeed, if any one person succeeded Lord Cecil as the embodiment of League principles, it was Briand. Yet his internationalist reputation partly obscured his nationalist record.

Born in 1860, Briand spent his early years in politics as a Socialist Party and anticlerical leader in the French Assembly. By World War I, he had moved considerably to the right, shedding his socialist principles and becoming a conservative who offered strong support to the army during the last

French Foreign Minister Aristide Briand championed the objectives of the Geneva Protocol on March 10, 1925, in one of the most memorable speeches ever delivered at the League of Nations.

days of peace. During the war, he was premier longer than any other Frenchman. Unlike his colleague Poincaré, he was not combative. He was more the conciliator than the antagonist, "an artist of compromise," according to Joel Blatt. He became one of the great survivors of the chaos called French politics during the Third Republic and went on to serve as premier eleven times and as foreign minister sixteen times. With a large, sad face and tremendous energy, Briand entered the 1920s as one of France's leading anti-German spokesmen. Whether out of personal principle or for political advantage, he drifted away from the conservative nationalists led by Poincaré and toward the left-oriented coalition around Herriot. This evolution led to his most notable foreign-policy triumph—the negotiations at Locarno, which transformed him into one of France's leading internationalists. Briand always subordinated consistency and principle to the preservation of French security and national interest. "The right to security is as vital as the right to bread," he once wrote. If French interests were best served by ordering troops into German cities, Briand would do so, as in March 1921, when Germany failed to make a reparations payment. If French interests were best served by ordering diplomats into Geneva, he would do that, too, even marching at the head of the line. He tempered his ideals to take advantage of his opportunities.

British Foreign Minister Austen Chamberlain helped refashion the diplomacy of Europe as an important participant at the conference that brought about the Locarno treaties in October 1925.

Of course, Briand did not negotiate the Locarno treaties alone. Playing equally important roles were Austen Chamberlain, the new British foreign minister, and Gustav Stresemann, the German foreign minister, as well as Viscount Edgar Vincent D'Abernon, the British ambassador to Germany. Chamberlain, the very model of an English aristocrat with his nineteenth-century monocle and exaggerated self-importance, was a moderate conservative who understood better than many other members of his government that European stability required British cooperation with both France and Germany. He was more sympathetic to the League than were most members of his cabinet and was less fearful of surrendering sovereignty to the Geneva organization. He had supported the use of League machinery to settle the Corfu crisis in 1923 and had thrown his weight behind Council efforts to resolve the Greco-Bulgarian dispute two years later.

Chamberlain's envoy in Berlin was Viscount Edgar Vincent D'Abernon. A shaggy giant who in appearance stood 180 degrees apart from the punctilious Chamberlain, D'Abernon was a diplomatic dynamo. His goal was to recreate the businesslike tone of European politics that existed during the Bismarckian era. More than any other Englishman, he persuaded Berlin and London to pursue what the French call a *rapprochement*, a resumption of good relations, which he hoped would help reintegrate Germany into the Western European community. He reasoned that Berlin would then have less reason to court the Bolsheviks, whom he despised. He was indifferent to the League, seeing it as an instrument that, at best, might occasionally serve British political or economic interests in Europe. Indeed, his contributions to the diplomacy leading up to Locarno were made without reference to Geneva. For that reason, it seems odd that Locarno opened the door to German membership in the League.

German Foreign Minister Gustav Stresemann completed the circle of statesmen who transformed European diplomacy from rivalry to cautious cooperation during the twenties. Like Chamberlain and D'Abernon,

German Foreign Minister Gustav Stresemann helped to carry his country into the mainstream of European life through his skilled participation at the Locarno talks October 5 through 16, 1925.

Stresemann was a nationalist and a conservative. Just as Chamberlain refused to be imprisoned by the memories and hostilities of World War I, so Stresemann overcame his earlier prejudices and helped to carry Germany into the mainstream of European life. Bald, much taller than Briand, with a ramrod backbone and a surprisingly good sense of humor, Stresemann had surrendered his youthful preoccupation with dueling and beer to rescue postwar German politics from the spirit of revenge so common on the right. He helped to establish a center-right party that drew enough support from both liberals and nationalists to dominate German foreign policy by the middle and late twenties. He himself remained a nationalist but not a militarist. Like Briand, he was a pragmatist when Europe sorely needed common sense.

The authors of both the Draft Treaty and the Geneva Protocol hoped to strengthen the League's war-prevention machinery. Paris's enthusiasm for these documents rested squarely on the French fear of war, and British opposition to both agreements left France feeling vulnerable. The French, therefore, worried; and this worry, in turn, gave birth to a willingness to consider new diplomatic directions. Certainly, the desire to prevent a rift between France and Britain became one of the main factors leading to Locarno, as was the change in leadership to Briand, Stresemann, and Chamberlain, a change that combined moderate nationalism with flexibility in Europe's three major capitals.

Locarno also resulted from some even more fundamental changes. For one, improvement in Europe's economic health had helped pave the way for political agreement. Although the Ruhr crisis of 1923 had led to a catastrophic inflation that threatened to bankrupt not only Germany but all of Europe, a masterful financial arrangement called the Dawes Plan, proposed in the spring of 1924 by American bankers who stood to lose billions in the event of a financial collapse, stabilized the fortunes of the Continent. The plan involved some important French concessions, including acceptance of binding arbitration in reparations disputes and a requirement that American loans, desperately needed by France as the European economy teetered, would be offered only if France regularized its political relationship with Germany.

And the Dawes Plan worked. By March 1925, even rejection of the Geneva Protocol did not dampen the belief that Germany and France might restructure their relationship in ways that would benefit all of Europe. However, while the officials who met at Locarno in October used humanitarian language, they did not act for humanitarian reasons. Stresemann sought an agreement in order to break the constraints of the Treaty of Versailles upon Germany, especially concerning France's military occupation of the Rhineland and disarmament. He also anticipated that peace with the West would allow Germany to advance to the East. Briand feared that unilateral French action against Germany, as had occurred during the Ruhr crisis, would isolate France even more. Although he understood what Stresemann was doing, he supported a *rapprochement* as a way to trap Germany in a mesh of diplomatic and political obligations that would help preserve French security. The British, meanwhile, believed an agreement would permit them to avoid choosing between France and Germany, while at the same time encouraging Germany to abandon its Rapallo ties with revolutionary Russia. They understood that Germany had turned toward Russia because the price that Paris demanded for improved German-French relations was too high for Berlin—namely, the preservation of even the most distasteful provisions (from the German perspective) of the Treaty of Versailles. London had already rejected two plans that would have guaranteed the peace via the League. If the British reached an accord with the Germans and French, London's future would be more secure. That would represent the real end of World War I.

The result was the Locarno treaties. Meeting at the Swiss resort town from October 5 through 16, representatives from the three major powers, along with Italian and Belgian officials, concluded an agreement whereby Britain and Italy would guarantee the borders of Germany's western neighbors. In other words, the French finally got from the British the promise of protection that had been lost in 1920 when the Americans failed to ratify the Covenant. With the French, Belgians, and Germans in agreement, the British could rest easy, and because the agreement said nothing about Germany's borders with Eastern Europe, the British incurred no dangerous obligations in that part of the Continent. England had again become the balance wheel in Europe. London agreed to guarantee the borders of both France and Germany against attack by the other, which meant that Great Britain would be obligated to militarily oppose France in the event of another Ruhr occupation. The price of stability was the end of the British-French entente.

Locarno meant something different for each signatory. Germany came away with the grand prize, for Locarno symbolized the formal end of French hegemony on the Continent. It confirmed German political and diplomatic equality. Berlin, it is true, reluctantly accepted what to many Germans were the distasteful disarmament terms of the Treaty of Versailles, but it did so *without* having to permit verification. In return, the French promised to evacuate German territory in the Rhineland near the city of Cologne. After six years of ostracism, Berlin returned to the thick of European diplomacy, without an obligation to respect the postwar status quo in Poland and Czechoslovakia. Fourteen years later, World War II would begin after German troops moved into those two countries, a legacy of what Locarno did *not* say.

Smaller powers have a saying: When elephants make love, the grass gets hurt. The states of Eastern Europe were the grass. Stresemann himself laughed that those states, the "servants" of France and England, "were dropped the moment there seemed a prospect of coming to an understanding with Germany." Curiously, some German nationalists objected to Locarno, too greedy to understand that Stresemann had achieved many of their most cherished objectives.

Although negotiated outside of Geneva and without the Covenant guarantees included in the Draft Treaty and the Protocol, Locarno directly affected the League in three important ways. First, the British approached Locarno with the intention of bringing Germany into the League. Here Chamberlain succeeded, for the treaty would not come into force until Germany formally took its seat in the Assembly. Locarno, therefore, brought the League closer to the original ideal of universality and made Germany a part of the global collective-security system. Second, Germany's membership, which on its face strengthened the collective character of the Geneva organization, paradoxically came as part of a regional, not universal, security arrangement. As former Under Secretary-General Frank P. Walters asked, "Was [the League] being treated, not as a living institution, universal in its scope . . . but as something that could be defined . . . to serve the purposes of a few great powers?" F. S. Northedge, an English historian strongly sympathetic to the League, recently complained that "Locarno was a sort of confidence trick," adding that it was "totally at variance with the League system." He overstated his case, but only slightly. Both he and Walters understood that German membership did not evolve from an innocent attempt to realize Wilsonian ideals.

Locarno affected the League in another way, too. The most important treaty concluded at Locarno was the Rhineland Security Pact, which required Germany, France, and Belgium to pledge not to attack one another. It also required Great Britain and Italy to guarantee the common borders of these three Rhine countries. Should one of the Rhine states break its pledge, a complaint would be brought to the League Council, which could then call for countermeasures. As in the Geneva Protocol, a state could be branded an "aggressor" if it failed to heed the recommendations of the Council or Council-appointed arbitrators. Did this strengthen the Covenant? Yes, but only superficially. On one level, the Rhineland Security Pact reinforced the Covenant by permitting the Council to order sanctions if a Locarno signatory resorted to aggression. But on another level, the Pact's use of Council authority to settle disputes peacefully, backed up by sanctions as defined in Article 16, placed the League squarely at the call of those states seeking to maintain the status quo in Western Europe—but *only* in Western Europe. By deliberately withholding from Germany's eastern neighbors the same type of protection given to France and Belgium, Locarno created a two-tier system of collective security that in the long run may have decreased political stability.

An examination of Germany's obligations—or, rather, lack of obligations—under Article 16 helps to clarify this. When Stresemann first raised the subject of German membership in the League in December 1924, he specifically requested a release from Article 16 obligations, claiming that the disarmament sections of the Treaty of Versailles made it impossible for Germany to participate in sanctions. (In reality, Germany was secretly rearming at this time.) Since none of Germany's World War I allies had made a similar request when seeking League membership, Secretary-General Drummond reacted coldly. Yet when Chamberlain and Briand approved German entry into the League in return for Berlin signing the Locarno treaties, both men agreed to soften Germany's Article 16 obligations. They borrowed the tepid language of the Geneva Protocol, making participation contingent upon a nation's "geographical position and its particular situation as regards armaments." In other words, any League member could decide for itself whether to contribute to the common effort. Locarno, then, did not strengthen collective security. It weakened it.

German Membership

Since the League's birth in 1919, the Germans had viewed the organization warily. Resentful over losing the war and over their treatment at Versailles, the Germans saw the organization as a "league of enemies," the visible embodiment of an unjust peace. Seeking a revision of the Treaty of Versailles, they feared that the League might be used by their enemies to freeze the status quo despite Article 19's call to eliminate "international conditions" that might endanger peace. Nevertheless, the Germans also saw League membership as a symbol of international equality and respectability. This, together with Stresemann's belief that the League might be used to revise objectionable features of the Versailles settlement, helped carry Germany into the organization as part of the package negotiated at Locarno. Most Germans quietly welcomed the change, but few celebrated. Right-wing nationalists, of course, called it treason.

Membership involved some unforeseen delays. A full year before Germany took its Assembly seat in September 1926, but just days before the Locarno treaties were to be signed, the German cabinet laid down its terms for entry. In addition to modifying Germany's obligation to participate in sanctions, the cabinet demanded a permanent seat on the Council, participation in the mandates system, and elimination of all references to German war guilt in future League deliberations. Briand and Chamberlain, needing German approval of the Locarno treaties, held their tongues, but others objected to this veiled ultimatum. Indeed, Berlin's demand for a Council seat nearly upset the proverbial apple cart.

According to the Covenant, the League Council had ten members, five permanent—in reality four, because the American seat remained vacant—and five temporary. As a Great Power, the Germans demanded one of the permanent seats, which opened a Pandora's box during February and March 1926. Poland, understandably suspicious of neighboring Germany, also demanded a permanent seat, as did Spain. With open season declared on permanent seats, Brazil then entered the hunt, complaining about League disregard for Latin America. Although many internationalists favored enlarging the Council to make it more representative, Berlin further confused the issue by announcing that it would refuse a seat if the Council was enlarged *prior* to German entry.

We may never know if this development simply reflected German nationalism or if it was part of a carefully planned strategy to prevent Poland from getting a permanent seat. What is clear is that it created a serious tangle just when the League would have basked in the glow of Locarno and the successful resolution of the Greco-Bulgarian dispute. Both Brazil and Spain threatened to withdraw from the organization if they were denied permanent representation, and China and Belgium announced their own candidacies for permanent seats as a way of advertising their regional importance. Facing paralysis, the Assembly acted predictably—it appointed two committees to buy time, then worked out a formula for Council membership.

At moments, it seemed as if the impasse might never be resolved. Only Drummond's skill, combined with concessions by diplomats from some uninvolved countries, helped to settle the issue. For example, Sweden gave its Council seat to Poland, partly to get the League back on track and partly in response to some complex diplomacy in the Baltic region that had nothing at all to do with the League. Some parties were never really satisfied. Brazil's claim to a permanent seat angered other Latin American republics, such as Argentina (unrepresented at Geneva since 1920) and Chile, both of which believed that they had as much right to representation as Brazil. Indeed, Brazil left the League on June 10 as a result of this snarl, becoming the first country to depart over a political issue. Spain then followed suit, announcing its withdrawal on September 11. (In March 1928, the Madrid government reversed its decision when the League promised it a semipermanent seat.) Political confusion began to look like political farce.

The Assembly finally adopted a formula that ended the controversy. It increased the Council from ten members to fourteen, of which five would be permanent; three, semipermanent; and six, nonpermanent. Members holding semipermanent seats were eligible for reelection to the Council by a two-thirds vote of the Assembly. Members holding nonpermanent seats had three-year, nonrenewable terms. Germany dropped its opposition to Polish representation on the Council, and in return, Poland agreed to a permanent seat for Germany. Brazil remained an outsider, highlighting the resentment over second-class citizenship felt by many of the Latin American delegates. Thereafter, Latin Americans would fill three of the six nonpermanent Council seats. But no one was completely happy except Drummond.

The fruit of all this maneuvering matured on September 8, 1926, when German delegates entered the Assembly for the first time. Noting that Germany and its former enemies were now meeting in "permanent and peaceful cooperation," Stresemann extolled the League as giving "new direction to the political development of mankind." Briand echoed his sentiments. The session resembled the love feast at Locarno. The British in particular appreciated it, for it meant the Germans had broken a promise made to the Bolsheviks in 1922. German representatives at that time had pledged that Berlin would never enter the League until Russia joined, a promise that was as meaningless as many other German pledges made between 1914 and 1939. Stresemann judged that Germany's real future required cooperation with the West; and London, Paris, and Warsaw all seconded the idea of keeping the Bolsheviks in the European doghouse, where they had been placed in 1918. The major Council members never considered the exclusion of Russia to be a critical problem. Regardless of the inflated rhetoric in Geneva, they gave only lip service to the ideal of universality. From the Draft Treaty to Berlin's pledge about Russian membership, the road to Locarno was littered with dead agreements.

Disarmament, Minorities, and Mandates

5

A few years ago, George Egerton, a Canadian historian who was assessing the League on its sixtieth anniversary, argued that the organization had been constructed on the "myth of collective security." According to Egerton, this myth became the foundation for all twentieth-century liberal internationalism. By "myth," Egerton did not mean make-believe ideas but rather deeply held ideals that come to symbolize a way of looking at the world; he meant a story—including all of its factual elements—that shapes that view. For Egerton, what was most important was that historians not accept the idea of collective security uncritically. Yet, he claimed, this is what most writers did, for they assumed that the collective-security ideal would have saved mankind from a second world war if only narrow-minded and tradition-bound politicians had given it a chance. Indeed, Egerton argued, League historians—most importantly Frank Walters in his two-volume history of the League and Lord Cecil in his memoirs—accepted this myth without ever realizing that it was not simple truth.

Egerton's observations on collective security can help to explain the approach of men like Wilson and Lord Cecil to designing the League. It can also help explain the approach of diplomats like Drummond and Briand to forging policy during the 1920s. To the extent that the League, its member governments, and the global public all identified the League with its collective-security functions, this myth had special relevance.

Collective security was not, however, the League's only valued work. The Covenant gave the League responsibility in other areas, too, and at least one of them—disarmament—also became the subject of myth. In one way, though, the myths of collective security and disarmament differed. While many post–World War II historians continued to believe in the collective-security myth, they came to view disarmament as a less important part of the machinery of peace. After Hitler, few historians continued to believe that arms alone cause war.

Disarmament

Article 8 of the Covenant stated, "The maintenance of peace requires the reduction of national armaments to the lowest point consistent with national safety. . . ." The authors of the Covenant considered disarmament so important that they addressed it even before they turned their attention to the enforcement obligations of Article 10. To the generation of 1919, disarmament had become a form of international gun control. Countless Europeans and Americans believed that another arms race like the pre–World War I naval race between Great Britain and Germany would *inevitably* result in conflict. It stood to reason, therefore, that disarmament—what today is called arms control—would minimize international insecurity. To interwar liberals, peace and disarmament became indivisible, joined together to form a powerful myth.

What this simple formula ignored was the possibility that armaments were a product of political rivalry and insecurity, not a cause. Just as sloppy thinking permitted many League supporters to believe that aggressor nations would never challenge the collective opinion of mankind, so, too, did it let many of them believe that disarmament would guarantee peace. The argument had grace, simplicity, and a certain logic on its side, and like all myths, it provided a persuasive and emotionally satisfying explanation for political behavior. Sadly, however, it also short-circuited the need to analyze post–World War I history.

The belief that peace required disarmament even found its way into the peace treaties. The Treaty of Versailles virtually disarmed Germany by stripping its army down to only 100,000 men and completely eliminating its navy and air force. Peace treaties with other defeated powers imposed similar restrictions. But to avoid charges that this constituted a victors' peace, the Allies proclaimed that the disarmament sections of these treaties were only a "first step" toward a general reduction of armaments among nations. Article 8, after all, did not just demand disarmament in principle; it authorized the Council to draft a comprehensive disarmament plan, which would be reviewed every ten years. Recognizing that the willingness of one government to disarm depended on what other governments did, it defined disarmament as an ongoing process.

Despite the high hopes of 1919, most League efforts at disarmament proved futile during the organization's first decade. The defection of the United States from the League undoubtedly had much to do with this, especially since Washington increased, not decreased, its naval expenditures in the immediate aftermath of World War I. Britain and Japan followed suit, creating fears of a replay of the unbridled naval competition that had preceded the war. In addition, Germany's vast military and economic potential made the French reluctant to convert their swords into plowshares. And if the French would not disarm, neither would the Italians, especially after Mussolini took power in 1922. That neither Turkey nor Bolshevik Russia belonged to the League accentuated uncertainty about disarmament; so did the involvement of both these countries in international and civil conflicts.

As a result, neither the Assembly nor the Council did much in this area during the early twenties. They did establish the inevitable committees. The Council created the Permanent Disarmament Committee in 1920. Composed of high-ranking military officers from the Great Powers, the Permanent Disarmament Committee focused on technical questions and proved quite cool to the concept of disarmament. To counter the committee's pro-military bias, the small countries filling the Assembly created, in February 1921, the Temporary Mixed Commission. Addressing the political rather than the technical side of the problem, the commission's membership included both military and civilian experts who turned out to be much more willing to take disarmament seriously. The Secretariat's Disarmament Section, organized in October 1921, played a surprisingly small role during this period, serving mainly to coordinate the activity of the Permanent Disarmament Committee.

To the extent that the major powers made any real progress in the disarmament field, these bodies were, in fact, largely irrelevant. The only serious negotiations materialized at the Washington Conference on the Limitation of Armaments, held from November 1921 to February 1922, a conference that directed attention to the sea, not the land. President Harding called the conference in order to end Washington's diplomatic isolation in the wake of the Senate's rejection of the Covenant. League officials watched uncomfortably as the Washington Conference established a precedent to reduce arms by means of percentage cuts in entire weapons categories. The success of the conference led to renewed arms discussions in Geneva, with the old excuses for inaction now making less sense. The United States had proven itself willing to cooperate; and even the Russians, who participated in the Genoa Conference just weeks after the Washington Conference adjourned, now called for serious negotiations.

Consequently, the Temporary Mixed Commission produced, in February 1922, its first serious effort and its first real failure. Lord Esher (Reginald Esher) of Great Britain tried to do for general disarmament what American Secretary of State Charles Evans Hughes had done for naval disarmament—to get things rolling, he proposed a dramatic and comprehensive cut in forces based on fixed ratios that would apply to all countries. Aware of France's insecurity complex, however, he proposed that France retain military superiority in Europe, with forces 50 percent larger than those of Italy and double those of Great Britain. Unfortunately, he really had not thought through his proposal, and except for the French, no one, not even his own government, had a good word to say about it. For example, the Italians had nearly refused to sign the recent Washington Naval Treaty even though it gave Italy theoretical *equality* with France in battleship strength. In no way would Rome approve the Esher Plan, which placed Italy in a position of *inferiority* regarding land forces. And Esher's arbitrary ratios satisfied other countries just about as much as they satisfied Italy. It made little difference that Esher had introduced his plan mainly to get the discussions off the ground. By July, the cascade of criticism grew so intense that even Esher favored shelving the proposal.

The failure of the Esher Plan in the spring of 1922 helped to uncover the raw disagreement over disarmament. Many Europeans believed that disarmament would guarantee peace, while many others believed there could be no disarmament until there was security. Unless this difference could be resolved, real progress toward arms limitation would stall. Of course, the disagreement never was resolved. For the most part, Germany's neighbors claimed that the size of an army reflected a country's insecurity, and they, therefore, insisted that security must precede disarmament. Furthermore, they argued, it was not enough to rely on the Covenant for protection. A strong aggressor might overwhelm a weak victim before the League Council even completed its deliberations under articles 11 through 15. Consequently, they argued, a government obligated to defend itself must not be forced to disarm unless it was confident of its security.

This was the kind of thinking that led the Assembly to adopt the famous "fourteenth resolution" on armaments in 1923. Resolution XIV became the foundation for much of the diplomacy of the mid-twenties, including the abortive Draft Treaty of Mutual Assistance and the Geneva Protocol, both of which required signatory states to join in disarmament efforts. The first thirteen resolutions concerned such things as extending the Washington Conference formula to additional countries and limiting the sale of arms by governments. The fourteenth resolution then addressed the fundamental issue of security. It required disarmament to be general, guaranteed security to all states by means of a Treaty of Mutual Guarantee, and demanded that states disarm before the guarantee became operational. In other words, once a state agreed to a disarmament plan, it would be eligible for assistance through strengthened collective-security arrangements. This was not pie-in-the-sky thinking, though it presented a paradox—it required the will to fight in defense of the Covenant by states that hoped the League's very existence made such fighting unnecessary. Britain's refusal to support the Draft Treaty and the Geneva Protocol, both inspired by Resolution XIV, shows clearly that political will was in short supply during the early twenties.

The failure of the Draft Treaty and of the Geneva Protocol meant, of course, that their disarmament provisions never went into effect. Not until the signing of the Locarno treaties did League officials feel confident enough to tackle the subject again. In December 1925, the Council established the Preparatory Commission for the World Disarmament Conference after the Assembly unanimously called for such action. The Preparatory Commission, as it came to be known, included all the major League members as well as Germany, the Soviet Union, and the United States. No longer could disarmament discussions be postponed by claims that a major power stood outside the framework of negotiations. With the good will from Locarno and the resolution of the Greco-Bulgarian dispute helping to lubricate the disarmament bandwagon, much was legitimately expected from the Preparatory Commission.

Once again, however, expectations turned into broken illusions. The Preparatory Commission became a welfare program for experts who sporadically produced draft agreements that were ignored by the very governments they were representing. The proposals to limit land armaments were undone by French fears of, and German demands for, military equality, while the naval proposals were overshadowed by conferences in 1927 and 1930 involving the United States, Great Britain, and Japan that finally extended the Washington Conference ratios to smaller ships.

But the main reason that the Preparatory Commission failed to produce more than hot air was the continuing distrust among the major powers during the late twenties. The spirit of Locarno proved weak. The French feared a German resurgence once Stresemann left the scene, while the British demanded that France reduce the size of its military forces. The Soviet Union was still an outsider among the capitalist countries. The Americans, with only a small standing army, refused to consider the kind of obligations that might lead to serious political commitments in Europe. And the Germans continued to resent the Versailles settlement. With some statesmen fearing catastrophe if arms were reduced and other statesmen predicting catastrophe if they were not, the technical gyrations of the Preparatory Commission had little meaning outside of Geneva. Indeed, the Preparatory Commission continued to spin its wheels until 1932, when it finally gave way to the long-awaited World Disarmament Conference. It had been five years of wasted effort, for the delegates to the World Disarmament Conference quickly resolved to ignore the drafts of the Preparatory Commission and cleared the deck for their own failure.

Minorities

If historians consider disarmament one of the League's notable failures, they give Geneva modestly higher marks for its efforts to protect minorities. To speak of minorities during the interwar period was, with few exceptions, to refer to population problems in Central and Eastern Europe. A country like Poland, for instance, housed not only the majority Poles but also Jews, Germans, Ukrainians, Lithuanians, Russians, and Czechs. Ethnic diversity would have created political headaches in the best of times; it presented special difficulties in the post–World War I period. The war had escalated nationalism. It had displaced and impoverished hundreds of thousands of men, women, and children across the Continent. The Paris Peace Conference had created new boundaries and redrawn others, not all of which made sense in the volatile postwar climate. The settling of old scores often created new ones. Woodrow Wilson and other internationalists expected that the League would eventually resolve the inevitable disputes.

Germany's postwar isolation and resurgent nationalism complicated the minorities mess. It was the victors, not Germany, who had redrawn the map of Europe, and ethnic Germans in areas like Alsace-Lorraine, where they constituted a small part of the population, and the Saar, where they were a majority, found themselves living as a "minority" under the French flag. In the Sudetenland, the majority Germans lived under the new Czechoslovakian flag. In Upper Silesia and Danzig, many Germans lived under Polish authority. And in Memel and East Prussia, Germans lived under Lithuanian rule. Had the leaders of the Weimar Republic, the postwar German state, been committed to preserving the Versailles settlement, all this might have made little difference because authorities in many of these areas went out of their way to protect minority rights. Unfortunately, the Weimar government did not place a priority on international stability. Resenting Versailles, German leaders, such as Field Marshal Paul von Hindenburg and even Stresemann, systematically used the minorities problem as a weapon to undermine the peace settlement. To the extent that the League had been a product of that settlement and had been designed to preserve—rather than change—the shape of postwar Europe, the League would face serious challenges in the area of minority affairs.

League procedures for dealing with minority disputes proved less controversial than the disputes themselves. In October 1920, the League

Council created a Minorities Section of the Secretariat to receive complaints, in the form of petitions, from anyone who felt that minority rights had been violated. The petitions could come from any source—a public official or a private citizen, a member of the aggrieved minority or a foreign sympathizer. To evaluate a petition, the Council president would appoint himself and two other Council representatives as a committee to investigate the matter, often in conjunction with Minorities Section officials. These Committees of Three, as they were called, compiled a surprisingly good record, although the confidentiality of committee discussions made complaints about League fairness inevitable.

The investigations of the nine-member Minorities Section paralleled the work of the Committees of Three. The section's first director, Erik Colban, was a Norwegian jurist and diplomat of unusual energy and tact. Highly respected as fair and humane, and dedicated to the ideals of postwar internationalism, self-determination, and equality, Colban embodied the spirit of the international civil service. He was in every sense an activist, rarely content to direct the Minorities Section from his desk. He frequently travelled to Central and Eastern Europe, the sites of most of the investigations. When he resigned in 1927 to lead the disarmament work of the League, he was replaced by Pablo de Azcárate of Spain, who served as director from 1930 to 1933. Like Colban, Azcárate won praise for impartiality and dedication, but his reputation never equalled that of his predecessor.

The League's work with minority problems exhibited a geographical unevenness. With only a single exception—Iraq in 1933—the Minorities Section targeted alleged abuses in Central and Eastern Europe. The peacemakers at Versailles had recognized that the new states emerging out of World War I contained potentially explosive ethnic mixes, charged with both historic animosities and modern nationalism. Because of this, these newly independent states were required to grant minority protection similar to that built into a 1919 treaty protecting ethnic minorities in Poland. This was a novel idea, for state sovereignty traditionally meant that a government had jurisdiction over *all* the elements of its domestic life. If a government permitted or encouraged the abuse of local minorities, that was unfortunate, but that was also its right. After the armistice, however, the Peace Conference insisted on placing limits on state mistreatment of minorities and turned supervision over to the League. Eventually, thirteen states joined Poland in submitting to League jursidiction regarding minorities. Some took their responsibilities seriously; others did not.

Certainly the Committees of Three and the Minorities Section took their responsibilities seriously. According to Richard Veatch, a Canadian scholar, League protection was never meant to cover an entire population suffering human rights abuses but only a genuine minority group subject to discriminatory action by a majority group. The League focused not only on run-of-the-mill political discrimination but also on questions of language, education, and culture. Veatch noted that both the Committees of Three and the Minorities Section erred on the side of accepting petitions rather than rejecting them, often to the distress of the accused governments. The League accepted approximately 55 percent of all petitions presented to it, which Veatch called "an unusually high proportion for this type of procedure." In concrete terms, this means that between 1922 and 1937, the

Committees of Three investigated 325 allegations of treaty violations.

The League Council had the right to consider petitions itself without referring them to a Committee of Three, but it rarely did. This was in part because the Council wanted to prevent minority questions from rising to the level of traditional international disputes that might trigger the use of the Covenant's Article 11. It was also because the Council routinely invited the alleged offending state to sit—and to vote—with the Council; an offender could then block the Council from resolving the minority dispute by casting a veto. True, the Council in theory had more authority than the committees did, but since that authority was subject to the veto, and since the committees—backed up by Colban or Azcárate—could negotiate a practical solution to a minority problem, most petitioners actually preferred going the committee route.

In light of this procedure, did the League effectively resolve most of the minority problems that were brought to its attention? The answer is a qualified yes. Veatch divided Europe into those states that were rarely the subject of a complaint, those that were cooperative when charged with a violation, those that were occasionally cooperative, and those that were flatly uncooperative. Only two states—Turkey and Lithuania—fell into the last category, while Poland, Greece, and Rumania usually improved their treatment of minorities in the face of real pressure. The remaining states bound by the treaties had reasonably good records. Most of them rarely discriminated against minorities and responded quickly to League recommendations. In addition, certain petitions accepted for investigation by the Council were of questionable validity. Some governments, such as Berlin, occasionally used minority issues for reasons that had little to do with protecting their ethnic brothers and sisters, and much to do with larger political objectives.

The political use and abuse of the minority issue constituted some of the League's most challenging work during the interwar years. Observers have noted that the vitality of the minority-protection system in Geneva reflected the vitality of the League itself. Few petitions arrived during the League's first two years; thereafter, petitions poured in until 1932, when the League was wounded by the Manchurian crisis and entered a period of decline. After the League failed to resolve the Italo-Ethiopian crisis in the mid-1930s, it developed a case of political rigor mortis. It is unsurprising that no minority petitions arrived after 1937. By then, the League, having suffered the withdrawal of Germany, Italy, and Japan as well as a general loss of confidence, could no longer protect abused minorities.

Yet even during the 1920s, when most of the minority petitions arrived in Geneva, League activity in this field cannot be understood without also recognizing the critical role played by Germany. Under Nobel Peace Prize-winning Foreign Minister Gustav Stresemann, Germany championed the German-speaking populations of Poland, Czechoslovakia, Lithuania, and France even before entering the League in 1926. Stresemann genuinely believed that German minorities in Eastern Europe and France were suffering unjustly in fields such as employment, education, and cultural expression. But Stresemann was not a sentimental man. He shrewdly calculated that defending minority rights could pay both international and domestic dividends for his government.

On the international side, Stresemann understood that the minority issue could be used to assert German claims to territories that the Treaty of Versailles had ceded to the new states in Eastern Europe. Unlike Hitler, Stresemann hoped to avoid using force to reassert Germany's title, but like most German nationalists, he also resented the treaty's grant of independence to Poland, Czechoslovakia, and Lithuania. Posing as the protector of German minorities in Eastern Europe, he kept German expansionist claims alive by charging that the new states were failing to live up to the standards established at Versailles. By publicizing violations of minority rights, he subtly discredited the new states and, by extension, the entire Versailles settlement. And publicize them he did. Stresemann was instrumental in providing financial and organizational support to German minorities in Eastern Europe. He helped to publish their newspapers and to sponsor their periodic congresses. He also encouraged them to submit petitions of protest to the League, firing up resentment in minority German communities from Rumania to France. Although millions of Germans opposed the League, they used its minority machinery to further their expansionist agenda.

Stresemann's policy also paid domestic dividends. During his tenure as foreign minister, from 1923 to 1929, his harshest critics came from the political right, the extreme nationalists who considered him too moderate and too willing to work within the political structure that had been constructed at Versailles. These nationalists hated the new states, hated France, hated internationalism, and hated the League. Stresemann shrewdly blunted their criticism of his Geneva policy by focusing on the minority issue. For underneath the minority issue ran powerful currents of German nationalism and expansionism, and his demagoguery helped to keep the German right on a tight leash until he left office at the end of the decade.

There was one final irony here. Ostensibly a champion of minority rights, Stresemann hoped to avoid charges of hypocrisy by defending the rights of non-German groups in his own country. He therefore endorsed legislation in the Reichstag giving full autonomy to Germany's "linguistic minorities," such as the Poles and Danes, though he did not extend such autonomy to assimilated groups, such as the German Jews. According to historian Carole Fink, who studied this neglected aspect of Stresemann's career, he only partly succeeded. He faced opposition from nationalists, who protested the mistreatment of ethnic Germans abroad but proved quite willing to abuse non-German minorities at home, and he encountered indifference from most other Germans. In actual fact, Stresemann had only limited influence in the area of domestic policy, and his successors quickly abandoned his efforts to protect non-German minorities within Germany. After the Nazi triumph in 1933, Berlin abruptly stopped using the League to protect German minorities elsewhere, a prelude to Hitler's decision to withdraw from the League in October of that year.

Although the League did not begin to decline for some years after he retired from politics, Stresemann contributed to the process by turning the League's minority machinery—created to diminish ethnic unrest in Eastern Europe and, therefore, to serve the status quo—into a tool for subverting the Geneva organization. He did not do this violently. Perhaps if Germany had had greater military might during the 1920s, he would have used the army rather than the League of Nations to protect German minorities.

Perhaps not. What he did do, however, was to use internationalism to serve German nationalism, and he tamed German extremists in order to reintegrate Germany into Europe and the League. It was a delicate balancing act. Successful during Stresemann's lifetime, it unintentionally prepared the way for the Nazis within four years of his death.

Mandates

Although the League could not end all abuse of minorities in Europe, it did achieve some success in this area before the advent of Hitler. Similarly, the mandate system administered by the League of Nations was also a story of partial success. Mandates represented a transition from nineteenth-century colonialism to twentieth-century self-determination. It was Woodrow Wilson at Versailles who articulated the self-determination ideal. He viewed the mandate system, the brainchild of South African General Jan Smuts, as a means to reach the ideal, for the system could help move people from colonial status to independence. It undoubtedly owed part of its existence to liberal idealism, but it also had roots in the imperial realities that existed at the time of the armistice.

Mandates involved administrative supervision by Great Powers of former colonial lands. Because nations, like individuals, rarely give up voluntarily what they do not have to give up, it came as no surprise that the Allies applied the new concept only to the former colonies of Germany. No British, French, Belgian, Japanese, or American colonies were included among the mandates. Indeed, the colonial powers among the former Allies saw their imperial authority increased, not decreased, as the Peace Conference granted them administrative control over the colonies of their former enemies. The Americans alone refused to participate in this post-colonial system.

The Allied Supreme Council, known simply as the Supreme Council, created the mandate system, but the League administered it. Article 22 of the Covenant stipulated that former colonies "inhabited by peoples not yet able to stand by themselves under the strenuous conditions of the modern world" would be placed under the tutelage of the "advanced" nations. But the Supreme Council, not the League, decided which former colonies would be included in the system and what the status of each would be. The colonies they designated as "A" mandates were all located in the Mideast and considered well along the road to independence. The "B" mandates included the sub-Sahara African territories except for South West Africa. The "C" mandates were those at the "lowest" stage of development; for them, independence was not seen as an option at all. Concerning this last group, the Supreme Council granted South Africa mandatory responsibility over formerly German South West Africa, and Australia over New Guinea. The following table shows the mandates supervised by League of Nations members. The mandates are grouped by developmental designation—"A," "B," or "C." The second column lists the mandates, and the third column names the supervisory powers.

In November 1920, the first League Assembly created the Permanent Mandates Commission to review the annual reports submitted by the supervisory powers. Known as the Mandates Commission, it was no ordinary commission. Its authority came directly from the Covenant, and as its name implied, it was a permanent body. Indeed, the Mandates Commission really administered the entire system, and its recommendations were routinely accepted by the Council and Assembly. Yet the commission's authority during the early twenties was surprisingly tenuous. It had no precedents upon which to base its work, and it had no power to enforce its edicts. Its authority was, in fact, quite fuzzy. Technically, the mandatory powers were not sovereign in the territories they supervised, but then the League itself had no sovereign power. The Mandates Commission, in Geneva, stood thousands of miles from its territories, and unlike the Minorities Section, it lacked the power to demand access to the mandates even when conducting investigations. During an investigation, the Mandates Commission had to rely on information supplied by the government holding the mandate. This was equivalent to doing cancer studies by relying exclusively on data supplied by tobacco companies.

That the commission was at least somewhat successful testifies to the quality of its staff, which was led by William E. Rappard of Switzerland. An outspoken internationalist, Rappard had an incisive mind and a willingness to speak honestly yet tactfully. In addition, it was to his advantage that he came from a neutral and noncolonial country. Unfortunately, his authority was circumscribed by that of the commission's chairman, Italy's Marchese Alberto Theodoli, a less impressive figure whose long tenure in Geneva stemmed from his unwillingness to challenge the Great Powers. But Theodoli's weakness was not so much personal as it was institutional; even if he had been replaced by Napoleon, the commission still would have possessed little real power. It could not even censure the mandatory states when

Mandates Supervised by League Members

	Mandate	Supervisor
"A"	Palestine	Britain
	Transjordan	Britain
	Iraq	Britain
	Syria	France
	Lebanon	France
"B"	Cameroons	France
	Cameroons	Britain
	Togoland	France
	Togoland	Britain
	Tanganyika	Britain
	Ruanda-Urundi	Belgium
"C"	North Pacific islands	Japan
	South West Africa	South Africa
	Western Samoa	New Zealand
	New Guinea	Australia
	Naura	Britain and Australia

they refused to provide the limited data it requested.

Like the Minorities Section, the Mandates Commission was only moderately effective. Two countries, France and Belgium, fully respected the recommendations of the commission. On the other hand, South Africa generally ignored the commission and exercised its authority in South West Africa as colonialism pure and simple; indeed, Smuts himself reportedly called Pretoria's mandate an "annexation in all but name." The other mandatory countries fell somewhere between these two extremes.

Certainly racism played an important part in the attitude of some of the mandatory powers. South Africa spent seven times more money on education for whites in a mandate where blacks outnumbered whites by a ratio of ten to one. And when South African officials ordered a shocking and bloody end to a minor revolt in 1922, they remained in office despite a blistering report issued by the Mandates Commission. Racism also played a part in Britain's reluctance to establish institutions of self-government in Central Africa, and the same criticism could be levelled against France and Japan. From San Francisco to Eastern Europe, Darwinian theory had convinced Caucasians that they were destined to rule over nonwhites, and the Japanese had their own version of this dogma. The result was racial condescension and fear-driven contempt. In light of all this, it is surprising that the mandate system worked as well as it did.

The most notable success of the mandate system came in 1929, when the British government recommended independence and League membership for Iraq. It took three more years before the Council, working through the Mandates Commission, established criteria for ending a mandate and assured itself that Iraq met those criteria (except in the area of protecting minority rights—in fact, during the Iran-Iraq War between 1980 and 1988, Iraq's use of poisonous gas to subjugate its Kurdish minority reminds us that the Mandates Commission long ago identified a painful problem). There was never any doubt that the commission would endorse the British recommendation. London's decision to end the mandate stemmed from its desire to avoid the sad experience of the French in nearby Lebanon and Syria, where Arab nationalism had violently disrupted orderly administration. The decision also followed Iraq's promise to give Britain access to both oil and airfields following the grant of independence.

But the Iraq mandate was a relatively simple matter compared to Britain's other "A" mandate in the Mideast—Palestine. Here, the Mandates Commission could no more guarantee order during the interwar years than a hot dog can bark. Palestine had lived under Turkish rule for centuries, and during the Great War, the British had shrewdly made promises to both the Jews and Arabs to undermine Turkey's influence. With the defeat of Turkey, which had been one of the Central Powers, Britain agreed to accept Palestine as a mandate. Now British officials had to make good on their contradictory promises. To the Jews, London had promised a homeland. To the Arabs, London had promised restrictions on Jewish immigration. When the Jewish population began to increase during the 1920s, the fears of Palestinian Arabs reinforced existing anti-Jewish prejudice. The result was predictable. In August 1929, destructive Arab attacks on Jewish communities signified the breakdown of order in Palestine. Investigations led to reports, which led to meetings of the Mandates Commission, which led to commission recommendations, which led to angry accusations. Britain, it seems, had failed to take even elementary precautions to prevent bloodshed.

The Palestine investigation was one of the few cases where the Mandates Commission sharply challenged a mandatory power. It mattered little. In 1933, violence flared once again, and the situation deteriorated steadily just when Nazi persecutions intensified demands for Jewish immigration into Palestine. The British tried to resolve the problem but failed, and by the end of the 1930s, London realized that a single state containing both Jews and Arabs had become an impossibility. Partitioning the state, never foreseen within the original mandate, became the new British policy shortly before Hitler plunged Europe into the Second World War. But the growth of Jewish and Arab nationalism during the subsequent years made a shambles of this policy, too. London finally walked away from the problem that its League of Nations mandate had complicated, not resolved.

To the End of the Decade 6

Even though the League continued to wrestle with the frustrating issues surrounding disarmament, minorities, and mandates, the early years of German membership turned out to be among the League's least troubled. French fears that Germany's entry into the League would demolish the status quo turned out to be unfounded. German membership not only increased the confidence and morale of League officials but also simplified League efforts in fields like minority protection. Secretary-General Sir Eric Drummond went out of his way to make the Germans feel at home by appointing a high-ranking (although ineffectual) German diplomat, Albert Freiherr Dufour-Féronce, as an under secretary-general. He also made room for a German on the Permanent Mandates Commission and appointed others elsewhere in the Secretariat. He generally accorded Berlin all the recognition he offered the other Great Powers, understanding that anything less would open the door to renewed German charges that the League was a tool of the former Allies.

Germany at Geneva

One problem, however, not only remained persistent but became even more troublesome for the League after Germany joined—Danzig. The relationship between the Germans and Poles in Danzig had not improved since the armistice, leading Drummond to steer a middle course through what James Barros called "a delicate situation." Drummond knew that France, an ally of Poland, and Germany were ready to use the Council to protect their interests in Danzig, so he sought to keep the matter off the Council's agenda while he pursued what a later generation would call damage control. The trivial quarrels in Danzig that claimed his attention have left historians wondering just what the fuss was about, but all of the questions—including the most technical—were actually loaded with political meaning. Drummond, often called a technician, had good political instincts, and he displayed them while trying to minimize the friction over Danzig.

For all Drummond's efforts, though, the Germans never did fit smoothly into the League system. During the immediate aftermath of Locarno, Stresemann was willing to work within the system in order to best serve his country's interests. His minorities campaign illustrated the German approach to Geneva during this period. But the foreign ministry in Berlin also tried to use the League to end German inferiority in the armaments field. Stresemann insisted on full military equality in order to reverse the verdict of the Peace Conference. In both fields, minorities and disarmament, Stresemann encountered delays and frustrations that eroded his position at home, where he already faced criticism by the nationalist right. But Stresemann had good reason not to alienate the British and French, and his willingness to remain a part of the Geneva system continued until he left office in 1929.

Yet even under Stresemann, German policy did weaken the League. In the months following Locarno, Stresemann conspired with his British and French counterparts to convert the permanent members of the League Council into an executive committee of Europe. Ignoring the Council's nonpermanent members, these Locarno statesmen met in highly publicized but private "tea parties" to discuss general European problems. By meeting outside of Geneva, they diminished the Council and even the League itself. Nevertheless, Germany under Stresemann remained moderate in its criticism of the League, and only after Stresemann left the scene did Germany become much less willing to compromise at Geneva. Once Stresemann retired, the far right, led by Hitler's brown-shirted Nazis, made the League a convenient scapegoat for German frustrations. The only wonder is why German membership remained constructive for as long as it did, because after 1919, Germany's main objective was always to revise the Treaty of Versailles even though the League had been created in large measure to preserve that settlement.

The Kellogg-Briand Pact

The bloom from the Locarno settlement soon faded. Continual efforts by Germany to revise the Treaty of Versailles prompted worried French officials to step up efforts to insure their security. If Briand had rested easier after Stresemann signed the Locarno treaties, within a year he understood that the agreements had strengthened Germany's ability to press for further revision of the postwar peace. Other developments deepened the sense of unease felt by Briand and his fellow internationalists. A 1927 naval conference, which organizers hoped would extend the limitations of the 1922 Washington Conference, produced one of the more depressing failures of the decade. The Americans and British agreed on nothing. Italy, meanwhile, made overtures to such Eastern European governments as Hungary and Albania, considered hostile to the Versailles settlement. Mussolini openly advertised his disdain for both the status quo and its guarantor, the League, by signing a pact of friendship with Hungary in April 1927. He then shipped his former enemy weapons prohibited by the 1920 Treaty of Trianon.

Mussolini's foray into Eastern Europe helped to persuade Briand that France must strengthen its mutual-security treaties with Poland and the Little Entente (Czechoslovakia, Yugoslavia, and Rumania). But Briand's continuing fear of German revival also led him to look west, to the United States, as a means of securing the French flank in the event of another war. Although the French foreign minister knew that the Americans had no interest in reconsidering membership in the League or in signing the same kind of mutual-security guarantee that linked France with its Eastern

European allies, he indirectly tried to lure the Americans into the French security system by means of a nonaggression pact. He proposed that the United States and France mutually pledge not to use force against each other. This would guarantee American neutrality in a war between France and any of its rivals, including Germany or even—implausibly—Great Britain. Washington knew that neither London nor Berlin would appreciate the United States slipping quietly into the French orbit, even if only as a distant star. But American Secretary of State Frank Kellogg, who represented an administration that took political isolation from Europe seriously, also understood that he could not simply reject what appeared to be a friendly statement of peaceful intentions. Kellogg's dilemma became even more acute when leaders of the American peace movement endorsed Briand's project.

To escape his predicament, Kellogg turned the diplomatic tables on the French, informing Briand that the Americans would sign an agreement only if other countries were invited to sign as well. In other words, he proposed a multilateral treaty, not just a bilateral treaty, to renounce war "as an instrument of national policy." When word of the plan reached the League, Drummond quickly recognized that it might help to bridge the gap between Washington and Geneva. He understood that the proposal was consistent in principle with the peaceful purposes of the League, though he also saw some problems. For instance, while the proposed treaty would renounce all wars, the Covenant permitted war if mediation efforts failed and a "cooling-off" period elapsed. Moreover, he worried that the Americans would insist on a clause permitting the use of force to defend the Monroe Doctrine, though he decided to remain silent on this subject as long as the Americans did not raise it publicly.

There is no question that League supporters of a pacifist persuasion favored the Kellogg-Briand proposal precisely because it appeared to "close the loophole" in the Covenant regarding legal war. Drummond, of course, appreciated this, but at the same time, he worried that the proposed treaty would actually complicate the League's work without drawing the Americans closer to Geneva. In the final analysis, however, his concerns were irrelevant. He came to understand, as did British Foreign Secretary Austen Chamberlain, that involving the League in the Kellogg-Briand negotiations would likely kill the project. Both men believed that Washington was already so nervous about an agreement with European states that any League involvement would produce an isolationist counterattack. Drummond was acutely aware of the weaknesses of the Kellogg-Briand proposal—it failed to define legal war, it lacked an enforcement mechanism, and it refused to call even for consultation in the event of its violation. Drummond was also aware of the inconsistencies between the Covenant and the Kellogg-Briand proposal. Nevertheless, he believed these inconsistencies were insubstantial when placed against the advantage of having the United States once again involved with Geneva.

Whatever Drummond's attitude, it was Washington and Paris, not Geneva, that made the key diplomatic moves to support the proposal. Kellogg, initially cool to Briand's plan, warmed up considerably because of popular support for the treaty combined with his personal interest in a Nobel Peace Prize. By the time he actually signed the treaty, he had even become enthusiastic about the whole thing. Ironically, Briand was beginning to lose his enthusiasm, but he could no longer back out. Besides, he hoped—wrongly, as it turned out—that the pact would signal the end of American isolation, and he hoped—correctly—that it would not conflict with the security provisions of the Covenant. In the end, the pact did not have the political significance that Briand had anticipated, but it did little harm beyond raising unrealistic expectations concerning the prospects for peace. And, of course, Briand, who had already won a Nobel Peace Prize for his Locarno diplomacy, shared with Kellogg the dream of winning one for his role as coauthor of the pact.

Signed by fifty-five nations on August 27, 1928, the Kellogg-Briand Pact generated so much euphoria that it was bound to disappoint its champions. Historians often claim that most governments simply ignored the pact, but this is an overly cynical judgment. For one thing, governments took note of the pact by their refusal to issue declarations of war when sending their young men into battle. In this fashion, they hoped to avoid the charge that they had illegally resorted to war. By not acting "illegally," they might avoid the collective-security machinery of the Covenant. Japan refused to issue a declaration of war when it invaded Manchuria in 1931; Italy followed suit in 1935 when it sent troops into Ethiopia.

American President Calvin Coolidge (seated, second from left) signs the Kellogg-Briand Pact on August 31, 1928. Next to Coolidge (seated, center) is American Secretary of State Frank B. Kellogg.

But the pact also contributed to another development of significance. It brought the United States and the League a bit closer. The small but articulate American internationalist community had pressured the State Department to coordinate the pact with the Covenant. The crux of the internationalist argument was that the United States should not take any action that might directly or indirectly aid a country violating the Kellogg-Briand Pact. In practical terms, this meant three things—the United States should not increase trade with an aggressor nation violating the pact if the League had already invoked economic sanctions; Washington should consult with all fifty governments that had signed both the pact and the Covenant in order to minimize any possibility that American action might unintentionally weaken the League; and the United States should announce both of these policies in advance so that League members could begin contingency planning before invoking the Covenant's Article 16. Henry L. Stimson, the American secretary of state between 1929 and 1933, was perhaps his country's most influential proponent of collective security and boldly endorsed all three points, but the State Department after 1933 retreated from his pro-League stance because the Great Depression and the growing fear of European war reinforced the isolationist tendencies of the American public.

Austria and Hungary

Fortunately for the League, the middle and late twenties were generally years of calm. The relative harmony of the period boosted the League's reputation, as did prosperity in Europe and North America. Prosperity came with the development of new technologies in the automobile, aircraft, electrical, and chemical industries, as well as with the return of consumer demand following the dislocations of World War I. But the economic revival also owed much to the 1924 Dawes financial program for Germany. By means of massive loans, the Dawes Plan helped to end Germany's ruinous inflation and contributed to the restoration of Europe's economic well-being.

Most historians are familiar with the results of the Dawes Plan. Few historians, however, realize that post–World War I League efforts to restore Austria to financial health served as its precedent. The historic Austro-Hungarian Empire had disintegrated in 1919, leaving a defeated country crippled by debt, dizzying inflation, and the loss of its imperial sources of wealth. Austria's financial weakness exceeded even that of Germany, worrying Allied officials, who feared that Vienna's economic collapse would ripple across Central Europe. Italy, Czechoslovakia, England, and France each extended loans to Austria between 1920 and 1922. When the Austrians proved unable to repay them, the Allied Supreme Council turned the problem over to the League Council.

In less than six weeks, the League's Financial Committee produced an imaginative proposal to bail Austria out of its predicament. Based on a protocol adopted on October 4, 1922, the League established a commission that, with Vienna's cooperation, drafted plans for a strict austerity program, streamlined the process for collecting revenues, and provided desperately needed loans guaranteed by other European governments. During the mid-1920s, Austria did what New York City would do during the 1970s—it carefully and painfully put its financial house back into order. Newly balanced budgets and reduced debt meant an end to the threat of economic chaos, at least for as long as prosperity lasted. But the plan came with conditions, including direct League supervision of the program and an Austrian promise not to seek political union with Germany. Austrian leaders grumbled about the supervision, while German nationalists resented the prohibition on a political union, but the League refused to back away from its responsibilities as defined in the 1922 protocol. On June 9, 1926, the League Council proudly announced that its objectives had been met, and it ended the commission's responsibilities at the end of that month.

Indeed, so promising was the Austrian program that the Council adopted a similar scheme for Hungary, the other part of the former Austro-Hungarian Empire. Prodded by Hungary's neighbors, the League adopted two protocols on March 14, 1924, providing loans to Hungary as well as a modified form of the supervision already established in Austria. Here, too, the program worked well enough for the Council to end direct League responsibility on the same day that it terminated supervision of the Austrian economy. The Allies had feared that the financial sickness of both Austria and Hungary would infect the more prosperous sections of Europe. Instead, by strictly supervising the two ailing economies, League commissions nursed both back to health. Once again, the League proved its usefulness, increasing optimism and economic security that in turn contributed to the spirit of Locarno. Unfortunately, these local remedies proved inadequate when the general economy of Europe collapsed during the next decade.

Russia

League successes during the mid-twenties were in large part limited to Europe. Germany joined the organization, but the United States did not, and Brazil even left in June 1926, at least indirectly because of Germany's membership. The other major nonmember during these years was the Soviet Union. The Bolsheviks had been excluded from the Peace Conference in 1919, in part because they had abandoned the Allied cause in 1918 and in part because they were sporting a program of revolutionary communism. Indeed, during the months when the Allies were drafting the Treaty of Versailles, Great Britain, France, Japan, and the United States joined "White Russian" armies to fight the Bolsheviks. Facing Allied military intervention and exclusion from the Peace Conference, the Bolsheviks unsurprisingly came to view the new League as a tool of the capitalist West. Lenin even condemned Wilson's League as just one more instrument of class oppression, while his foreign minister, Georgi Chicherin, denounced it as "a coalition of victor-Powers [*sic*] created in order to secure their acquisitions and conquests."

Outwardly at least, the Russian position remained unchanged during the 1920s. Postwar cooperation between Germany and the USSR, begun in 1922 at Rapallo, predictably hardened the anti-Soviet attitudes of both London and Paris. It was not just that the Allies excluded Russia from Geneva. They also isolated the Soviet government in general, with London and Washington refusing to extend even diplomatic recognition to Moscow. Although the British Labour government finally exchanged ambassadors with Moscow in February 1924, the publication in London of a letter purportedly written by Soviet authorities advocating revolution in England led to a major conservative election victory and the severance, once again, of diplomatic relations. Indeed, as noted earlier, British Foreign Secretary Austen Chamberlain's enthusiasm for the Locarno Pact stemmed in part from his desire to wean Germany away from the USSR. The League was still a long way from being universal.

Yet relations between Moscow and Geneva did exist, for the League's technical work served as a bridge between the two cities. In 1924, delegates from the League's Health Committee visited Moscow, while Soviet military officials met with a League-sponsored committee in Rome to discuss naval limitation. Then, in 1927, regular contact was established despite a nasty quarrel between the Soviets and the Swiss that had earlier led to Moscow's refusal to send even unofficial delegates to Geneva. Historian Frank Walters believed that Moscow might have established an unofficial office in Geneva had it not been for this quarrel, called the Vorovsky affair. The affair had begun on May 10, 1923, with the assassination, on Swiss soil, of Mechislav Vorovsky, the Soviet representative to the Lausanne Conference. The Soviets demanded that the Swiss apologize for the incident and guarantee the safety of all other Soviet citizens visiting Switzerland under League auspices. The dispute finally ended in 1927, although the Swiss public remained extremely hostile to the Russians for many years thereafter.

Communist setbacks in China and Great Britain, along with growing confidence at home, may also have prompted Moscow to accept a number of League invitations in 1927. Soviet delegates participated in disarmament discussions and in the League's first economic conference. They also agreed to attend a session of the Communication and Transit Organization (but never did make it). By December of that year, the number-two man in the Soviet foreign ministry, Maxim Litvinov, himself headed the Russian delegation to the Preparatory Disarmament Conference. Litvinov continued to visit Geneva annually, even after he became foreign minister in 1930. He established a reputation as one of the League's most remarkable characters, renowned for his sharp wit, undiplomatic honesty, and superb debating ability. A pragmatic communist, he had what Frank Walters called a "repellant and bewildering" accent, but his brilliance, his dedication to working-class ideals, and his affection for the League left an indelible imprint on those who worked with him. With Litvinov's influence in Moscow growing after 1927, Russia's knee-jerk hostility toward the League gradually ended. Although Litvinov did not formulate Soviet foreign policy alone, his sympathy for collective security, along with Stalin's belief during the mid-thirties that the Soviets needed allies to resist fascism, led to Russia's membership in the League after Hitler became chancellor of Germany. By 1934, however, both Germany and Japan had quit the organization, leaving the League further from universal membership than it had been when Litvinov first arrived.

Maxim Litvinov, the number-two man in the Soviet foreign ministry, was one of the League's most remarkable characters. His sympathy for collective security led to Soviet membership in the organization in 1934.

Vilna—Again

Improved Soviet-League relations paid a dividend when the League tried to resolve a stubborn dispute toward the end of the twenties. The League thrived during these years because no crisis as serious as the Corfu incident or the later Manchurian affair tested its Covenant. But the quiet was broken when two old rivals, Poland and Lithuania, became embroiled in yet another confrontation over Vilna.

Since 1921, Vilna had been divided into Polish and Lithuanian sectors, an arrangement formalized by the League Council in February 1923 and endorsed by the Conference of Ambassadors a few weeks later. Formalized or not, the Lithuanian government refused to reconcile itself to any boundary that gave Poland even partial control of Vilna. Although the Lithuanians did not take up arms during the mid-twenties, they nursed their hatred and remained technically in a state of war with their neighbor to the west. They initially rejected political contact, then cut all communications and commerce with Poland. As a League member, Lithuania had placed itself in a peculiar position. While some countries fought but refused to declare war, Lithuania declared war but refused to fight.

As long as the guns remained silent, League officials prayed that the Vilna controversy would somehow settle itself. Their prayers failed. In the fall of 1927, the dispute flared up once again after Poland accused Lithuania of mistreating ethnic Poles in Vilna. Poland had grown increasingly resentful over both Lithuania's refusal to accept the division of Vilna and its severing of all commercial ties. Growing militarily stronger, Poland now hinted it might overthrow the Lithuanian government and install a regime more agreeable to Warsaw.

Marshal Jozef Pilsudski, dictatorial leader of Poland since 1926, helped to create the confusion over Vilna in 1927.

In hindsight, it is still difficult to determine how real the Polish threat was. Marshal Jozef Pilsudski, the dictatorial Polish leader who took power in a 1926 military coup, blew hot and cold rhetoric over Vilna. Though he formally denied that he would violate the Covenant, the Lithuanians took his threats seriously and appealed to the League even though they, not the Poles, claimed to be in a long-standing state of war. It made for a confusing situation, which was further complicated when the Russians (allied with Lithuania) and the French (allied with Poland) joined in, hurling charges and countercharges.

The French played a particularly crafty game. Briand recognized that France's membership on the League Council required Paris to appear neutral, yet he delayed Council action to give Poland a chance to strengthen its military position before the next Council session. His maneuvering paid off, aided by Soviet demands that Lithuania settle the matter short of war. With Paris deep in negotiations over the Kellogg-Briand Pact and with Moscow edging closer to the League, neither the French nor the Russians really wanted a war in Eastern Europe. They, therefore, encouraged both the Polish and Lithuanian dictators to present their cases before the Council. With Chamberlain, Briand, and Stresemann guiding the proceedings, the Council succeeded in drafting an acceptable compromise after subjecting both sides to some strategic arm-twisting. The Poles agreed to recognize the independence of Lithuania, while the Lithuanians agreed to end their state of war against Poland. A League committee would examine the latest complaints about Lithuanian mistreatment of Polish subjects, and both governments would, for the first time, hold direct talks. Unfortunately, these talks led nowhere, for Lithuania never reconciled itself to any Polish authority in Vilna. Underlying hatreds continued to poison relations between the two countries. In short, although the League may have prevented war in 1927, it did not establish real peace.

The Chaco

The League, in theory universal, in fact never applied its peace-keeping authority outside of Europe until 1928. When, in December of that year, Paraguayan troops attacked a Bolivian outpost in a remote area called the Gran Chaco, few League officials had ever heard of the place. Their ignorance said a lot about the League in Latin America.

With the notable exception of Mexico, most of the Latin American states had joined the League following the Peace Conference. Their influence, however, remained limited; none of the sixteen Latin American countries was given a permanent seat on the Council, and Spanish was rejected as an official language of the League. Then, after the first Assembly in 1920, one of the more important Latin American states, Argentina, suspended its membership until 1933. Bolivia, Peru, and Honduras absented themselves for most of the first decade. Costa Rica formally withdrew in 1925, claiming inability to pay its $5000 assessment. And Brazil left during the confused battle over German membership on the Council. Unlike Spain, which also withdrew at that time yet quietly returned in less than two years, Brazil stayed out.

The American rejection of the Covenant undoubtedly complicated the role of the Latin American states at Geneva. On one level, many of these nations feared offending the United States, while on another level, they joined the League to advertise their independence from the United States. Certainly many Latin American officials resented the Covenant's Article 21, which required the League to respect the validity of the Monroe Doctrine; Article 21 had been inserted into the Covenant for no other reason than to lure the Americans into the League. After Warren Harding became president of the United States, reports reached Geneva suggesting that Washington officials were encouraging the Latin American governments to ignore their League obligations in favor of Pan American Union commitments. The activities of the union, an intergovernmental group of twenty-one Western Hemisphere nations that was favored by the United States, frequently paralleled the work of the League. Washington denied the reports, and there is no solid evidence to substantiate them, but they were certainly consistent with the attitude of many State Department officials during the 1920s.

Latin American problems, therefore, required a cautious and respectful approach by the League in general and by Sir Eric Drummond in particular. The League had first encountered the hazards of Latin American diplomacy in 1920, when it addressed the Tacna-Arica controversy. This dispute had grown out of a long-simmering frontier quarrel between Chile on one side and Peru and Bolivia on the other. While Chile had flatly opposed League involvement, Bolivia and Peru had asked the League Assembly in November 1920 not only to consider the matter under the Covenant's Article 15 but also to modify an existing 1883 treaty. This could be done under the authority of Article 19, which called for the reconsideration of agreements that might endanger the peace. When the Assembly had refused to modify the earlier agreement, claiming that changes could be made only by the countries involved and not by the League as an institution, both Peru and Bolivia had angrily left Geneva, not to return until 1929. This incident hardly increased Drummond's desire to tackle future Latin American disputes, like the Chaco controversy.

The Chaco, like Vilna, sat in an unsettled region characterized by poorly delineated boundaries. Both Bolivia and Paraguay had fortifications and border patrols in the area. The first reports of trouble appeared vague and unreliable, reminding League officials of the early days of the Greco-Bulgarian dispute. It appeared that Paraguayan troops had attacked a Bolivian outpost on December 5, 1928. Bolivian officials immediately responded by preparing their army to counterattack. Bolivia also appealed to the League, placing the Chaco controversy on the secretary-general's desk on December 6.

Drummond, along with his colleagues in Geneva, had learned a lot during the decade. Instead of protecting the League behind a legal fog, as he had done in 1920 with the Tacna-Arica dispute, Drummond himself brought the matter to the Council's attention. He asked Briand, the Council president, to call a special session if fighting should break out again, and he gave a stern lecture to the Bolivian minister to Switzerland about the need to resolve disputes peacefully. A few years earlier, Drummond almost certainly would have proceeded more cautiously. He would likely have waited for a member state of the League to place the dispute before the Council.

Former American Secretary of State Charles Evans Hughes (seated, second from right) presides over a 1928 session of the Pan American Union, which helped to end the hostilities in the Chaco controversy in 1929.

Article 4, however, allowed the Council to discuss *any* matter that threatened the peace, and by 1928, Drummond was more than willing to bring such matters to the Council's attention, at least when the quarreling countries were smaller powers.

But Drummond offered more than empty sentiments. After mastering the details of the situation, he informed the Bolivian envoy that under Article 13, Bolivia could request reparations from Paraguay. This was a key point because Bolivia was threatening to walk away from mediation sponsored by the Pan American Union unless Paraguay compensated Bolivia for losses suffered in the frontier skirmishing. Because mediation held real promise for settling the dispute, Drummond used the League to facilitate non-League talks. And Drummond also made it clear that the League would step aside completely if both parties preferred to use the International Conference of American States on Conciliation and Arbitration to resolve the dispute. He displayed both wisdom and flexibility. Indeed, the Pan American group helped to end the hostilities in early 1929 and appointed a neutral commission to negotiate a permanent settlement. Unfortunately, neither the League nor the neutral commission could resolve the underlying issues; as a result, the Chaco controversy evolved into Latin America's most bitter quarrel during the next decade.

Drummond's Pessimism

While historians view the 1920s as the League's golden age—as a decade of hope—League officials enjoyed no such perspective. To the secretary-general and his colleagues, routine problems hardly looked ordinary. The League's landscape was cluttered with German demands concerning Danzig, minority complaints throughout Eastern Europe, unrest in Latin America, stalemate on the disarmament front, and rising demands for higher tariffs. Drummond, in a reflective memo written in 1929, said that "we have reached, or shall shortly reach, a time when we may expect, taking all League activities into account, stagnation if not retrogression." His pessimism may strike some as curious, but events soon proved it to be anything but foolish.

Drummond's assessment of the League's future was not a ploy to persuade member governments to increase their annual contributions. Rather, it was contained in an internal document circulated only to those officials whose commitment to the League was no less strong than his own. He described the outlook as gloomy but then suggested an escape from what he saw as a darkening storm. That escape was along the path of universality: "If the United States could be induced in any way to become a Member of the League," he wrote, "the future would be assured. . . ." Drummond firmly believed that American membership would return Brazil and Argentina to full participation, would induce Mexico to join, would make the League in China "infinitely more effective," and would "silence the opposition" to the League in all countries. If the United States did not join, Drummond then predicted the real demise of the League in the Western Hemisphere and, therefore, as a universal institution. Would the United States reconsider its membership? Under the right conditions, which included the elimination of articles 10 and 16 and the substitution of conferences for sanctions, Drummond thought that it would. For that reason, he called for a "great international conference" to "reconcile" Washington and Geneva.

Drummond articulated in his memo the "myth of universality," a kissing cousin to the "myth of collective security." It is doubtful, however, especially during the early years of the Great Depression, that any changes in the Covenant would have brought the United States into the League. It is equally doubtful that American membership could have reconstructed the collective-security machinery of articles 10 and 16. The real problem with the League was never the Covenant's force provisions but rather the unwillingness of member countries to subordinate their sovereignty, to commit themselves to action in conflicts that did not threaten their own vital interests. Drummond correctly foresaw the danger to the League. He just never figured out a way to avoid it.

Nevertheless, Drummond's pessimism obscured something important about the League at the end of the decade. Focusing on the League's ability to prevent war, which he believed necessitated American membership, the secretary-general's memo ignored any serious consideration of the League's success in developing other ingredients of twentieth-century internationalism. These ingredients emerged from less visible corners of Geneva, from the specialized bureaus rather than the Council and Assembly chambers. They were the organization's major legacy to future generations.

The Nonpolitical Agencies 7

When historians evaluate the modest successes and failures of the League during the 1920s, they usually confine their attention to the collective-security efforts reported on the front pages of the world's newspapers. But Geneva's activities were much more wide-ranging, stretching into a number of areas that are usually, though inaccurately, called nonpolitical. These activities include the protection of political refugees, the financial and economic reconstruction of postwar Europe and China, attempts to eradicate the trade in drugs and prostitution, the development of international judicial procedures, and improvements in labor conditions. Some of this work involved bureaus that were agencies of the League, while other activities involved bureaus that were autonomous, such as the World Court, or semi-autonomous, such as the International Labour Organisation. This "less political" work constituted the heart of the League's contribution to internationalism.

Most of the League's economic and social activities had international roots extending well back into the nineteenth century. The shock of World War I, though, convinced even many conservative governments that war could result from social conflict and that the way to end war was to guarantee social and economic justice in all corners of the globe. This notion was eventually built into the Treaty of Versailles' proclamation that peace can only be "based upon social justice," an idea that was restated in the preamble to articles 23 and 24 of the Covenant. Article 23 committed the new organization to a broad range of activities, from guaranteeing freedom of transit to directing medical efforts for the prevention of disease; from supervising agreements dealing with the "white slave trade" to improving labor standards; from controlling the arms trade to providing justice for native populations in areas administered by League members.

The political work of the League was, by its very nature, passive, triggered only when a country violated a specific provision of the Covenant. Article 23, on the other hand, envisioned a fundamentally active League, what modern conservatives might call an "international busybody." Curiously, during a period when many governments jealously guarded their sovereignty in ways that undermined the League's political success, Geneva's economic and social work expanded rapidly.

F. S. Northedge, an English internationalist, identified an important irony in his history of the League. He claimed that the organization sprang from the social and political ideology of nineteenth-century liberalism, which idealized peace, free trade, and free expression. This optimistic ideology foresaw not the dependence of countries but their interdependence, not the dependence of peoples on government but their independence from government. The state would trust in the good sense of its people and in the benefits of a free market. This world view encouraged governments to become less intrusive in the lives of their citizens and permitted the League to act as a watchdog to ensure that no single state corrupted the system. For instance, the League might leap into action if a state increased tariffs in opposition to the Covenant's free-trade philosophy or if a state violated the League's commitment to universal freedom of transit.

Northedge perceptively noted that all this occurred at the beginning of an intensely nationalistic century, when both democracies and dictatorships pursued policies of economic and political nationalism, not internationalism. Consequently, the League's liberal principles swam against the tide. What puzzles historians is that the League's economic and social activities occasionally succeeded in spite of this nationalism. Less puzzling is that these occasional successes occurred mainly during the twenties, before the Great Depression and the arrival of fascism in Germany and Japan turned the world in an even more nationalistic direction.

Refugees

Of the League's nonpolitical work, aiding refugees proved to have the most immediate value. While many wars have produced the sad, familiar images of families fleeing from their homes, World War I produced so many refugees as to create a major international tragedy. Between 1914 and 1920, the war dislocated as many as 3 million Europeans, who sought refuge in new lands where they were neither understood nor wanted. They often lacked homes, schools, jobs, even food. The magnitude of the problem overwhelmed the private groups that tried to help. At the same time, few governments were anxious to spend their scarce resources on improving conditions for refugees.

Given the international scope of the crisis, League involvement should come as no surprise. Yet it was not inevitable; Article 23 said nothing about refugees, and refugees usually had no well-known spokesmen to plead their cause. Nevertheless, their plight could not be ignored, especially after 1920, when Gustave Ador, the president of the International Red Cross, proposed that the League tackle the problem. Asserting that voluntary agencies simply could not marshal enough resources, he argued that the League was the logical alternative.

With only a tiny treasury and no experience, League officials were afraid to take on this responsibility. Yet Ador's request could not easily be ignored. Article 25 called for the League to cooperate with the Red Cross, and the huge number of refugees fleeing the Russian civil war added a sense of urgency. Consequently, in February 1921, the Council appointed a High Commissioner to direct League efforts to aid Russian refugees. After Ador himself refused to accept the post, Sir Eric Drummond offered it to the man who would eventually become as closely linked to the refugee issue as Martin Luther King would be to civil rights—Fridtjof Nansen of Norway.

Nansen had already served effectively as head of the League's effort to return war prisoners to their homelands and as codirector, with American Herbert Hoover, of efforts to feed starving Europeans. Having largely completed both of these tasks, he now took on the refugee assignment.

It was a happy choice for both the League and Nansen. During the twenty years of the League's life, no one served internationalism more unselfishly or more energetically than did this dedicated Norwegian. Experienced in working with recalcitrant governments from his attempts to resolve the prisoner-of-war and food issues, Nansen brought physical stamina, patience, single-mindedness, ingenuity, and fairness to his task. Coming from a small and neutral country, he avoided accusations of favoritism. He also benefitted from an international reputation that he had established before undertaking his humanitarian efforts—he had received worldwide acclaim for his expeditions to the North Pole. Although he had never quite reached the pole, he contributed valuable information to at least ten scientific fields, ranging from astronomy to paleontology. Unfortunately, he would discover that persuading governments to aid refugees was an even more elusive goal than reaching the pole; certainly some of the government officials with whom he dealt turned out to be nearly as frigid as the arctic temperature. Nevertheless, he refused to surrender neither his enthusiasm nor his dedication to helping the refugees, and his death in 1930 at the age of sixty-eight took from the League one of its truly great leaders.

Fridtjof Nansen of Norway served internationalism with unselfishness and energy as High Commissioner for Refugees.

Yet even Nansen's efforts proved inadequate to the task. As many as 2 million Russian refugees were joined by thousands of others, including Armenians and Greeks fleeing Turkey, Turks fleeing Greece, and Jews fleeing Rumania and Poland. Homeless, destitute, fearful, hungry, and vulnerable to disease and malnutrition, these groups were in danger of becoming the forgotten men and women of Europe, stateless people on a continent increasingly defined by nationalism and nationhood. But Nansen did not let the world forget them, although many of the nations at Geneva would have preferred to do just that. His efforts to touch the conscience of Europe stand as testimony to his perseverance. As historian Elmer Bendiner put it, the members of the League "squirmed and temporized" on the refugee problem. They tried to divert attention by referral—refugee health issues to the Health Committee, refugee labor issues to the International Labour Organisation, other problems to other committees. Nansen refused to acquiesce in this fraud. He cried "foul," and sometimes people listened.

Nansen's greatest success related to his efforts to provide "passports" for these so-called stateless persons. An official passport permits an individual to cross international borders and retain rights recognized under international law. Because most refugees lacked a formal passport, they also had no recognized rights. Nansen proposed a "certificate of identity" for the Russian refugees. Eventually recognized by fifty-two countries, these "Nansen passports" would be given by the end of the decade to virtually any refugee who wanted one. In the late twenties, the League granted Nansen, as its High Commissioner for Refugees, the right to determine who was a refugee, a status that theoretically made a person eligible for political asylum. Unfortunately, only one country, France, fully accepted the Nansen passport, though most countries extended it at least partial recognition. Some, including the nonmember United States, technically recognized the passport but still restricted immigration. Refugees needed to read the passport's fine print.

In the final analysis, the League never mirrored Nansen's own commitment and effort. What the refugees needed went far beyond passports; they needed food, jobs, money for resettlement, and guarantees of police protection. Politically and financially fragile during the early twenties, the League could not provide these things. Dependent on modest assessments to cover its own considerable needs, it could allocate only enough resources to cover administrative expenses, such as funding the High Commissioner's office. When private fundraising through churches and the Red Cross also proved inadequate, Nansen set up the independent Nansen Relief Organization to raise funds. He also leaned on member governments for special contributions to finance refugee resettlement, but these, too, proved inadequate, in part because Drummond himself had other priorities. Not even Nansen's eloquence could shame member governments or the League Secretariat into making more strenuous efforts to aid the refugees. Historians have labelled Nansen "the League's conscience"; his contemporaries awarded him the Nobel Peace Prize in 1922. But he was not Superman. In spite of his heroic efforts, League refugee work remained anemic.

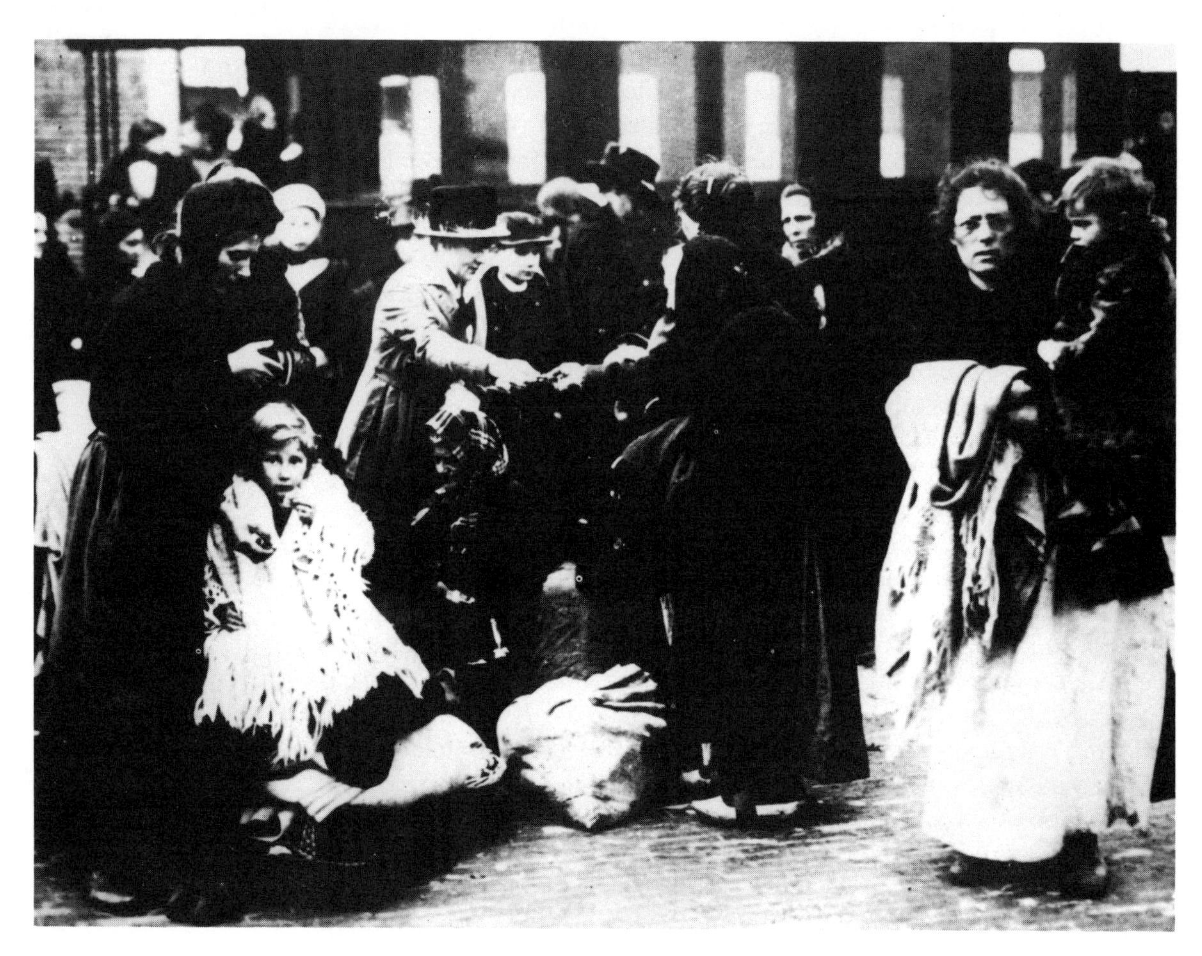

Millions of people were displaced from their homes during and after World War I. Here, a group of refugees returns from Holland in 1918.

Economics and Finance

Karl Marx argued during the nineteenth century that war is the product of economic rivalry and inequality, an idea accepted in 1914 by millions of liberals as well as Marxists. Therefore, it was no surprise that the authors of the Covenant included, in Article 23, both equitable treatment in commerce and freedom of transit. Indeed, Woodrow Wilson's highly publicized commitment to free trade, one of his famous Fourteen Points, made it almost inevitable that the League would become involved in this area. When the League was organized, it included the Economics and Financial Section, headed by Sir Arthur Salter, an ambitious English economist. Salter had extensive international experience, having served as secretary of the Allied Maritime Transport Council, which had coordinated English and American shipping during the war.

Salter, like Marx, was convinced that war stemmed from economic rivalry. He hoped to make his organization into a genuinely international decision-making body, rather than merely a channel through which individual governments would coordinate their own economic programs. As early as 1919, he proposed that representatives from different countries be allowed to meet without interference from their home governments. But others in the League Secretariat, including Drummond, were much less inclined to grant the specialized agencies such autonomy. They feared that the major powers might be threatened enough by the kind of organization proposed by Salter to curtail their support of the League in general. Salter's energetic internationalism would significantly influence League developments during the entire interwar period, but his temporary service as director of the Reparations Commission between 1920 and 1922 deprived the Economics and Financial Section of his leadership when it was most needed.

The dislocations caused by the war made it necessary for the Economics and Financial Section to begin its work almost immediately. Drummond ordered the section to focus first on the rebuilding of national finances, especially in those areas of Europe most seriously injured by the war. The new section was also expected to collect and review statistics bearing on the critical economic development of Europe during the postwar years. This task necessitated close cooperation between the section and the various public and private groups already compiling this data outside of Geneva.

The League Council gave the enterprise additional shape at the end of 1920 by establishing the Joint Economic and Financial Committee. Originally a "provisional" committee composed of two ten-member sections—one economic and the other financial—it achieved "permanent" status within three years. Both sections were staffed with experts from governments represented on the Council. Although these experts were technically volunteers who worked only for the League, they in fact retained close ties with their home governments. This, of course, often biased their recommendations, but it also minimized disagreements between Geneva and the European capitals. Did this politicize the work of the committee? Yes, but it also increased the committee's influence. And with economic nationalism lurking just below the surface of international politics, the ability of the committee to influence both large and small states paid real dividends. Historian A. Alexander Menzies, writing perceptively about the committee, noted that an unusual amount of continuity existed among the staff members in each section. He viewed the committee as a "club," with a respected membership dominated by bankers and economists. Their prestige steadily increased the committee's influence among the other organs of the League.

Of the two sections within the Joint Economic and Financial Committee, the financial section was initially the more successful after it drafted its highly publicized plans for rescuing the Austrian and Hungarian economies. By arranging loans and creating a mechanism to supervise expenditures, it revived the two sagging economies and ensured that it would be asked to do similar work during the Great Depression. Unfortunately, it was less successful the second time around. The other branch, the economic section, had a much more complicated career, with some notable achievements and some equally notable failures. It organized a number of economic conferences, including the Brussels Conference in 1920, the Genoa Conference in 1922, and the World Economic Conferences of 1927 in Geneva and 1933 in London. The Brussels Conference established a model for future meetings but accomplished little in the way of real reform during the immediate post–World War I depression. Historians generally consider the Genoa, Geneva, and London conferences to have been failures. Indeed, the Genoa and London conferences did little more than advertise that the major powers were unwilling to surrender their independence in the economic arena.

The failure to resolve problems in areas that were politically sensitive and economically critical—such as reparations, tariffs, and currency stabilization—suggests that the goals of most states remained highly nationalistic during the decade. On the other hand, the economic section did successfully encourage cooperation in less important areas. It sponsored agreements for publicizing tariff changes, disseminating statistical information, clarifying customs terminology, and accepting uniform laws covering financial transactions by international checks and bills of exchange. It also facilitated agreements requiring the use of arbitration to resolve economic disputes and the simplification of customs procedures. The League made the occasional specialized economic conferences of the early 1920s into routine events by the end of the decade.

In short, the Joint Economic and Financial Committee compiled a good record on technical issues. But when technical questions shaded into political questions, the committee encountered frustrations similar to the ones that were faced by League officials working on refugee aid and minority affairs. By the end of the thirties, hindsight made clear that the committee had performed respectably during the twenties, though even Salter understood that it might have done a lot better. The committee also taught the world that Marx's view of politics as merely a function of economics could easily be stood on its head, for the political suspicions of postwar Europe often caused governments to resist economic cooperation as proposed by the League. Notwithstanding the occasional failures and frustrations, the leaders of the Joint Economic and Financial Committee lived to see their agency's functions built securely into the structure of the United Nations.

Communications and Transit

League efforts to facilitate international travel and communications composed some of the more technical and less visible activity of the Geneva organization during the twenties. The splintering of Eastern Europe into new states following the armistice added urgency to this work. Governments were already familiar with the benefits of cooperation because of several prewar agreements. Immediately after the war, the French-sponsored Commission of Enquiry on Freedom of Communication and Transit proposed a series of conventions to give direction to the League's activity, and in 1921, the General Conference on Communications and Transit established an organizational framework in the communications area. The delegates at the conference in Barcelona created the Transit Committee to oversee routine League responsibilities and to arrange general conferences every four years. Its secretariat was headed by Robert Haas, a Frenchman described by the head of the League's Disarmament Section, Salvador de Madariaga, as "an ugly man" who had "one of the keenest brains and one of the kindest hearts I have known."

Unlike the Economics and Financial Section, which was wholly a League organ, the Transit Committee held an in-between status. Its budget was part of the League budget, but the Transit Committee itself had more autonomy than did the Economics and Financial Section. The committee had its own secretariat, and states could be members even if they rejected membership in the League. Germany and Brazil joined during the years they stood outside the League, but the United States, the Soviet Union, and Turkey did not, although they did participate in some of the committee's conferences.

As with the other technical groups, the success of the Transit Committee was patchy. On one hand, it did well at solving problems connected with passports, the transmission of electric power across borders, the establishment of a transportation system for China, and navigation in deep-water ports. On the other hand, it failed to secure cooperation concerning new technologies like radio and air travel. Although these failures may have resulted in part from the absence of several important states from the committee, they also stemmed from the highly sensitive political and military uses for these technologies, including propaganda, reconnaissance, and espionage. Not until after World War II would governments successfully tackle these subjects within an international framework.

Health and Vice

Epidemic disease has afflicted mankind since time immemorial. Aside from ordering an occasional quarantine, however, governments generally ignored the problem for lack of anything that they could do about it. Only after Louis Pasteur, the great French chemist, publicized his germ theory of disease in the mid-nineteenth century did real improvement in public health become possible. The implications of Pasteur's work led, in the 1860s, to the establishment of agencies that gradually turned health into a state responsibility. International efforts to control disease soon followed, including the founding of the International Health Office (IHO) in 1907. The IHO served as a clearing-house for information among its thirty-one members.

The evolution of international public health agencies was greatly affected by World War I. The historic link between war and disease affected millions of people between 1914 and 1918. Typhus, cholera, dysentery, and smallpox thrived amid the filth of trench warfare and the breakdown of existing health-care systems. At the end of the war, a worldwide influenza epidemic killed more people than had died in battle. The dramatic effects of these epidemics prompted internationalists at the Paris Peace Conference to include health among the responsibilities of the new League. IHO officials subsequently proposed that the League absorb their own agency, which was serving exclusively as an information service. They also proposed that the League establish a separate health committee to expand medical action services, like prenatal programs and smallpox prevention, and set up a health section in the Secretariat.

These IHO proposals were sensible, but they could not be divorced from the politics of the League. Anti-League groups in the United States protested, as did a number of governments that believed the League might exceed its authority by moving directly into the health field. Caught in the middle of this crossfire, the League Council backed off. It instead created a temporary Epidemics Commission to coordinate and improve the work of the various national agencies in the health field and then a provisional Health Committee to provide executive direction. The Epidemics Commission organized the Warsaw Conference of 1922, undoubtedly the most important meeting of the decade. Out of Warsaw emerged direct communication between the League and the national health services, as well as between the various national offices themselves. The momentum from Warsaw helped the League to both transform the temporary Health Committee into a permanent body and establish the Health Organization of the League.

The League's Health Organization was an umbrella body including both the Health Committee and the Secretariat's Health Section. Its twelve members selected Ludwik Rajchman of Poland, already chairman of the Health Committee, as its chairman. Facing continued opposition from the United States and some other quarters, the organization might have drifted ineffectively were it not for Rajchman. This Pole was no ordinary civil servant. Described by Madariaga as having a thin face with "eyes, nose, lips honed to a cutting edge," he also had a mind with a cutting edge. He was trained as a bacteriologist, but he became an imaginative and strong-willed administrator with extraordinary energy and the ability to argue a case superbly. He had the idealism of Nansen and the political instincts of Clemenceau. His committee, expected in 1921 to last for only one year, was still going strong in 1939. After World War II, the League's Health Organization evolved into the World Health Organization, one of the semi-independent agencies of the United Nations.

Some historians consider Rajchman's Health Organization the most successful of all the nonpolitical agencies of the League. Its accomplishments almost certainly stemmed in part from its genuinely nonpolitical character. It made its presence known on every continent. Even those governments that stood outside the League system eagerly cooperated with it. Underfunded like most League agencies, Rajchman's organization nevertheless managed to attract supplemental grants from private sources such as the Rockefeller Foundation and occasionally from countries that hosted its projects.

The Health Organization stood atop what political scientist Martin Dubin described as an elaborate structure of specialized councils and agencies composed of medical experts, governmental officials, and representatives of private agencies. It sponsored educational campaigns, reorganized national offices for controlling epidemic disease, distributed medicines, trained local health officials, established clinics for pediatric care, and provided help to establish or reorganize public health services. Its greatest successes occurred during the 1930s, especially in China, where it virtually took over the public health system. The applause was nearly universal. Only the growth of anti-Semitism after 1933 marred the picture; like a number of other high-level League officials, Rajchman was a Jew and hence drew fire from the new Nazi government in Berlin. By 1939, the League Council succumbed to fascist pressure and dismissed Rajchman from his post. Nevertheless, the many professionals working together under the auspices of the Health Section were probably less burdened with interference from national governments than were the members of any other League body.

In addition to its work with health concerns, the League also sponsored efforts to stem the traffic in both narcotics and prostitution. In light of our current failures to end the drug trade, it is unsurprising that the League was frustrated in this area. Narcotics in 1920 meant mainly, though not exclusively, opium. Grown largely in the Far East, opium was smoked, eaten, or traded on a worldwide scale. More than many governments would admit, it was a significant part of the economic life of many farmers and of a number of countries. In a period when moralistic reform swept through many Western governments, it was almost inevitable that the League would seek to contain, if not eradicate, the opium trade.

An international convention to stop the drug trade was signed in 1912, but it did not achieve legal standing until the 1918 armistice. More importantly, the League created the Advisory Committee on Opium and Other Dangerous Drugs (Opium Committee) to enforce the provisions of the 1912 convention. The convention, however, did not prohibit the production of opium, only its import and export. Furthermore, the extent to which reformers demanded a halt to the manufacture of "other dangerous drugs" led some industrial countries to lose their enthusiasm for the convention. Frank Walters noted that Switzerland, a leading chemical manufacturer, refused even to sign the 1912 convention until the mid-twenties because officials feared the effects of the convention on the Swiss economy.

In the end, the League's Opium Committee—initially composed of representatives from Asian and European countries having a direct stake in the trade—paid what Walters described as "too much attention to the material interests of the governments and too little to the social and moral aspects of the problem." In other words, the committee did next to nothing,

The League created the Advisory Committee on Opium and Other Dangerous Drugs on February 21, 1921, to combat the spread and abuse of narcotics. Here, two men smoke opium, the most popular narcotic of the interwar years.

leading to recrimination that embarrassed the League. The Council eventually altered the composition of the committee to improve its public image, and the committee did indeed swing into action. It sponsored studies that revealed the prevalence of drug addiction, which led to sensational exposés, which led to more conventions and more committees. This all provided the appearance of reform, but not one ounce of hard evidence exists that the League actually prevented the production or distribution of opium, heroin, cocaine, or any other drug covered by the 1912 convention. The Opium Committee publicized the problem. It did not solve it.

Defenders of the League's nonpolitical work probably would argue that the League could never have "solved" such problems anyway. The League could only point the way to solutions, then leave the rest to the governments. In this view, Geneva publicized issues that most governments preferred not to address at all. (For an in-depth discussion of one of these issues, see "The Question of Slavery," on page 105.) The League's misfortune was that it came into being when the public actually believed that such problems were, in fact, solvable. During the 1920s, the public increasingly relied on the advice of "experts," so the League brought experts to Geneva in record numbers. Ironically, a strength of the League—its willingness to bring natural and social scientists, military experts, and other specialists together for common discussions—turned into a weakness in this case because these experts often raised public expectations beyond what could be reasonably accomplished.

The Question of Slavery

Antislavery sentiment swept across the Western world during the nineteenth century. In 1833, the British government freed all slaves in its empire. By 1861, the winds of liberal reform swept across Russia, prompting Czar Alexander II to liberate millions of agricultural serfs. Two years later, Abraham Lincoln, by means of a civil war, emancipated the American slaves. And in 1888, Brazil, the last well-known bastion of slavery, followed Lincoln's example.

By the twentieth century, most people believed that slavery had disappeared into the pages of history textbooks. But that assumption was wrong. Sir Arthur Steel-Maitland, a British delegate to the Assembly, demanded a League campaign against the pockets of slavery that continued to exist in Africa. Subsequent investigation revealed that the ancient institution persisted mainly in Ethiopia and, ironically, in Liberia, a nation founded in the 1830s by freed American slaves.

Although the League Covenant said nothing about slavery specifically, articles 22 and 23 laid the foundation for work in this area. Article 22 established the mandate system, based on the "principle of well being and development" forming "a sacred trust of civilization." Article 23 was even more direct, obligating League members to secure "fair and humane conditions of labour" and "just treatment of native inhabitants."

It was the early work of the Permanent Mandates Commission that initially brought the slavery problem to Steel-Maitland's attention. After reviewing disturbing though incomplete data about the status of labor collected by the commission, Steel-Maitland reported to the Assembly in 1922. At this point, the story of Steel-Maitland's campaign against slavery becomes mainly a story of committee action. More allegations than information had been coming in, so League officials referred the matter to the Assembly's Sixth Committee, placed the subject on the Assembly's agenda for September 1923, and requested that the Council order a Secretariat report on the subject. Unfortunately, the Secretariat suffered from the same lack of hard information as did the Assembly. Therefore, it prepared a questionnaire for submission to various agencies in Africa (the League made questionnaires a central part of international life), and the data it collected was inserted into its report to the Assembly.

According to theory, all this should have worked well, but in practice, it did not. None of the mandatory powers wanted to advertise their problems, and the native officials in the mandates feared losing their jobs if local conditions embarrassed their superiors. Thus, the information requested by the League often reached Geneva in fragmentary and misleading form. To add to the problem, the societies suspected of tolerating slavery had high rates of illiteracy along with inefficient administrative systems, which further prevented Geneva from getting the information it needed.

In the midst of all this, Ethiopia applied for admission to the League in 1923 and was accepted by the Assembly on condition that it strictly apply the existing conventions prohibiting slavery. This was more easily demanded than done. The Assembly's condition presumed that the Ethiopian government not only *wanted* to apply the antislavery conventions (it probably did) but *could* apply them (it could not). Slavery, therefore, lingered on, and a decade later, when Mussolini launched his imperialistic adventures, he used Ethiopia's slavery as a justification to conquer that land. Mussolini apparently thought that one barbarity justified another.

In any case, facts conflicting with allegations continued to be a problem for the League. Shortly before the 1924 Assembly adjourned, Western delegates resolved to undertake still another inquiry, this time relying both on information supplied by governments and on data gathered by private organizations. The Assembly's Sixth Committee then divided the responsibility further, forming a subcommittee to collect yet more data—data that turned out to be inconclusive. Then, after the Sixth Committee reported back to the Council, the Council president proposed still another committee, an eight-member Temporary Committee on Slavery to include representatives from the Permanent Mandates Commission, some former colonial officials, an ILO official, Haiti's delegate to the League, and an Italian cultural official. All this persistence paid off, and by the fall of 1925, the Assembly had enough information to draft its long-awaited convention on slavery.

The Slavery Convention was drafted by the Sixth Committee of the 1925 Assembly. It was adopted by the full Assembly on September 25, 1926, and then circulated by the Council to all governments for signing and ratification. The convention instructed the League Council to send annually all laws and regulations concerning the suppression of slavery to the Assembly and then to all signatories. It also supplemented earlier agreements seeking to end slavery, most importantly the Brussels Convention of 1889 and the Treaty of St. Germain of 1919. The convention prohibited not only slavery but also the slave trade, and it defined slavery in broad terms that included not only traditional slavery but serfdom, peonage, and forced labor unless done for public purposes. It said that even publicly ordered forced labor could be employed only in exceptional circumstances, with the laborers protected against removal from their home areas and guaranteed adequate compensation. In sum, the convention addressed the conditions that would appear in Hitler's Germany and Stalin's Russia no less than the conditions in Ethiopia.

The Slavery Convention became law on March 9, 1927. It was hardly revolutionary in its impact, even though, by the end of 1929, thirty League members had ratified it. Its main problem was that it ignored the necessity for enforcement machinery in case a signatory violated its terms. The League, therefore, did not end slavery. It did, however, concentrate attention on a disturbing remnant of pre-industrial life and clarified the link between traditional slavery and its twentieth-century descendants. To that extent, the League modestly contributed to an important internationalist theme—humanitarian values are not limited by national boundaries.

This may also help explain the public's disappointment with League efforts to halt the traffic in women and the exploitation of children. Both issues stood among the more popular causes after the turn of the century. Paralleling the Opium Committee was the Advisory Committee on the Traffic in Women and Children. This Advisory Committee functioned in reality as two separate committees, one focusing on the "white slave trade," the other on child abuse. As with the Opium Committee, it produced exposés that lent themselves to more sensational treatment than one would ordinarily associate with the League's technical work. And as with the drug experts, the Advisory Committee's experts promised more than they were ever capable of delivering, although their efforts were by no means futile. The Advisory Committee, cooperating with the ILO's Child Welfare Committee and functioning under the direction of the League's Social Affairs Section, helped to draft conventions for the protection of indigent children and those held away from their parents in foreign custody. Prodded by the Advisory Committee, a few governments adopted legislation to raise the minimum age for both marriage and sexual consent. And increasingly, Western governments either regulated or prohibited prostitution; the commercial and often involuntary movement of women across national boundaries for sexual purposes was thus curtailed although not eradicated. As with drugs, it is difficult to measure the adequacy of League efforts in contrast to strictly national measures, but they certainly had some effect.

Intellectual Cooperation

In Geneva today is a large building that houses the Organization for Intellectual Cooperation. This organization has its roots in the League's Committee for Intellectual Cooperation, founded in 1922 to serve the economic and legal needs of writers, critics, artists, and others who "trade" in ideas. It aimed to bring intellectuals from around the world into contact with each other in order to generate cultural exchange and to mobilize their energies to serve the cause of peace. The genesis of some of this work predates 1919, but the war and improvements in communications gave a more practical meaning to such cooperation.

The League considered the Committee for Intellectual Cooperation to be one of its most novel projects. The committee was initially composed of twelve leading intellectuals, including German physicist Albert Einstein, French chemist Marie Curie, French philosopher Henri Bergson, and English classical scholar Sir Gilbert Murray. It drafted its own agenda, which ranged from organizing university exchanges to instituting copyright protection to preserving archeological treasures. Additionally, the committee dabbled in areas such as making Esperanto an official international language, coordinating bibliographies, translating important literary works, and educating the public about the League's many activities.

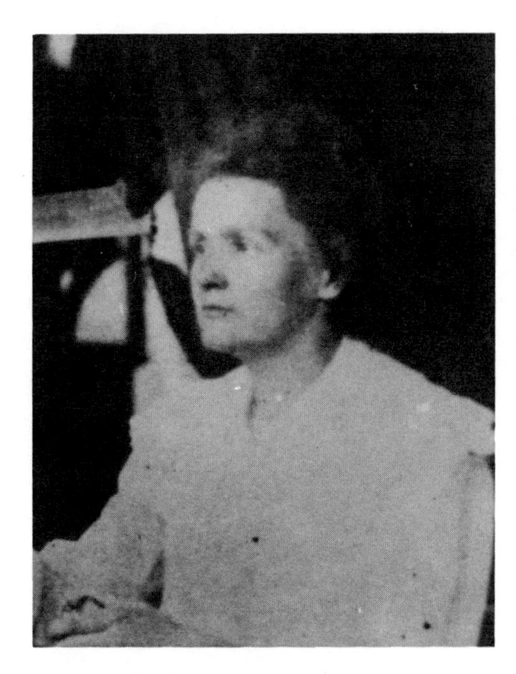

French chemist Marie Curie (above) and German physicist Albert Einstein (below) were prominent members of the Committee for Intellectual Cooperation, created by the Council on May 15, 1922.

However worthy its goals, the committee accomplished little. It suffered from a number of problems, including poor administrative leadership, intellectual rivalries, chauvinism, and the Assembly's reluctance to place a high priority on its work. It also suffered from the absence of organizational and bureacratic machinery that could transform good ideas into good works. Thanks to the urging of the French, the Assembly in 1924 approved creation of the International Institute for Intellectual Cooperation. With most other governments displaying varying degrees of indifference, Paris in the summer of 1925 appropriated funds for the institute with the proviso that the institute would be located in the French capital. Until World War II, the institute would serve, not always effectively, as the administrative arm of the committee.

With or without the institute, funding intellectual cooperation remained a critical problem, especially during the lean 1930s. The bottom line was the bottom line—the Assembly refused to allocate more than a token amount of money for the committee (and the institute), while French financial support dwindled. Without adequate funding, the committee could do little. It had no Rajchman to drum up independent support and no Nansen to touch the conscience of mankind. The intellectuals on the committee wrote much but communicated little, for they mainly talked only to each other. The growth of fascism made anti-intellectualism fashionable. Not until after World War II when the United Nations Educational, Scientific and Cultural Organization (UNESCO) appeared would this area of international activity again be taken seriously.

Labor

The 1919 peace treaties all included the League Covenant in their texts. They also incorporated the Constitution of the International Labour Organisation (ILO). Unlike the Health Organization and the Economics and Financial Section, the ILO, while technically a part of the League, was really autonomous. It even held its first meeting before the League itself was organized and included as members some countries that were not members of the parent League. In addition, it had a separate headquarters in Geneva.

The organizational structure of the International Labour Organisation was similar to that of the League but not identical with it. It consisted of the International Labour Office, which was equivalent to the League Secretariat; the International Labour Conference, which was parallel to the League Assembly; and the Governing Body, which consisted of twenty-four members and was comparable to the League Council. Unlike the Council, however, only half the members of the Governing Body represented governments; the other half represented employers and labor unions. The League Council did have some influence here, for it selected two-thirds of the membership of the Governing Body, while the International Labour Conference selected the other third. League influence was also reflected in a number of other ways. The ILO was located in Geneva "as part of the organization of the League." The League Assembly approved its budget and provided its revenues. And the ILO's director-general—although, for the most part, independent—reported directly to Sir Eric Drummond on budgetary matters. Beyond this authority, League influence was limited. The Governing Body alone selected the director-general, and of equal importance, it set the ILO's agenda. By the end of the 1920s, the ILO rivalled the League in size, and it continued to grow in prestige well after the League entered its period of decline.

The relationship between the League and the ILO was greatly influenced by the ILO's director-general, Albert Thomas. A forty-two-year-old French Socialist in 1919, Thomas gave the organization its independent character, quickly marking it with his own stamp. Short and powerfully built, he neither looked nor acted like a traditional diplomat in the city that symbolized diplomacy. Red-faced, street-smart, and blunt, he came from a working-class background and never forgot it. Madariaga noted his spontaneity, his "rebellious looks," his appearance of "natural force." Thomas combined imagination and physical energy. Drummond never felt comfortable with him, in the way that aristocrats rarely feel comfortable with commoners, a condition aggravated by Thomas's refusal both to defer to his betters and to abide by the diplomatic expectations of the 1920s. Thomas was the true democrat at Geneva, free of the doctrinaire Marxism that rendered so many other socialists ineffective when negotiating with the conservative governments of that age.

The ILO did not emerge spontaneously in 1919 but owed its birth to a Swiss-based group called the International Association for Labour Legislation, which for years had demanded better wages, shorter hours, and increased occupational safety for the working class. The outbreak of war had interrupted this type of international cooperation, but the substantial contribution of labor unions to the war efforts of the United States, Great Britain, and France left union leaders in a strong bargaining position. Wartime coalition governments often included labor or socialist support, as in France, where Thomas served as Munitions Minister. The ILO was the price that labor had demanded for its loyalty.

So quickly did the ILO materialize at the Peace Conference that its first organizing conference convened in Washington even before the peace treaty was ratified. Unfortunately, the American capital in October 1919 was hardly an ideal place for the conference. American opposition to the League co-existed with growing antiradical sentiments that blurred the distinction between socialism and communism, a development that contributed to the Red Scare of 1919. American officials, therefore, became extremely nervous about hosting the conference. Nevertheless, the meeting underscored for Americans the reality of the League and left no permanent scars on either the ILO or United States.

The United States' rejection of the Covenant also meant it refused to join the ILO, since League members automatically became ILO members. Thomas worried about American abstention from his organization much less than Drummond fretted about it for the League. He simply invited unofficial observers from the American business and labor communities to join ILO meetings, after which he proposed a dynamic ILO agenda that in just three years resulted in the adoption of sixteen conventions and eighteen important recommendations. The Washington meeting had already recommended reductions in working hours. Subsequent meetings addressed the problems of workers in different industries and were followed by conferences on workman's compensation, minimum wages, and compulsory labor.

Thomas mobilized the resources of the ILO in a way that Drummond failed to do at the League. As a result, the ILO by 1930 had built a reputation for accomplishment and innovation that dwarfed the reputation of the parent organization. This does not mean that the ILO *always* translated recommendations into law or *dramatically* improved conditions of labor throughout the world. Nevertheless, it set clear and reasonable standards that served the interests of both employers and employees in member countries.

In 1920, some conservative officials had feared that Thomas's organization would bring revolution to the West, that the ILO masked the evils of socialism and class conflict. But revolutionary Russia had refused to join precisely because the organization was *not* revolutionary. In fact, the Soviet Union remained Thomas's harshest critic until the day he died. The ILO was committed to social harmony, and its constituency of government officials, employers, and labor representatives virtually guaranteed moderation and compromise. The degree to which interwar officials valued the ILO's work can be judged by examining ILO membership. Countries might drop out of the League, as Brazil did in 1926 and Japan and Germany did in the early thirties, but they usually remained in the ILO. Even the United States eventually joined. In spite of the Great Depression and Thomas's premature death in 1932, the ILO was here to stay.

The World Court

The last of the important League organs was the Permanent Court of International Justice (PCIJ), commonly called the World Court. Although not a political body, it addressed political issues to a much greater degree than did most of the League's other specialized bodies. Its jurisdiction theoretically extended to virtually all international issues, from traditional political disputes to commercial quarrels. Like the Minorities Section committees, it remained vigorous only as long as the League did. When the League declined after 1931, the Court weakened, too.

The Court, like the ILO, had its roots in the prewar period. The Hague Conference in 1899 had established an international mechanism for arbitration of disputes. The World Court grew from this precedent, although its functions as a court of international law went far beyond arbitration alone. Of course, the Court also respected the Hague precedent in another way—it always met in the Dutch capital, never in Geneva.

Like the League, the World Court was a product of the Peace Conference. But although it was a part of the League, it was not subordinate to it. Its authority stemmed from a League resolution passed in 1920 that granted it a wholly separate statute. This was no small matter, for it meant that the Court was independent and did not have to answer to the League. However, as with the ILO, the League funded the Court and elected its fifteen judges by means of simultaneous votes of the Council and Assembly. This gave even smaller states a voice in the selection process. In all other ways, the Court operated independently. Although Covenant procedures required the submission of certain types of cases to the Court, the Court could also be asked to hear disputes submitted by states outside the League. Indeed, about 600 treaties and conventions eventually required the submission of international disputes to The Hague.

More than any other branch of the League, the World Court symbolized the rule of international law, although many internationalists were acutely aware by the mid-twenties that the Court had not lived up to expectations. Even friends of the PCIJ were troubled by its limited jurisdiction. The most serious problem was that the Court could hear a case only if *both* parties to the dispute were willing to submit to its authority. And usually, both parties agreed only if neither had "vital interests"—things worth fighting to protect—at stake. Moreover, the Court issued as many "advisory opinions" as it did formal judgments (sixteen of each); these advisory opinions, although frequently useful to the disputing parties, lacked the full force of law.

Contributing further to doubts about the Court's value was the inability of the Court to enforce its decisions. In theory, Article 16 sanctions were available as the ultimate enforcement mechanism, but they were never invoked during the 1920s. In short, the Court's very limited ability to preserve international peace highlighted the inadequacy of a strictly legalistic approach to world order, a point frequently noted by proponents of collective security. And these collective-security proponents often added that the ineffective Court was really what many British and American internationalists had originally hoped the League would be—primarily a legal institution without the force machinery of articles 10 and 16.

League Authority Versus Agency Autonomy

Beyond the question of judicial procedure versus collective security was an important administrative issue common to all the League's technical and nonpolitical agencies. The debates of 1919 and 1920 had never fully addressed the degree to which these agencies stood independent of the parent body, the League. The independence of the World Court and of the ILO became quickly apparent, though League officials did not always appreciate it. But if the League could do little about the independence of those two organizations, it wasted little time discouraging independent activity by the other agencies. On May 19, 1920, the Council passed a resolution specifying that the secretariats of the specialized agencies would be subordinate to the League Secretariat, warning that the ILO's autonomy would not serve as a precedent for any other technical organ of the League.

This was more than just a quarrel over turf. It highlighted competing visions of international organization. Drummond spoke for the primacy of the Secretariat over the agencies and saw the League as fundamentally a collective-security organization; he believed the League should be the conduit for action by its member governments. Others felt the agencies should evolve into much more independent bureaus, relying on experts from around the globe to make decisions free from the political constraints often imposed by governments. This latter view expressed the spirit of twentieth-century internationalism transcending the narrow objectives of collective security. With few exceptions during the interwar years, Drummond's view, supported by most governments with representatives on the Council, triumphed—the League remained primarily a collective-security organization limited by a traditional conception of sovereignty. Not even Hiroshima would seriously undermine this concept as the League evolved into the United Nations.

Success Within Failure 8

Most observers agree that the League failed. It failed, they believe, because it could not prevent a second world war, the war that collective security was supposed to prevent. Yet this conventional view does not do the League justice because, in an important sense, the League actually succeeded. It initiated and organized international cooperation in many social and technical areas. International activities attempted before the formation of the League had been carried out haphazardly. Badly administered and poorly coordinated, they had commanded little respect. The League changed much of this. Nevertheless, it is important that we not exaggerate the success of the League's nonpolitical work, for the League's record, like that of the prewar internationalists, was spotty. What does bear special attention, though, is the size of the record. By 1929, the League's nonpolitical work rivalled its collective-security activity in scope and importance, although contemporaries may not have realized this.

Moreover, the attention that contemporaries directed toward the collective-security functions of the League obscured something else of importance—the development of the *idea* of international cooperation, really a set of ideas that today we call internationalism. The League was in part a product of these ideas, but it also helped to organize and legitimize them. The League gave internationalism both shape and substance. However imperfect the League's performance may have been, the League conferred a kind of reality on international cooperation that did not exist before 1919. Today, we take such cooperation for granted, which is a mark of Geneva's success.

The Twilight of Internationalism

Some writers recently have bemoaned what the president of the Carnegie Endowment for International Peace called "the twilight of internationalism" in the late twentieth century. By this, the Carnegie president meant developments such as the failure of the United Nations to prevent hostilities in places like Vietnam, Afghanistan, the Persian Gulf, Somalia, and the former Yugoslavia. But this view may be too narrow. Internationalism, after all, is a concept that is much broader than collective security, and the League of Nations, building on earlier precedents, helped to institutionalize cooperation in many areas that will continue regardless of the future of collective security. At the same time, collective security cannot be ignored. It did, after all, constitute the heart of the Covenant.

At the end of the League's first decade, most literate people associated the League of Nations with its collective-security functions, not its nonpolitical activities. No one could have predicted that the collective-security ideal would shortly be subject to devastating attack. By 1930, it is true, the bloom had worn off the League's celebrated success with the Greco-Bulgarian dispute. The Locarno Pact had slowed, but not prevented, the rise of German nationalism. Nevertheless, no major crisis had yet proved that collective security was only a pipe dream. The Wall Street Crash had barely begun to sour the world's economic climate, and outside of the United States and Canada, few economists were predicting that the stock-market debacle heralded a depression. Even if they had, they probably would have comforted themselves with the thought that capitalist economies always experience periods of boom and bust. Hardly anyone believed that the Crash threatened the existence of capitalism itself. In short, the world appeared to be in pretty good shape in 1930. The League had few detractors, apart from extreme nationalists. Even communists had softened their opposition to the organization.

There were, however, some critics. Together with a few of the League's best friends, like Drummond and Salter, they continually lamented that the United States had remained apart from the organization. Still, the League had survived American absence, and the frigid relationship between Geneva and Washington during the early twenties had warmed up by the end of the decade. By 1930, American envoys routinely attended League-sponsored meetings in both the political and the technical areas, acting occasionally as voting participants, more often as "unofficial observers" whom one cynic called "something between a guest and a spy." But at least the Americans were taking Geneva seriously. Though careful to refrain from anything that might suggest membership, they reorganized their consulate in Geneva in order to facilitate reporting on League-related developments. They even considered joining affiliated bodies. Every American president and secretary of state during the 1920s endorsed membership in the World Court, and increasing American interest in the ILO led to membership in that organization in 1934. In short, the relationship between the United States and Geneva had become so complex and interdependent that critics could not write off the League simply because Washington remained a nonmember.

Yet American nonmembership was part of a broader and more disturbing pattern. The League may have hoped for universal membership during the 1920s, but it could never attain it as long as Russia, Turkey, Germany, and Brazil, each an important country in its own right, stood outside the Geneva orbit. While some of them eventually joined, states such as Japan and Italy later left. For collective security to work as its Wilsonian proponents had hoped, no single state would have dared to challenge the combined might of all the other states. Sadly, however, the history of the League reveals that the nonmembers tended to be powerful states, not militarily weak ones, which helps to explain the League's failure during the thirties. It also helps to explain why, during the twenties, collective security existed more in theory than in practice. It was never really employed during that first decade because many internationalists continued to believe that the mere *threat* of collective force would deter a country from violating the Covenant.

Of course, except for Italy during the Corfu crisis, no major country actually challenged the League system before 1930. The decade was peaceful, at least in comparison to what preceded and followed it, though not because governments were intimidated by the Covenant's force provisions. Peace stemmed from the more fundamental features of the twenties—the postwar exhaustion of Europe; the isolation of Soviet Russia; the military weakness of Germany; the failure of France's occupation of the Ruhr, which prepared the way for Locarno; and the extensive involvement of American banks in propping up the European economy before October 1929. In other words, the League benefited from the economic and political climate of the twenties, not the other way around.

The Problem of Consensus

There were also some less obvious problems during the twenties. Too often we view the League as if it had a mind and a will of its own. It had neither. Unfortunately for the cause of internationalism, the League suffered from a lack of consensus even during its best decade. The French government, after all, never viewed the League as anything more than a mechanism to maintain the status quo in order to preserve the anti-German provisions of the Treaty of Versailles. Not even Briand endorsed the lofty ideals of international harmony when they did not serve French security interests. The British were more optimistic; they viewed the League as an institution that would reintegrate the Germans into the European political and economic structure. The Germans, resentful over being initially excluded from the League, tried to convert the organization into an instrument to alter the Versailles settlement. The Italians certainly did not share the French view of the League, especially after Mussolini launched his revisionist policy in 1923. And Japan remained uninterested, though not unfriendly, toward the League, leaning more toward the British than the French conception of the organization during the 1920s.

Then came the smaller powers. In general, they seemed to view the League in a somewhat schizophrenic manner. Many applauded the collective-security provisions of the Covenant, which they hoped would protect them from their more powerful neighbors. At the same time, however, they reduced their own obligations under Article 16, fearing that sanctions would expose them to the hazards of war. Furthermore, some of the smaller countries—such as Poland, Lithuania, and Greece—had territorial designs of their own. Thus, during the 1920s, the commitment of the smaller states to League principles never quite measured up to expectations.

In other words, no consensus ever existed about the League's most important objectives. The issue was never really "peace" but rather the British conception of peace as opposed to the French conception of peace, as opposed to the German conception, and so on. Therefore, if peace required revising the Versailles settlement for the British, Germans, and Italians while preserving it for the French, then the League's goal of collective security would necessarily be thrown into doubt. After all, the Covenant merely spelled out a means to attain an end. With disagreement over the ends, there was little reason to believe that articles 10 through 16 could ever be effectively invoked in disputes involving the major powers.

An Active Assembly

The authors of the Covenant had not foreseen a development that significantly affected the operation of the League during the twenties. The Covenant called for a Council composed of the most important states and an Assembly with universal membership; and most observers, including the statesmen who drafted the Covenant, presumed that the smaller Council would efficiently address the potentially explosive questions of war and peace, while the larger Assembly would be more an instrument to mobilize world opinion. Articles 11 through 16 clearly indicated that the founders expected the Council, not the Assembly, to be the more active branch of the League when a country violated the Covenant.

Yet the founders did not give the Council *exclusive* authority in matters of war and peace. The Covenant specified, in articles 3 and 4, that both bodies "may deal at its meetings with any matter within the sphere of action of the League or affecting the peace of the world." This identical wording gave the Assembly potentially greater authority than any observer had anticipated in 1919. Perhaps the drafters of the Covenant permitted appeals to the Assembly because, as political scientist Jean Siotis suggested, they suspected that a Council member might refuse to take action against an ally violating the Covenant. Additional articles also enhanced the authority of the Assembly. Article 11 permitted any League member the "friendly right" to bring a matter affecting the peace to the attention of either body. Article 15 allowed the Council itself to transfer consideration of a dispute to the Assembly.

The growth of the Assembly's authority also stemmed from two other developments. First, the drafters of the Covenant had not planned for the Assembly to hold annual meetings, yet the Assembly not only met each year but did so with many of the world's leading statesmen in attendance. Second, the Assembly, in 1920, assumed control of the League's financial affairs, even though the Covenant did not spell out its authority to do this. The Assembly soon voted the annual budget of not only the League itself but also of affiliated bodies like the International Labour Organisation and the World Court. It also required all other League organs to report back to it annually. These developments substantially increased the Assembly's authority and prestige.

From the earliest days of the League, therefore, the Assembly joined the Council in being actively involved in League efforts to keep the peace. Yet Assembly consideration of collective-security issues never amounted to much. The powerful states, all enjoying Council membership, remained the most influential. Purity of intentions, abundantly found among the smaller states in the Assembly, counted for little—not for nothing, just for little.

First-Rate People

If the Assembly's involvement with collective security exceeded the expectations of the founders of the League, so, too, did the role of the secretary-general. Sir Eric Drummond proved to be a fair-minded and capable official. As James Barros has shown, Drummond was a good deal more political than he wanted people to think, but he was far from being a narrow British partisan. He knew that a nonpolitical appearance would enhance both his prestige and his effectiveness during the 1920s. Lacking the flair and the force of Albert Thomas at the ILO, Drummond still guided the League through some thorny problems, such as German membership and the Spanish threat to withdraw. His influence in creating a genuinely international civil service lasted not only beyond his term but beyond the life of the League itself.

Furthermore, the quality of the men whom Drummond brought into the technical agencies of the League, as well as the quality of those he placed throughout the Secretariat, was high. It is often said that first-rate people surround themselves with first-rate people, while second-rate people surround themselves with third-rate people. To his credit, Drummond surrounded himself with mainly first-rate people, which was a mark of his own confidence and stature. He may have lacked color, but he did not lack competence.

The Final Analysis

There is little reason to believe that different men or women could have substantially improved the League's record during the twenties. Perhaps a more aggressive secretary-general might have made a marginal difference in some cases. Perhaps not. The League might have been better off had it not been burdened with the direct administration of Danzig and the Saar. Countless hours were spent trying to resolve quarrels in both localities that were really unresolvable; the results were hardly commensurate with the effort. Yet the League had little choice. The Saar and Danzig had been handed to it by the Peace Conference, and for the League to walk away from them would have very likely and very quickly compromised its authority. Moreover, the League's efforts in both of these contentious areas ended up drawing favorable reviews by historians, regardless of the drain on time and resources.

In the final analysis, the League's main problems during the twenties related not to what it did but to what it could not do. It could not require the Americans to join. It could not require the Germans to give up their desires to expand into Eastern Europe. It could not require the British to prepare their African colonies for independence. It could not require the Canadians and Scandinavians to risk their armed forces under Article 16 to defend the principle of collective security. It could not be more than the sum of its parts. The League existed in a world that still worshipped national sovereignty, and it possessed extremely limited power just when technology was making the centuries-old concept of sovereignty increasingly dangerous. The next decade would starkly reveal just how weak the League was when it came to preventing war.

In assessing the League's modest record during the twenties, it is important to recognize that the young organization faced not just impersonal hurdles like the concept of sovereignty, but real nationalist and isolationist enemies who strove to turn the League into a global scapegoat. Even those who championed the League contributed to the problem, for they often raised unrealistically high expectations about collective security. Of course, without the enthusiasm of those champions, the League might never have even gotten a chance to fail. But although we probably learn from our failures more than we do from our successes, the twenties did not reveal enough failure—did not confront enough crisis—for the League to learn just how weak it really was. This would be left for the final ten years, but by then it was too late.

Chronology

1919

JANUARY

3 Henry Cabot Lodge, chairman of the Foreign Relations Committee of the U.S. Senate, declares that planning for a league should follow the signing of a peace treaty.

The Bolsheviks, together with their Lithuanian allies, take Vilna from the Poles.

5–15 The Spartacist (radical left) Revolt in Berlin dramatizes the instability of postwar Germany.

9 England's Viscount Robert Cecil of Chelwood (Lord Cecil) suggests that the formation of a league should be the first task of the Paris Peace Conference.

11 British Prime Minister David Lloyd George raises the possibility of an American mandate over Armenia, where the Turks have driven thousands from their homes.

14 Cecil produces a draft of a league covenant, which includes some provisions to enforce league decisions but does not include universal membership.

18 French Premier Georges Clemenceau rejects German membership in a postwar league of nations, a theme of French policy for the next six years.

20 American President Woodrow Wilson presents a draft covenant for the league. At the same time, Cecil criticizes the idea of universal membership.

25 The plenary session of the Peace Conference endorses Woodrow Wilson's recommendation to create the League of Nations and forms a commission to draft the Covenant. It also creates a commission on international labor legislation, which leads to the formation of the International Labour Organisation (ILO).

27 The Peace Conference elects a committee to draft the Covenant of the League of Nations. Cecil and American legal adviser David Hunter Miller submit a plan for the League to the League Commission.

FEBRUARY

1–2 Miller and British legalist Cecil Hurst make and submit a revised draft to the League Commission. Drawing from ideas in many other plans, it defines the Secretariat as more administrative and less political.

3 Chaired by Wilson, the League Commission holds its first formal session and considers a variety of proposals.

The Reparations Commission holds its first session.

6 The League Commission assigns four seats on the League Council to the smaller states, who had protested their lack of Council representation.

American President Woodrow Wilson and wife arrive in Dover, England, in January 1919 on their way to the Paris Peace Conference.

8 The Council of Ten, representing the major states at the Peace Conference, creates the Supreme Economic Council to deal with everything from the economic effects of the Allied blockade of Germany to the price of food and raw materials.

11 Léon Bourgeois of France attacks the broad disarmament features of the Miller-Hurst plan. French opposition to disarmament, one of Wilson's Fourteen Points, becomes clear.

13 Japan asks for a Covenant commitment to racial equality, which leads to British and American opposition. The United States and Britain also oppose a French suggestion to create a League military organization.

Maurice Hankey, secretary to the British Cabinet, is asked to become secretary-general, a nonpolitical position.

15 Wilson returns home from Paris, temporarily suspending his direct involvement at the Peace Conference.

MARCH

2 Lenin establishes the Third International, which Western nations use to justify their policy of nonrecognition of Russia.

Thirty-nine American senators sign a round-robin statement saying that a league of nations should *follow* a peace treaty rather than be *included* in a treaty.

8 The International Conference of League of Nations Societies, meeting in Berne, Switzerland, asks that smaller nations also be represented in the League.

10 The Peace Conference votes to limit the German army to 100,000 men.

12 The Peace Conference resolves to permanently disband the German air force. In addition, the conference's Polish Committee recommends that Upper Silesia, the Corridor, and Danzig be transferred to Poland.

The conference agrees to permit nations that were neutral during the war to comment on the draft of the peace treaty.

The Austrian assembly votes to make Austria an integral part of Germany. The Allies object.

15 The Peace Conference's Labor Commission presents its draft of the ILO charter.

17 The Peace Conference agrees to make the Covenant a part of the peace treaty, thereby linking them in the public eye. Any nation rejecting the treaty therefore also rejects the Covenant.

20 The Allies award Hungary's Transylvania region to Rumania. Hungarian resentment continues to the present day.

21 The Hungarian revolution begins, resulting in the formation of a communist government under Béla Kun.

23 Benito Mussolini organizes his first fascist units in Italy.

24 The Council of Ten at the Peace Conference ends its regular meetings. It is succeeded by the Council of Four, which is composed of Great Britain, France, Italy, and the United States.

26 British Labour Party leader James Ramsay MacDonald says that the Bolsheviks may create a radical league of nations in opposition to the league being formed in Paris.

30 Following a two-month debate, American international lawyer Elihu Root proposes an amendment to the Covenant to protect the Monroe Doctrine. The Allies reluctantly accept it as the price of American support for the Covenant.

APRIL

1 Woodrow Wilson, back in France, joins David Lloyd George to make Germany's Danzig into a "free city." The League is given the responsibility to protect Danzig's status, leading to years of controversy. The decision is formalized on November 9.

American lawyer Elihu Root proposed an amendment to the Covenant on March 30, 1919, to protect the Monroe Doctrine.

3 Geneva is chosen as the site of the League.

4 **–May 1** A communist government is established in Bavaria following an uprising.

5 The Council of Four places the responsibility for the war on Germany.

A *Literary Digest* poll in the United States shows overwhelming support for the League among American newspapers.

7 Woodrow Wilson threatens to return home from the Peace Conference after facing French opposition on issues relating to reparations, the Saar, and the Rhineland.

9 Wilson introduces his plan for the Saar, the third largest coal-producing area in Europe. The plan involves a League trusteeship.

10 The League Commission adopts a clause permitting withdrawal from the League after a two-year notice.

Rumania invades Hungary to prevent a Hungarian reconquest of Transylvania.

11 Britain, responding to pressure from its Dominions, joins the

United States to eliminate the racial-equality clause from the draft treaty. Japanese officials express strong resentment.

After the United States and Britain block a French plan for a League military staff, the League Commission approves a revised draft of the Covenant.

The Peace Conference accepts Wilson's plan for a fifteen-year League trusteeship of the Saar, to be followed by a plebiscite to determine if the Saar will return to German rule or remain French.

The League Commission selects Geneva as the headquarters for the new organization.

14 Wilson rejects Italy's claim to Fiume, and on April 24, Italy temporarily withdraws from the Peace Conference in protest.

14 **–29** The British and Americans discuss and accept a Treaty of Guarantee for the Rhineland that mandates a gradual withdrawal of French troops over a period of fifteen years.

17 Hankey rejects the post of secretary-general.

19 Polish General Jozef Pilsudski recaptures Vilna from the Bolsheviks, but his victory leads to a decade-long feud with the Lithuanians, who ally themselves with the Russians.

22 **–23** Sir Eric Drummond considers and accepts the post of secretary-general.

26 Wilson says that the military clauses of the peace treaty are dependent upon German disarmament.

28 The Peace Conference approves the final League draft.

MAY

1 Wilson proposes a plan to protect minorities, which prompts the Council of Four to establish the Committee on New States and the Protection of Minorities.

5 Italy returns to the Peace Conference.

14 Lloyd George drafts a proposal for an American mandate over Russian and Turkish Armenia.

21 League opponents in the U.S. Senate begin a campaign to amend the Covenant.

30 The Yugoslavians reject a compromise on Fiume to make the city into a buffer between Yugoslavia and Italy.

JUNE

1 A Rhineland republic is formed under French influence, but it collapses within weeks when confronted by local opposition.

10 The Secretariat is set up in London.

13 ILO conventions go into effect on industrial work hours, pregnancy protection, night work for women and youths, and industrial minimum wages.

20 The German government resigns rather than sign the Treaty of Versailles, which it calls a diktat.

21 Germany scuttles its fleet at Scapa Flow and ends French plans for even more stringent disarmament restrictions.

26 The Council of Four agrees to consider the Saar frontier dispute.

27 Wilson expresses support for the idea of a United States mandate over Armenia, but he says that the American people must make the final decision.

28 The Treaty of Versailles is signed; its first section contains the League Covenant. Poland and the Allies sign a separate treaty, which contains a minorities section that becomes a model for other newly independent countries emerging from the war.

29 The Italian-Greek Treaty gives Italy a protectorate over Albania.

JULY

2 Raymond Fosdick, an American, agrees to become an under secretary-general of the League. He remains in office until it becomes clear that the United States will not join the organization.

10 Wilson submits the Treaty of Versailles to the Senate for ratification.

12 The Allied naval blockade of Germany is lifted, ending a period of near-starvation for tens of thousands of Germans.

22 Reports circulate that Japan will finally drop its demand for racial equality in return for political concessions in Shantung province, a former German sphere of influence in China.

31 The Germans adopt the Weimar constitution, ending the monarchy.

AUGUST

1 Béla Kun flees Hungary as his communist experiment is crushed by Rumania.

4 **–February 25, 1920** The Rumanians confiscate huge amounts of property during their occupation of Hungary. Hungarian claims concerning this property occupy the League and the World Court throughout the twenties.

18 The Poles engineer a revolt in Upper Silesia and take control of much of the region.

19 Wilson tells the Senate Foreign Relations Committee that he will oppose all but interpretative amendments to the Covenant, setting the stage for a major political confrontation over the League.

24 The Communist Party newspaper *Pravda* announces Russian opposition to the League. Russia does not join the organization until 1934.

27 Drummond suspends all appointments to League posts in order to defuse potential opposition from American enemies of the organization.

28 The Senate Foreign Relations Committee approves a resolution demanding that American voting power at the League be equal to the combined vote of all the British Dominions.

SEPTEMBER

4 The Senate Foreign Relations Committee adopts its reservation to the Covenant's Article 10. It also adopts reservations relating to the right to withdraw and to the Monroe Doctrine.

10 The Treaty of St. Germain-en-Laye ends the war with Austria. It contains sections protecting minorities and barring an Austrian union with Germany.

12 Italian nationalists led by Gabriele D'Annunzio occupy Fiume, precipitating a major crisis between Yugoslavia and Italy.

27 The Allied Supreme Council authorizes a plebiscite for the Teschen area, claimed by both Poland and Czechoslovakia.

OCTOBER

6 The Allies force Germany to withdraw troops occupying Latvia.

NOVEMBER

1–19 The Senate Foreign Relations Committee discusses and approves many additional reservations to the Covenant, including one permitting the United States to increase its armaments without the consent of the League.

16 The French elections produce a victory for the Bloc National, led by Georges Clemenceau, Raymond Poincaré, and Aristide Briand.

Poet Gabriele D'Annunzio led Italian nationalists in a September 12, 1919, occupation of Fiume.

19 In the first of two votes, the U.S. Senate refuses to ratify the Treaty of Versailles by 38 to 53.

27 The Treaty of Neuilly-sur-Seine formally ends World War I with Bulgaria.

28 Twelve neutral nations announce that they will defer their acceptance of League membership pending ratification of the Treaty of Versailles by the U.S. Senate.

DECEMBER

1 Eighteen nations attend the Brussels Preliminary Conference to plan League operations and agencies.

8 The Allied Supreme Council approves the Curzon Line as Poland's eastern frontier. Vilna is awarded to Lithuania.

12 Lloyd George announces the end of British military efforts to overthrow the Bolsheviks.

1920

JANUARY

1 The publication of John Maynard Keynes' *The Economic Consequences of the Peace,* highly critical of the Versailles settlement, hurts the prospects for American support of the Covenant.

Paris marks the first anniversary of Armistice Day in 1919 with an exhibition of junked cannons and other weapons of war.

10 The Treaty of Versailles takes force, and the League of Nations is born. Lord Cecil calls for the early admission of the defeated powers.

16 Wilson convenes the first meeting of the Council.

The Saar Basin Governing Commission sets the new boundary for the formerly German coal-producing district.

17 French conservatives, claiming that the Treaty of Versailles is too lenient, remove Clemenceau from the presidency. Paul Deschanel replaces him.

29 The Peruvian assembly votes to submit its dispute with Bolivia over Tacna-Arica to the Council, but the Council refuses to accept responsibility for settling the matter. The dispute flares again a decade later.

FEBRUARY

2 The Dorpat Treaty establishes peace between Russia and Estonia.

10 Wilson orders American officials to ask the Conference of Ambassadors to support the Balfour Declaration, which calls for a Jewish homeland in Palestine.

11 Neutral Switzerland joins the League, subject to a final plebiscite.

The Saar Basin Governing Commission appoints a French chairman, Victor Rault.

12 The Council appoints a High Commissioner to Danzig and defines his duties.

An Allied commission and French forces take control of Upper Silesia.

13 The Council begins supervising the minority section of the Polish treaty. Thereafter, it takes direct responsibility for the protection of European minorities.

MARCH

3 Venezuela joins the League as Latin American reservations about membership appear to fade.

12 The League refuses the Allied Supreme Council's request that it assume a mandate over Armenia.

16 Allied armies, composed of units from Greece, Great Britain, France, and Italy, march into Constantinople, hoping to end a conflict between Greece and Turkey that began after the war. Although the Allies force Turkey, a nonmember of the League and former German ally, to sign the harsh Treaty of Sèvres on August 20, 1920, Western attempts to dismember the country lead to a nationalist uprising led by Kemal Ataturk. League efforts to end the crisis fail. By 1923, Turkey defeats the Allies and restores its authority over all of Asia Minor, leaving the Allies little choice but to replace the Treaty of Sèvres with the more respectful Treaty of Lausanne.

19 The U.S. Senate, by a vote of 49 to 35, just 7 votes shy of a two-thirds majority, rejects the Treaty of Versailles for the last time.

APRIL

4–May 17 The French occupy Frankfurt after Germany orders troops into the Ruhr to suppress a domestic rebellion.

8 Portugal joins the League.

9–11 The Council hears reports on the Danzig elections, the repatriation of prisoners in Siberia, and the protection of Turkish minorities.

10 The Council declines to consider a German appeal to end the Frankfurt occupation.

13–17 The International Health Conference, meeting in London, drafts a plan to create the League's Health Organization.

18–26 European leaders meet in San Remo, Italy, to select "A" mandates, which will be administered by Allied governments until they are granted independence.

19 The League asks the United States to send a delegation to the Brussels International Financial Congress, scheduled for September.

20 A convention on waterway transit is signed at the Barcelona Conference of the League's Transit and Communications Section.

25 Poland launches an offensive against Russia to take the Ukraine. It fails, persuading many Polish commanders that the war cannot be won.

MAY

5 Moscow ignores Drummond's request to welcome a League committee of investigation regarding aid to Polish and Ukrainian refugees.

15 The Council directs that all petitions relating to the Saar should go to the Saar Basin Governing Commission.

16 Despite Switzerland's long-standing policy of neutrality, a national plebiscite favors League membership.

19 The Persians make an appeal to the Council under articles 10 and 11 one day after the Russians attack anti-Bolshevik forces in Persia's Enzeli area.

The Council approves a resolution to place all of the League's specialized agencies, except the ILO, under the authority of the secretary-general.

The League establishes the Epidemics Commission in response to the spread of disease, especially influenza, in the wake of the war.

The Council requires agencies affiliated with the League to report directly to the Secretariat, thereby subordinating their authority to the League itself.

21 Cecil creates a furor in London when he charges that the British government is only lukewarm in its support of the League.

JUNE

4 Hungary signs the Treaty of Trianon with the Allies. The treaty transfers a significant amount of territory from Hungary to Rumania and two new states,

Czechoslovakia and the Kingdom of the Serbs, Croats, and Slovenes (Yugoslavia).

5 The Bolsheviks regain control of Vilna, driving the Polish forces out.

6 The Germans elect a new coalition government and replace the National Assembly with the Reichstag.

14 Persia tells the Council that the Russians must evacuate their troops from Enzeli in advance of direct negotiations.

16 The Council postpones discussing the Enzeli dispute pending direct talks between the Russians and Persians. The talks produce a settlement, relieving the League of further responsibility.

16 **–July 24** A meeting at The Hague produces a draft statute for the Permanent Court of International Justice (PCIJ), commonly known as the World Court.

19 Great Britain uses Article 11 to bring the Aaland Islands controversy, between Finland and Sweden, to the League Council.

20 American jurist Elihu Root submits his influential plan for the PCIJ.

24 The Treaty of St. Germain, between the Allies and Austria, goes into force.

Lloyd George says that Germany can join the League when Berlin demonstrates its willingness to fully accept the terms of the Treaty of Versailles.

25 The Hague is selected as the site for the World Court.

26 Sweden agrees to submit the Aaland Islands dispute to the Council. The Council then forms a Commission of Inquiry.

JULY

5 **–16** During the Spa Conference, Germany agrees to disarm in return for needed coal imports.

League of Nations Members

The following table lists all the members of the League of Nations. The second column shows if they were an original member or, if not an original member, their date of entry. The third column shows when they tended their notice of withdrawal, if they did so.

Member	Date of Entry	Notice of Withdrawal *(Effective after two years)*
Afghanistan	September 1934	
Union of South Africa	*Original member*	
Albania	December 1920	*Annexed by Italy, April 1939*
Argentine Republic	*Original member*	
Australia	*Original member*	
Austria	December 1920	*Annexed by Germany, March 1938*
Belgium	*Original member*	
Bolivia	*Original member*	
Brazil	*Original member*	June 1926
United Kingdom of Great Britain and Northern Ireland	*Original member*	
Bulgaria	December 1920	
Canada	*Original member*	
Chile	*Original member*	June 1938
China	*Original member*	
Colombia	*Original member*	
Costa Rica	December 1920	January 1925
Cuba	*Original member*	
Czechoslovakia	*Original member*	
Denmark	*Original member*	
Dominican Republic	September 1924	
Ecuador	September 1934	
Egypt	May 1937	
Estonia	September 1921	
Ethiopia	September 1923	
Finland	December 1920	
France	*Original member*	
Germany	September 1926	October 1933
Greece	*Original member*	
Guatemala	*Original member*	May 1936
Haiti	*Original member*	April 1942
Honduras	*Original member*	July 1936
Hungary	September 1922	April 1939
India	*Original member*	
Iraq	October 1932	

Member	Date of Entry	Notice of Withdrawal *(Effective after two years)*
Ireland	September 1923	
Italy	*Original member*	December 1937
Japan	*Original member*	March 1933
Latvia	September 1921	
Liberia	*Original member*	
Lithuania	September 1921	
Luxemburg	December 1920	
Mexico	September 1931	
Netherlands	*Original member*	
New Zealand	*Original member*	
Nicaragua	*Original member*	June 1936
Norway	*Original member*	
Panama	*Original member*	
Paraguay	*Original member*	February 1935
Persia	*Original member*	
Peru	*Original member*	April 1939
Poland	*Original member*	
Portugal	*Original member*	
Rumania	*Original member*	July 1940
Salvador	*Original member*	August 1937
Siam	*Original member*	
Spain	*Original member*	May 1939
Sweden	*Original member*	
Switzerland	*Original member*	
Turkey	July 1932	
Union of Soviet Socialist Republics	September 1934	*Declared by Council resolution to no longer be a League member, December 14, 1939*
Uruguay	*Original member*	
Venezuela	*Original member*	July 1938
Yugoslavia	*Original member*	

6 Russia drives the last Polish troops from the Ukraine and begins an advance that nearly captures Warsaw.

On the same day, the Russians assail the League for not being universal in membership.

8 The commissioners drafting the PCIJ statute agree that judges from the Hague Court of Arbitration should help select the judges for the World Court.

12 The Council appoints a Commission of Jurists to consider the legal issues surrounding the Aaland Islands controversy.

20 The Lithuanians and Russians sign a peace treaty in Moscow that reflects the anti-Polish positions of both countries. Russia recognizes Lithuania's sovereignty over Vilna, formerly Russian but now claimed by Poland.

28 The Conference of Ambassadors divides the Teschen district between Poland and Czechoslovakia following disorders that lasted from March to May 1920.

29 **–August 5** The Council meets in San Sebastian, Spain. It considers the admission of Germany and creates the Permanent Mandates Commission.

AUGUST

2 Italy agrees to evacuate its military forces from Albania but continues to view Albania as a field for its political and economic influence.

4 The Council agrees to hold the first meeting of the Assembly in Geneva, confirming the decision to make Geneva, not Brussels, the home of the League.

10 Italy and Greece sign a treaty that includes turning over the island of Rhodes to Greece.

11 The Russians and Latvians sign a peace treaty at Riga.

14 The Czechs and Yugoslavs conclude an alliance, a prelude to the Little Entente. Both countries agree to enforce Hungarian compliance with the peace treaties and to prevent the restoration of the Austrian Empire.

14 **–16** The Poles defeat a Russian advance in fighting around Warsaw.

18 The Scandinavians propose to amend the Covenant to weaken the obligations of smaller countries to participate in League-sponsored sanctions under Article 16.

22 The ILO agrees to investigate labor conditions in Russia, but the Russians denounce the ILO's action, calling the organization a "front" for Western capitalism.

24 The Bolsheviks, implementing the terms of the Russian-Lithuanian treaty of July 20, 1920, turn over Vilna to Lithuania, setting the stage for years of conflict between Lithuania and Poland.

SEPTEMBER

5 The Commission of Jurists examining the Aaland Islands case rules that Finland does not have exclusive domestic jurisdiction over the territory and that historic demilitarization obligations relating to the Islands should, therefore, remain in force.

Poland asks the Council to prevent war with Lithuania over Vilna.

7 France and Belgium sign a military accord that forms the basis of their interwar alliance.

15 French President Deschanel resigns because of ill health.

16 **–20** The Council meets in Paris. It hears both parties to the Aaland Islands dispute and appoints a Commission of Inquiry to further study the controversy.

18 The Council begins considering the dispute over Vilna between Poland and Lithuania. On September 20, it passes a resolution calling for an end to hostilities, which is accepted by both parties.

19 The Council passes a resolution supporting "equitable treatment" in international commerce.

20 Over German protests, the Council recognizes the transfer of Eupen and Malamedy to Belgium, as specified by the Treaty of Versailles and reaffirmed on February 21, 1921.

The Council formally approves Geneva as the headquarters of the League, endorsing its earlier action.

21 The Swiss government agrees to free the League of all taxes.

24 Alexandre Millerand becomes president of France, serving until June 11, 1924.

24 **–October 8** The Brussels International Financial Conference hosts unofficial delegations from the United States and Germany.

OCTOBER

4 The Council accepts the Curzon Line as the Polish-Lithuanian border and appoints a military control commission to oversee the frontier.

7 The Brussels International Financial Congress calls for arms reductions in order to relieve some of the pressure on the international financial structure.

8 The Suwalki Agreement between Poland and Lithuania formally establishes a line to separate their armies. The agreement lasts one day.

9 A maverick Polish army general, Lucian Zeligowski, marches on Vilna and proclaims the new state of Central Lithuania.

12 An armistice is signed between Russia and Poland, ending three years of intermittent war.

14 The Russians and Finns sign a peace treaty at Tartu. Russia is fully at peace for the first time since 1914.

15 **–21** The International Passport Conference meets in Paris.

16 The United States agrees to sit on the Aaland Islands Commission of Inquiry.

20 **–28** The Council meets in Brussels. It agrees to submit the Vilna dispute to the Assembly.

26 **– November 1** The Secretariat staff moves from London to Geneva.

30 The Polish cabinet agrees to a plebiscite in Vilna to determine who will have control of that city. Lithuania first rejects the plebiscite, fearing that Vilna will decide to affiliate with Poland. However, it then reverses its decision, afraid that its rejection will undercut its claim to international support.

NOVEMBER

1 The Tacna-Arica controversy spills over to involve Bolivia and Chile (Bolivia has been involved in its own quarrel with Peru). Bolivia asks the Council, under Article 19, to revise the 1904 treaty with Chile that established the old boundary.

2 Warren Harding is elected president of the United States. His campaign had rejected Wilson's League of Nations but offered vague support for an "association of nations."

11 The Council appoints a commission to look into the Vilna dispute between Lithuania and Poland, and subsequently proposes a plebiscite to resolve the issue of jurisdiction.

12 The Italians and Yugoslavs sign a treaty at Rapallo, resolving the dispute over Fiume.

14 **–December 18** The Council meets in Geneva. It approves the statute of the PCIJ and chooses the members of the Permanent Mandates Commission.

15 **–December 18** The first session of the Assembly creates committees to deal with mandates, disarmament, and other areas of nonpolitical activity.

17 The Council accepts an obligation to protect the constitution of Danzig, thereby guaranteeing the free status of that city. The League's responsibilities toward Danzig are explained in a report by Viscount Kikujiro Ishii of Japan.

The League nominates members to the Economic and Financial Committee, which becomes two separate committees in 1921.

18 The League resolves to send troops to Vilna to supervise the plebiscite.

20 Nineteen nations ask that Spanish be made an official language

of the League, but on November 30, the request is rejected.

22 The League accepts a British proposal to condemn pogroms against Jews in Eastern Europe.

27 At a meeting of the League Disarmament Commission, Britain and France reject the demand for arms reductions made by the smaller countries.

Bulgaria signs the Treaty of Neuilly.

28 An Assembly committee gives the Council exclusive authority to order economic sanctions by blockade.

29 Poland and Lithuania sign the Kovno Protocol for Vilna, setting up a second neutral zone under the auspices of a military control commission.

30 Wilson informs the Council that the Senate has rejected an American mandate over Armenia.

DECEMBER

1 The Council gives its final approval to the appointment of the Permanent Mandates Commission.

Italian poet and adventurer Gabriele D'Annunzio declares war on Italy.

2 The Assembly gives its preliminary approval to the Draft Statute of the PCIJ.

3 Fearing that its collective-security obligations under Article 10 might involve it in a war without the support of its American neighbor, Canada proposes the elimination of the article.

4 Argentina walks out of the Assembly after its proposed amendments to the Covenant, which include one on the compulsory arbitration of disputes, are not accepted. Argentina does not send another delegation to the League until 1933, but its government occasionally pays dues after 1924.

6 The Assembly sends Canada's proposal to eliminate Article 10 to a special committee.

7 A Council report recommends that League members not blockade one another without Council approval.

8 In light of Harding's victory, President Wilson refuses to send an American delegation to the disarmament discussions, even in an advisory capacity.

9 The Lithuanians, having agreed to a plebiscite in Vilna, ask for an eight-month delay.

The League sections for health, economics and finance, and transit and communications are established. They are to be responsible to both the Assembly and Council.

10 The Assembly, following its discussion of an "international language," recommends that public schools around the world teach Esperanto.

12 The Soviet government protests the sending of an international force to Vilna.

The Council assigns Poland the responsibility for the military defense of Danzig's free-city status.

13 The Assembly gives its final approval to the Draft Statute of the PCIJ.

14 The Assembly asks the Council to appoint a commission that later becomes the Temporary Mixed Commission on Armaments.

15 Austria becomes the first member of the former Central Powers to gain admission to the League. China is voted a seat on the Council, but some observers interpret this as an anti-Japanese statement by the League.

16–17 Following discussions, the Assembly approves the admission of Luxemburg, Finland, Bulgaria, Costa Rica, and Albania to the League but rejects the applications of the Baltic states.

20 The League establishes the Committee on Allocation of Expenses to create a formula for setting members' dues. In 1925, a new "unit" system is adopted in which each country is assigned a number of units based on its ability to pay. Under this system, Britain pays just over 10 percent of the League's budget; France and later Germany each pay about 8 percent; Italy and Japan, 6 percent; and other countries, correspondingly less. The United States usually pays for the expenses related to the meetings it attends.

22 Lloyd George says there will be no disarmament until all states join in the League discussions.

27 Italian troops expel D'Annunzio from Fiume.

1921

JANUARY

11 The United States withdraws from all meetings of the Conference of Ambassadors and the Allied Supreme Council.

17 Wilson appoints a representative to the International Commission on Migration, but the representative is withdrawn two months later by President Harding.

20 Wilson rejects a League invitation to mediate between Turkey and Armenia. He claims that the Armenian problem is merely one part of the greater problem of Russia.

24 The Supreme Council asks the League to devise a financial plan to rescue Austria.

FEBRUARY

8 South Africa is granted a mandate over former German South West Africa, which today is Namibia.

12 The League protests a Swiss decision not to permit an international force heading to Vilna to cross neutral Swiss territory.

17 **–March 8** The United States and the League quarrel over Japanese mandates in the Pacific, with the Americans refusing to recognize Japanese administration of the island of Yap.

18 The United States withdraws its representative to the Reparations Commission, as well as all its representatives to League subcommittees.

19 France and Poland sign an anti-German military alliance.

20 Claiming financial stringency, the League refuses to appoint a commissioner for Russian refugees. Instead, it urges the International Red Cross to take on the responsibility.

21 **–March 3** At the twelfth session of the Council, held in Paris, Gastao da Cunha of Brazil is the first non-European Council president.

21 The Council appoints the Advisory Committee on Opium and Other Dangerous Drugs (Opium Committee), composed of the eight signatories of the Opium Convention. It also invites the signatories of the 1904 and 1910 conventions on the traffic in women to attend a meeting from June 30 to July 5 that creates, by September, the Advisory Committee on the Traffic in Women and Children.

25 The Council establishes the Temporary Mixed Commission on Armaments, chaired by French President René Viviani.

26 The Council wrestles with Switzerland's refusal to permit international troops to cross Swiss territory to serve in Vilna.

27 Communists and fascists clash in Florence, beginning a period of continual violence in Italy that does not end until Mussolini seizes power in 1922.

MARCH

3 The League-sponsored plebiscite in Vilna is cancelled.

Poland and Rumania sign a mutual-assistance treaty.

4 The Council meets in a special session to consider Costa Rica's seizure of land in Panama's Coto region. On March 10, the League accepts American plans for mediation, and two days later, the dispute is settled.

Warren Harding is inaugurated as president of the United States.

8 France and Belgium occupy Dusseldorf and two other German cities.

10 **–April 20** The first General Conference on Communications and Transit, held in Barcelona (and known as the Barcelona Conference), is considered a great success after it drafts two major treaties—the Convention on Freedom of Transit and the Convention on the Regime of International Waterways.

17 Lenin announces Russia's New Economic Policy and, on March 18, signs a peace treaty with Poland.

18 **–19** The League dismisses Germany's protests against the penalties assessed for nonpayment of its reparations because the Council claims that only a League member can present a protest.

20 A League-sponsored plebiscite in Upper Silesia shows that 60 percent of all Silesians support incorporation into Germany, while the industrial southeast favors Polish rule.

24 The Reparations Commission declares Germany to be in default of its treaty obligations.

30 The League's Financial Committee asks all countries to suspend their monetary claims against Austria for fifteen years. On April 1, it submits a plan for Austrian relief to the Allied Supreme Council.

APRIL

23 Nicaragua announces its withdrawal from the League, calling it mainly a European organization.

Rumania signs a treaty with Czechoslovakia, which is part of the Little Entente.

24 A plebiscite in the Austrian Tyrol shows that the district favors union with Germany.

25 Because of vigorous protest from the United States and some other countries, the International Public Health Office decides to retain its separate existence instead of merging with the League. The League then forms a provisional Health Committee, which becomes a permanent bureau on July 7, 1923, when the International Health Organization is formally created.

29 Albania appeals to the League under Article 11, protesting the occupation of its territory by Greek troops. On June 15, Albania again uses Article 11 to protest military occupation of its soil, this time by Yugoslavia. These appeals, stemming from the failure to define Albania's borders when the country received independence in 1913, embroil the League in Albanian border controversies for the next four years.

The London Conference on reparations hands a huge bill to Germany and threatens to occupy the Ruhr unless it is paid.

MAY

1 A civil war between the Poles and Germans erupts in Upper Silesia.

10 The Aaland Islands Commission of Inquiry recommends Finnish sovereignty, with guarantees for the Swedish culture and language. On June 14, the Council accepts the recommendation.

11 Vast borrowing lets the Germans meet the Allies' reparations terms, preparing the way for the withdrawal of Allied troops from the Ruhr.

19 George Harvey, the American ambassador to Great Britain, announces that the United States will reject all contact with the League. Officials in Washington give him what *The New York Times* calls "silent approval."

24 W. Cameron Forbes, an American, declines an invitation to sit on the Permanent Mandates Commission.

25 France and Britain agree to a twenty-year delay in pressing Austria for financial claims.

28 Hungary, a former member of the Central Powers, notifies the League of its plans to request admission.

29 The residents of Salzburg, Austria, vote for union with Germany.

JUNE

1 The League considers eleven amendments to the Covenant, submitted by ten states.

7 Yugoslavia and Rumania sign a treaty, completing the formation of the Little Entente.

Austria complains to the Council that Yugoslavia threatened to confiscate the property of Austrian citizens in Yugoslavia unless Vienna pays its war debts in Yugoslav currency.

18 The Council submits the Barcelona Conference conventions concerning free transit and navigation to the states for signing.

19 The Council asks four prominent American jurists to nominate an American to sit on the World Court. However, responding to State Department pressure, they refuse.

21 Despite German protests, the Council approves the transfer of certain state insurance funds from Germany to France. The French claimed these funds after acquiring the formerly German Alsace-Lorraine region as a result of the war.

22 **–23** The Council discusses and reaffirms its 1920 decision that Poland is responsible for the defense of Danzig. It also reaffirms an earlier decision freeing Danzig of military responsibilities, including the storing of munitions.

23 The German commander in Upper Silesia accepts the plan to withdraw troops.

25 The Council refuses to address the question of Yugoslavia's occupation of Albanian territory as long as the matter is also before the Conference of Ambassadors. Albania then appeals to the Assembly, which asks the Council to appoint a Commission of Inquiry.

27 Finland and Sweden agree on guarantees for the Aaland Island Swedes, including protection of the Swedish culture and language.

28 The Council hears both sides of the quarrel over Yugoslavia's confiscation of property from Austrian citizens. Yugoslavia proposes direct negotiations, and the Council orders that no confiscation take place during the talks, which begin in September.

30 Thirty-four nations attend the International Conference on the Traffic in Women and Children, held in Geneva.

JULY

7 President Harding announces that the United States will host the Washington Conference on the Limitation of Armaments. On August 11, the invitations are sent out.

15 Lithuania initially refuses to attend the meetings on the Vilna controversy because Poland has not guaranteed the withdrawal of General Zeligowski's army. The meetings finally begin on August 27.

16 **–19** The first meeting of the Temporary Mixed Commission on Armaments is held in Paris.

17 The Council approves the transfer of state insurance funds from Germany to Poland.

After the League complains that the United States refuses even to acknowledge the receipt of League communications, adverse publicity forces the State Department to reverse its policy of no contact.

18 A subcommittee of the Temporary Mixed Commission addressing the subject of the traffic in arms asserts that the American absence from the commission is impeding progress.

23 The citizens of Helgoland petition the League, asking for either neutralization or annexation to Great Britain.

26 The Treaty of Trianon comes into force.

AUGUST

12 Prompted by British Prime Minister David Lloyd George, the Allied Supreme Council asks the League to define the German-Polish border in Upper Silesia, even though Article 89 of the Treaty of Versailles grants this responsibility to the Allies. On August 29, the League accepts, offering hope that the results of the March 1920 plebiscite will be implemented.

22 **–24** The Conference on Assisting Russian Refugees meets in Geneva.

24 **–25** The United States signs peace treaties with Germany and Austria, thus formally ending its participation in the Great War.

30 **–October 12** The Council is preoccupied with the Vilna dispute between Poland and Lithuania.

SEPTEMBER

1 The Council appoints a committee—composed of Belgium, China, Brazil, and Spain—to study the Upper Silesian boundary.

2 The Permanent Court of International Justice comes into force. American jurist Elihu Root declines a position on it.

3 The Council discusses a proposal to eliminate the Covenant's Article 10, which many proponents of collective security consider to be the heart of the document. On September 17, the Amendment Commission recommends retaining the article.

5 **–October 5** The second session of the Assembly meets, chaired by Jonikheer van Karnebeek of the Netherlands.

12 The Council defers consideration of a border dispute between Austria and Hungary.

22 The Assembly admits Estonia, Latvia, and Lithuania to the League but rejects Montenegro.

A Swiss court upholds the diplomatic status of League employees.

24 Bolivia threatens to leave the League as a result of its dispute with Paraguay.

25 The Assembly resolves that no foreign women should be employed as prostitutes in licensed houses in member countries.

28 Bolivia withdraws its request for Council revision of its 1904 treaty with Chile. It had made the request on November 1, 1920.

The Disarmament Commission recommends against the use of poisonous gas in war and endorses the American call for a conference on naval limitation.

30 A lack of funds prompts the Assembly to "disengage" the League from aiding Russian refugees.

OCTOBER

2 The Assembly instructs the Council to appoint a three-person commission on the Albanian border dispute.

3 The Assembly adopts an amendment to Article 26 that requires unanimous consent to amend the Covenant.

5 The Assembly votes to amend Article 16 to deny a veto over League sanctions to a state accused of violating the Covenant. In addition, it accepts a Scandinavian amendment to Article 16 that weakens the mandatory provisions for states participating in sanctions. Neither amendment is formally approved when submitted to the member states for ratification.

10 **–20** The Baltic states hold the Conference on the Neutralization (and demilitarization) of the Aaland Islands under League auspices.

12 The Council committee on Upper Silesian issues reports that it has delineated the Polish-German frontier, has stated the principles for the administration of the area as a single unit, and recommends the protection of minority rights. These terms are incorporated into a Council resolution passed on March 15, 1922.

20 The Conference of Ambassadors accepts the reports on Upper Silesia and invites the Council to appoint a leader for the Polish-German negotiations.

The Aaland Islands convention is signed in Geneva, confirming the Islands' neutrality and prohibiting Finland from fortifying them. It goes into effect on April 6, 1922.

Former King Karl IV of Hungary fails in his attempt to march on Budapest when the Czechs and Yugoslavs mobilize.

24 **–November 19** The third meeting of the ILO focuses on agricultural labor.

NOVEMBER

7 Great Britain asks for a Council meeting in order to consider invoking Article 16 against Yugoslavia, which is threatening to annex northern Albania. On November 16, the Council meets and establishes a Commission of Inquiry, which bases its investigation on the Conference of Ambassadors' action of November 9, 1921. Eventually, Yugoslavia withdraws its troops because of Allied pressure, not League action.

8 Britain objects to a French decree requiring all persons born in Tunisia or Morocco to hold either a Tunisian or French passport. Claiming that the issue is international and not domestic in character, the British take their case to the World Court.

9 The Conference of Ambassadors reaffirms Albania's 1913 border, but the issue contributes to the Corfu crisis of 1923.

12 **–February 6, 1922** The Washington Conference, an attempt by the United States to break out of the isolation caused by its abstention from the League, meets. Its focus is on naval limitation and stability in the western Pacific.

9 The Conference of Ambassadors reaffirms Albania's 1913 border, but the issue contributes to the Corfu crisis of 1923.

12 **–February 6, 1922** The Washington Conference, an attempt by the United States to break out of the isolation caused by its abstention from the League, meets. Its focus is on naval limitation and stability in the western Pacific.

23 **–26** German and Polish officials meet to resolve their problems in Upper Silesia.

25 Great Britain declares that the inhabitants of mandates do not have the status of subjects, although some states, including Great Britain, often treat them as if they do.

DECEMBER

2 As Bolivia did earlier, Peru withdraws its request to have the Council revise its 1883 treaty with Chile. However, it reserves the right to resubmit the request.

12 The United States and Japan settle their dispute over the administration of Yap when Tokyo guarantees Washington economic rights in the mandated Pacific islands equivalent to those of the League powers. A treaty is signed on February 11, 1922.

12 **–14** The International Conference on Standardization of Sera and Serological Tests meets in London.

14 Czechoslovakia and Poland agree to submit their future disputes to compulsory arbitration.

28 Lithuania rejects a proposed settlement of the Vilna dispute. Relying on Russian support, it instead demands the removal of all Polish authority from the district.

American Secretary of State Charles Evans Hughes (second from right) leads delegates to the Washington Naval Conference, intended to bring about naval limitation and stability in the western Pacific. The conference was hosted by the United States from November 12, 1921, to February 6, 1922.

1922

JANUARY

8 After a plebiscite in Vilna held by General Lucian Zeligowski shows that the majority of the population favors Poland, Vilna's diet votes to unite with Poland. Lithuania protests.

11 The Council accepts responsibility for seeing that the Aaland Islands convention is executed in a lawful manner.

13 To resolve the Vilna problem, the Council establishes a provisional line of demarcation for judicial and civil administrative matters. The line is formally approved on May 17, 1922.

Finland appeals to the Council under articles 11 and 17, protesting Russian actions in eastern Karelia. Russia, a nonmember of the League and diplomatically isolated, rejects League competence over the problem.

14 The Council expands the Advisory Committee on the Traffic in Women and Children.

Armenia asks the League for ships to transport 100,000 refugees from Turkey, where many Armenians were recently massacred.

15 Raymond Poincaré takes office as France's new premier. Pursuing a nationalist and anti-German foreign policy, he serves until June 1, 1924.

18 Leon Trotsky attacks the League as a capitalist instrument.

22 The first session of the PCIJ convenes.

30 The ILO asks the World Court to rule on the legality of establishing an eight-hour day for agricultural workers. The Court agrees to hear the issue.

FEBRUARY

6 The delegates to the Washington Conference sign the Five Power

Raymond Poincaré became French premier on January 15, 1922.

Leon Trotsky, Russian revolutionary and Soviet statesman, accused the League of being a capitalist tool on January 18, 1922.

Naval Limitation Treaty, the Four Power Treaty for Pacific Stability, and the Nine Power Treaty on China.

15 The PCIJ moves into the Carnegie Peace Palace at The Hague.

20 Lord Esher (Reginald Esher) of Great Britain presents his plan for land-armament reduction to the Temporary Mixed Commission. He calls for percentage reductions roughly based on the formulas used at the Washington Conference. The plan is soon rejected.

MARCH

3 A fascist coup overturns the government in Fiume, and on March 17, Italian troops enter the city.

11 The League notes that twenty-one countries are late in paying their dues. Except for Argentina, they pay their assessments by the end of the year.

15 Italy and France ask that implementation of the military clauses of the Treaty of Versailles be the responsibility of the League.

17 Poland signs neutrality treaties with Estonia, Latvia, and Finland.

20 **–28** The Epidemics Commission convenes a European Health Conference in Warsaw. Twenty-seven nations meet to establish the first effective international response to epidemic disease.

24 The U.S. Senate ratifies the Four Power Treaty for Pacific Stability.

The Council authorizes the creation of a local advisory committee (Landsrat) in the Saar to soften criticism of the League administration.

26 The Council accepts Armenia as a special responsibility of the League.

29 The U.S. Senate ratifies the Five Power Naval Limitation Treaty.

APRIL

3 The United States refuses to sign a League convention on the white slave trade because it conflicts with the police provisions of some of its states.

8 Vilna becomes part of Poland. Lithuania refuses to recognize the change and closes its frontier with Poland. This lasts until the state of war is ended in 1927.

10 **–May 24** The Genoa Conference meets to discuss the economic revival of Europe. Although Germany and Russia attend, little real progress is made because France both fears a German revival and demands that the Bolsheviks pay the debts of the czar. The French also refuse to permit arms-limitation discussions.

15 Seeking to conciliate the German population, the League authorizes a new parliament in the Saar.

16 The Rapallo Treaty allows Russia and Germany to break out of their postwar isolation.

MAY

1 Latvia's constitution goes into effect.

3 A Polish commissioner, General Adalbert Korfanty, leads an uprising in Upper Silesia with covert help from France. Polish control is restored, thereby reversing the settlement achieved with the 1921 plebiscite.

11 **–17** The Council meets in Geneva and establishes a South American bureau.

12 Lithuania declares that it will protect minorities, but it compiles a poor record in this area.

15 In the wake of the Korfanty uprising, Germany and Poland sign an Upper Silesian convention that provides for a complex system of economic and social administration by both countries. The convention goes into force on June 3, 1922.

The Council creates the Committee for Intellectual Cooperation, one of the League's most novel ventures.

16 The Council refuses to launch an inquiry into the Russian famine.

17 Czechoslovakia grants the League authority to act as an arbitrator in the event of a loan default.

The Council supports Germany's protest against the treatment of Germans in Poland.

The Council declares that nonmembers of the League must promise, prior to appearing before the World Court, to abide by the Court's decision.

18 Hope for disarmament diminishes when only twenty countries reply to a League arms questionnaire.

31 Over French objections, the Reparations Commission grants Germany a one-year moratorium due to fears of a German economic collapse.

JUNE

2 The Conference of Ambassadors asks the Council to recommend a settlement for a border dispute over Burgenland, situated between Austria and Hungary. On June 18, the Council complies.

JULY

2 Hungary asks the Council to confirm a Delimitation Commission ruling on its boundary with Yugoslavia in territory north of the River Mur.

3 Lord Cecil proposes the Draft Treaty of Mutual Assistance to the Temporary Mixed Commission on Armaments.

3–5 A Conference on Identity Certificates for Russian Refugees meets in London.

6 Japan ratifies the Washington Conference treaties.

17–24 The Council meets in London.

18 The Council, approving a resolution to halt Balkan frontier raids by Bulgarian bandits, creates a mixed Yugoslavian-Bulgarian commission.

19 The Council successfully persuades Yugoslavia, Greece, and Rumania to seek a claims settlement against Bulgaria for the frontier raids. The Bulgarians had first brought the controversy to the Council under Article 11.

20 The Council orders the Secretariat to join other experts to study the River Mur dispute between Hungary and Yugoslavia, and to make recommendations for a settlement. Yugoslavia later refuses to accept the recommendations.

The Rockefeller Foundation gives its first major grant to the League's Health Committee.

AUGUST

1 Lord Balfour (Arthur Balfour), the British foreign secretary, proposes a comprehensive reparations settlement to free Germany from its debt obligations. American officials, fearing they might have to forgive Britain's debts to the United States, refuse to consider the idea.

The German mark begins to collapse under the weight of the economic strains brought on by reparations.

Lithuania adopts a constitution and becomes a democratic republic.

3–4 The Milan city government falls to the fascists.

7–14 The London Conference on reparations fails when the British and French cannot reach a comprehensive settlement.

12 At its first ordinary session, the World Court bars the ILO from regulating agricultural labor.

14 The Allied Supreme Council again asks the League to take responsibility for stabilizing Austrian finances.

29 The Conference of Ambassadors refers the Upper Silesian controversy to the League Council. A partition eventually places 60 percent of the population under German administration but most of the mineral and industrial wealth in Polish hands.

British Foreign Secretary Lord Balfour (Arthur Balfour) proposed a reparations settlement to free Germany from its debt, but American officials nixed the plan.

31 The Advisory and Technical Committee for Communications and Transit establishes an investigatory committee to settle a dispute over railroad traffic to and from the Saar. Germany argues that the traffic falls under German domestic jurisdiction, but France challenges this position.

31–October 4 The Council meets in Geneva and focuses on Austrian finances.

SEPTEMBER

1 Britain's Lord Balfour proposes that the League protect the Holy Places in Palestine.

2 Germany protests the presence of French troops in the Saar.

4 Justice John Clarke resigns from the U.S. Supreme Court to work for American membership in the League.

4–30 The Assembly meets.

Hungary becomes the third member of the Central Powers admitted to the League.

8 Peru announces that it will not participate in League activities until the United States joins.

Citing recent massacres of Armenians, Britain asks the League to protect minorities in Asia Minor.

9 France reaffirms its opposition to German membership in the League.

12 Spain threatens to withdraw from the League if it is denied a seat on the Council.

13 The smaller Council members discuss ways of reducing the pull of the Great Powers on that body. Among their suggestions is increasing the number of smaller states on the Council. On September 21, the Council adds two nonpermanent seats, raising the number to six.

The Disarmament Commission drafts a treaty based on Lord Cecil's proposal for regional pacts.

Marcus Garvey, an American black separatist leader, asks the League to establish a mandate over South Africa.

19 The Council transmits its decision in the Burgenland case to the Conference of Ambassadors.

20 The League authorizes a loan to Austria as part of its financial plan for that country.

Bolivia asks the League to arbitrate a 1904 treaty with Chile.

23 Lloyd George proposes that the League supervise transit through the Bosporus and the Dardanelles.

25–27 A League-sponsored Serology Conference meets in London.

27 The Assembly adopts Resolution XIV, laying a basis for the Draft Treaty of Mutual Assistance and the Geneva Protocol for the Pacific Settlement of International Disputes.

28 The Assembly asks the Council to assist in finding employment for Russian refugees.

30 Admitting failure at gaining Yugoslavian cooperation, the Council suspends its efforts to settle the Hungarian-Yugoslavian dispute over the River Mur.

Annex III.

RESOLUTION XIV OF THE THIRD COMMITTEE
OF THE THIRD ASSEMBLY.

(a) The Assembly having considered the report of the Temporary Mixed Commission on the question of a general Treaty of Mutual Guarantee, being of opinion that this report can in no way affect the complete validity of all the Treaties of Peace or other agreements which are known to exist between States; and considering that this report contains valuable suggestions as to the methods by which a Treaty of Mutual Guarantee could be made effective, is of opinion that:

1. No scheme for the reduction of armaments, within the meaning of Article 8 of the Covenant, can be fully successful unless it is general.

2. In the present state of the world many Governments would be unable to accept the responsibility for a serious reduction of armaments unless they received in exchange a satisfactory guarantee of the safety of their country.

3. Such a guarantee can be found in a defensive agreement which should be open to all countries, binding them to provide immediate and effective assistance in accordance with a prearranged plan in the event of one of them being attacked, provided that the obligation to render assistance to a country attacked shall be limited in principle to those countries situated in the same part of the globe. In cases, however, where, for historical, geographical, or other reasons, a country is in special danger of attack, detailed arrangements should be made for its defence [*sic*] in accordance with the above-mentioned plan.

4. As a general reduction of armaments is the object of the three preceding statements, and the Treaty of Mutual Guarantee the means of achieving that object, previous consent to this reduction is therefore the first condition of the Treaty.

This reduction could be carried out either by means of a general treaty, which is the most desirable plan, or by means of partial treaties designed to be extended and open to all countries.

In the former case, the Treaty will carry with it a general reduction of armaments. In the latter case, the reduction should be proportionate to the guarantees afforded by the Treaty.

The Council of the League, after having taken the advice of the Temporary Mixed Commission, which will examine how each of these two systems could be carried out, should further formulate and submit to the Governments for their consideration and sovereign decision the plan of the machinery, both political and military, necessary to bring them clearly into effect.

(b) The Assembly requests the Council to submit to the various Governments the above proposals for their observations, and requests the Temporary Mixed Commission to continue its investigations, and, in order to give precision to the above statements, to prepare a draft treaty embodying the principles contained therein.

OCTOBER

2 At the Council, Britain and France agree to ask the PCIJ to issue an advisory opinion on the question of the Tunisian passport falling under domestic or international law. The Court later rules that it is a French domestic matter.

4 The Geneva Protocol for Austrian Financial Reconstruction is signed. It later forms the basis for one of the League's major achievements.

4–30 The Assembly meets, with Sir Augustin Edwards of Chile as presiding officer.

9 German President Friedrich Ebert says that his country will not join the League until the United States does.

11 Iraq and Great Britain sign a treaty making Iraq into a modified mandate of the League.

19 Lloyd George falls as British prime minister, leading to the ministry of Andrew Bonar Law, who serves from October 23, 1922, to May 20, 1923.

25 The Irish government adopts a constitution.

28 Mussolini's March on Rome brings his fascist government to power.

31 Italian King Victor Emmanuel III calls on Mussolini to form a cabinet. Similar to Adolph Hitler eleven years later, Mussolini takes office legally, despite the violent methods of his fascists.

NOVEMBER

14 Germany's economic problems lead to the fall of the Joseph Wirth government and to its replacement with the cabinet of Wilhelm Cuno.

15 A general election in Great Britain produces a conservative (Unionist) victory, as the liberals split and the Labour Party becomes the official opposition for the first time.

The March on Rome on October 28, 1922, brought Mussolini's fascist government to power.

16 Hungary asks the Council to mediate a minor dispute with Czechoslovakia over the border near the Salgo-Tarjan coal basin.

20–February 4, 1923 The first Lausanne Conference is held and concludes peace between Turkey and Greece after years of conflict. To protect its oil interests, the United States attends the conference.

25 Mussolini is given dictatorial powers, as Italian authorities feel he is the key to maintaining order.

DECEMBER

9–11 The second London Conference on reparations is held. Another French and British failure to reach a settlement leaves Germany financially vulnerable.

13 The League announces that its plans to protect minorities in Turkey are now in force. On December 18, however, Turkey announces its own plan.

18 Russia denounces Lloyd George's plan to put the League in control of sea traffic through the Bosporus and Dardanelles.

26 The Reparations Commission again declares Germany to be in default. French nationalists on the commission demand that Germany comply to the letter with all agreements.

30 Soviet Russia reorganizes as the Union of Soviet Socialist Republics (USSR), a federation of socialist republics.

1923

JANUARY

6 Albert Thomas, director-general of the ILO, states that he deplores American abstention from the League and the ILO.

The Reparations Commission grants Danzig a twelve-month moratorium on its debt payments.

8–14 The Opium Committee discusses and approves a resolution calling for all nations to exchange information about drug trafficking.

9 The Ruhr crisis begins when the Reparations Commission declares a German default on coal deliveries to France and Belgium.

10 Lithuania occupies Memel following a local pro-Lithuanian uprising and establishes a provisional government.

11 Following Germany's default, Premier Raymond Poincaré orders French troops into the Ruhr industrial area of Germany. Britain refuses to participate in the occupation.

13 Germany suspends all reparation payments to France and Belgium.

19 The Germans begin passive resistance in the Ruhr district.

25 Lord Curzon (George Curzon) of the British Foreign Office asks the Council to consider, under Article 11, the boundary quarrel between Turkey and Iraq.

29 **–February 3** The Council meets in Paris and creates rules for minority petitions.

30 A Greek-Turkish agreement on the exchange of minority populations is signed.

President Harding agrees that the United States will act as mediator in the Tacna-Arica dispute.

31 Hungary and Czechoslovakia accept Council-sponsored arbitration of their border dispute in the Salgo-Tarjan area, which leads to a settlement embodied in a Council resolution on April 23, 1923.

The Council asks the Permanent Advisory Commission on Armaments to report on Resolution XIV, preparing the way for the Draft Treaty of Mutual Assistance.

FEBRUARY

2 The Council refers German complaints about Polish treatment to the PCIJ.

Lord Curzon (George Curzon) of the British Foreign Office brought the boundary quarrel between Turkey and Iraq before the Council on January 25, 1923.

3 The Council, citing Article 15, permits Poland and Lithuania to establish administrative authority in separate sections of the neutral zone around Vilna. Poland accepts the resolution, but Lithuania does not.

5 Switzerland agrees to provide the ILO with a new home overlooking Lake Geneva.

A bitter three-month strike in the Saar begins, ostensibly over wages but in fact against the French occupation of the Ruhr.

7 The PCIJ issues an advisory opinion upholding Great Britain's contention that the Tunisian passport dispute is fundamentally international in character and, therefore, can be referred to the League for resolution. On May 24, the French and British settle the dispute by mutual consent.

10 Lithuania asks for an advisory opinion from the PCIJ regarding Council procedures to settle the Vilna controversy.

12 The ILO reports on comparative cost-of-living standards.

16 The Conference of Ambassadors assigns formerly German Memel to Lithuania as an autonomous state. Lithuania incorporates Memel on May 8, 1924.

24 President Harding and Secretary of State Charles Evans Hughes jointly call for the United States' entry into the World Court.

27 The Burgenland dispute between Austria and Hungary is settled. Hungary agrees to pay Austria 3 million Swiss francs as reparations for the damage caused by Magyar raiders.

MARCH

1 **–17** In accord with a Council resolution of July 19, 1922, a mixed commission settles the Bulgarian-Yugoslavian border dispute by drawing a clearer frontier line.

4 The United States agrees to cooperate with the Opium Committee.

13 Chaim Weizmann, a leader of the Zionist movement, proposes Jerusalem as the seat of the League.

14 Acting on a Polish request from February 26, the Conference of Ambassadors officially recognizes the Curzon Line as the new Polish-Lithuanian boundary. Since it gives Vilna to Poland, Lithuania protests.

Secretary of State Charles Evans Hughes called for American entry into the World Court on February 24, 1923.

15 Appealing under Article 15, Hungary asks the Council to protect Hungarian farmers in Rumania from property-confiscation decrees and to declare that Rumanian agrarian law is in violation of treaties.

Léon Bourgeois resigns as president of the French Senate in order to devote his remaining years to support of the League.

APRIL

17 **–23** The Council meets in Geneva and asks the United States to join the disarmament talks.

21 With reference to the eastern Karelia dispute between Finland and the USSR, the Council asks the PCIJ to rule on the applicability of the 1920 Dorpat Treaty.

22 The Council approves a major loan to Austria.

23 After hearings, the Council adopts a report on the Hungarian-Rumanian farm case, which requires negotiations under the guidance of the Council. The negotiations fail, as Hungary raises new objections to Rumanian conduct.

The Council asks High Commissioner for Refugees Fridtjof Nansen to draft a plan to aid Greek refugees.

23 **–July 24** The second Lausanne Conference discusses and finally produces a treaty with Turkey.

26 The U.S. Senate Foreign Relations Committee chairman, William Borah, announces his opposition to American membership in the World Court.

27 Lord Cecil again calls for German membership in the League.

MAY

4 The French Senate Finance Committee criticizes the League for "lavishness."

5 Austria and Hungary sign an arbitration pact.

10 Mechislav Vorovsky, a Soviet delegate to the Lausanne Conference, is murdered by anticommunists in Switzerland. The Swiss ignore Moscow's demand that they guarantee the safety of all Soviet representatives in Switzerland and begin a boycott of League meetings that lasts until the late twenties.

16 The Argentine president urges his country's re-entry into the League.

19 Hungarian and Rumanian officials discuss their quarrel over the Hungarian-owned farms confiscated by the Rumanian government.

22 Stanley Baldwin takes over as head of Britain's conservative cabinet, with Lord Curzon as foreign secretary. Baldwin serves until January 22, 1924.

24 **–June 6** The Opium Conference is held. An American plan to restrict the production of opium is accepted.

JUNE

6 The Health Committee adopts a convention on the sanitary control of inland waterways.

16 The Soviet government announces that it refuses to cooperate in the PCIJ's consideration of the eastern Karelia case.

JULY

2 **–7** The Council meets in Geneva and is preoccupied with Canada's attack on Article 10, a move supported by Austria.

2 The Council expresses its satisfaction at the pace of Austria's financial reconstruction.

5 The Council continues to seek a settlement in the Hungarian-Rumanian farm dispute. It asks Hungary to reassure its nationals and Rumania to live up to its treaty obligations.

Sir Eric Drummond answers critics of the League's finances. Although he asserts that further budget reductions are not possible, France demands more cuts.

Stanley Baldwin became prime minister of Great Britain on May 22, 1923.

6 The Council backs a Greek loan to refugees in Asia Minor.

7 The League's Health Organization, provisionally organized in 1921, becomes a permanent agency.

15 **–16** Experts meet at The Hague to discuss bills of exchange.

20 The League agrees on reduced dues for Central American republics in order to keep them as members.

23 The PCIJ refuses to rule on the eastern Karelia case unless the Soviets agree to submit the case to the Court.

24 A peace treaty replacing the Treaty of Sèvres and ending World War I with Turkey is signed at Lausanne, resulting in hundreds of thousands of Greeks and Turks being forced from their homes in a population exchange.

25 Britain's Lord Curzon recommends a League-sponsored loan to Hungary similar to the Austrian loan.

26 The Council asks the PCIJ to render an advisory opinion concerning the German minority in Poland.

AUGUST

2 Vice President Calvin Coolidge becomes the American president upon Warren Harding's death.

7 The Disarmament Commission completes its Draft Treaty of Mutual Assistance, making aggressive war an international crime.

12 Gustav Stresemann, supported by the socialists and the center parties, becomes Germany's chancellor as the Wilhelm Cuno cabinet falls.

18 The Conference of Ambassadors asks the Council if the terms of a delimitation agreement setting the Czech-Polish frontier near Teschen can be altered under Article 11. On August 27, the Council asks the PCIJ for an advisory opinion, which is delivered on December 6, 1923.

23 The United States agrees to attend the upcoming conference on opium. American internationalists become more optimistic as the American Bar Association, on August 31, calls for full membership in the League.

27 The murder of Italian General Enrico Tellini, who was investigating the Albanian-Greek border dispute for the Conference of Ambassadors, begins the Corfu affair.

29 An Italian ultimatum to Greece demands punishment of Tellini's murderers, a 50-million-lire indemnity, and other concessions.

30 Greece rejects the Italian ultimatum, while Mussolini joins the Conference of Ambassadors' protest regarding Tellini's murder.

31 Twenty-one Italian vessels attack Corfu, killing sixteen people and wounding thirty-five. The Italians then occupy the Greek island. The Conference of Ambassadors formally asks Greece to investigate the Tellini murder.

Calvin Coolidge became president of the United States on August 2, 1923, when Warren Harding died.

31 –September 29 The Council is preoccupied with the Corfu crisis, especially after Greece, on September 1, appeals to the League under articles 12 and 15.

SEPTEMBER

1 An earthquake in Tokyo kills 200,000 people and levels the city.

2 Greece proposes an international investigation of Tellini's assassination under the auspices of the Council.

3 –29 The fourth meeting of the Assembly is presided over by Sir Cosme de la Torriente y Perasa of Cuba.

Ethiopia and Ireland are admitted to full membership.

The Canadian effort to weaken Article 16 is supported 29 to 1, but Persia's opposition technically kills it because of the veto rule.

4 French Premier Poincaré declares that the Council will state the facts of the Greek-Italian dispute but will avoid the issue of jurisdiction as long as the dispute is being considered by the Conference of Ambassadors.

Italy loses in all elections for Assembly committee posts.

5 Greek delegate Nicolas Politis reminds the Council of its responsibility in the Tellini affair under articles 10, 12, and 15, but Italy's foreign minister refuses to accept the authority of the League. The Conference of Ambassadors declares that Greece is responsible for the incident because the murders occurred on Greek soil.

6 The Council approves a Conference of Ambassadors recommendation that Greece pay an indemnity to Italy. The approval is embodied in an eight-point resolution that the Council forwards to the Conference of Ambassadors.

7 The Conference of Ambassadors accepts the Council's eight-point resolution.

Brazil, having threatened to withdraw from the League if Italy withdraws, reverses itself when given a nonpermanent seat on the Council.

8 The Conference of Ambassadors sends its demands to Athens. The demands are based on the Council's eight-point resolution.

9 The Greek government agrees to the Conference of Ambassadors' demands for an indemnity and reparations, thereby relieving the Council of the need to threaten Italy with sanctions.

11 The PCIJ rules in favor of the German minority in Poland.

Press reports circulate that international banks will extend loans to Germany if France withdraws from the Ruhr.

11 –12 Italian representative Romano Avezzana backpedals on his government's pledge to evacuate Corfu by September 27, nearly collapsing the settlement.

12 The Draft Treaty of Mutual Assistance is approved by the Assembly and submitted to the League members for ratification.

13 Mussolini finally accepts the plan to evacuate Corfu.

General Miguel Primo de Rivera takes power in Spain in a military coup.

Like Mussolini, he is unsympathetic to the League.

14 The Conference of Ambassadors sets September 22 as the deadline for the Commission of Inquiry to report on the Tellini murder.

Mexico again rejects League membership.

15 The Assembly adopts a resolution calling for the end of the traffic in women.

18 Italy continues to question the authority of the League in the Corfu dispute and asks for a formal interpretation of Article 15. The Council accepts the primacy of the Conference of Ambassadors in the affair.

20 The League agrees to consider extending the principles of the Washington Conference to nonsignatory nations.

Ethiopia's admission to the League is held up by a debate over Ethiopian slavery.

22 The Commission of Inquiry submits a report to the Conference of Ambassadors that fails to identify the murderers of Tellini.

23 The Conference of Ambassadors refers to the Council, under Article 11, Lithuania's refusal to accept conditions for the transfer of Memel to Lithuania. The Council appoints a commission to study the issue and to prepare a new draft convention.

25 The Conference of Ambassadors awards Italy the full 50-million-lire indemnity, basing its decision on Greece's failure to identify and punish Tellini's murderers.

26 German passive resistance in the Ruhr ends. Economic panic sweeps through Europe as the German mark collapses and the French franc falls approximately 25 percent.

27 Italy withdraws its troops from Corfu.

28 The Council submits to a Commission of Jurists five questions relating to the authority of the League in political disputes such as the Corfu affair.

Ethiopia is admitted to the League despite the evidence of slavery there.

29 Greece pays its indemnity under protest.

The League receives its first formal request for a financial program for Hungary similar to the Austrian program. The request comes from Hungary's reparations creditors.

30 The Commission of Inquiry's second report completes the indecisive factual record of the Corfu affair.

China hints at withdrawal from the League because of its failure to be given a Council seat.

OCTOBER

6 In the wake of Ethiopia's entry, the League announces plans for a campaign to eliminate slavery from countries where it still exists.

27 The PCIJ hears arguments in the Czech-Polish border dispute.

29 The League's High Commissioner for the Austrian financial program says that the plan could be duplicated elsewhere.

NOVEMBER

6 Drummond says that Mussolini is again ready to support the League.

7 Fridtjof Nansen calls for a League-sponsored loan to Germany along the lines of the Austrian loan. He declares that the League is the only hope for distressed economies such as those of Germany and Greece.

8 **–11** Hitler attempts his Beer Hall Putsch in Munich but fails.

10 The Reparations Commission unveils its plans to reconstruct the Hungarian economy.

12 The PCIJ holds an extraordinary session to discuss the Czech-Polish border dispute.

14 A new Italian election law allows Mussolini to extend and consolidate his power.

15 **–December 9** The League holds its second General Conference on Communications and Transit.

16 A military coup in Lithuania succeeds in overthrowing the government.

17 Great Britain supports American demands for equal commercial opportunity in mandated territories.

20 An ILO convention on minimum wages for certain categories of industrial work goes into force.

The German currency stabilizes after the ruinous inflation stemming from the Ruhr occupation.

20 **–26** The second International Conference on Standardization of Sera and Seralogical Tests meets in Paris.

23 Stresemann falls as chancellor of Germany but takes over the Ministry for Foreign Affairs.

26 The Commission of Jurists begins deliberations in its study of the Covenant in response to the problems encountered during the Corfu incident.

29 League members are asked to sign a protocol to make arbitration a part of all commercial treaties.

30 Committees are formed to study the relationship between Germany's economic instability and the reparations accords.

DECEMBER

6 The PCIJ issues an advisory opinion, requested on August 18, that there be no deviation from the findings of the Delimitation Commission in the Czech-Polish boundary dispute.

The British general election sharply reduces the Conservative Party's dominance, but Stanley Baldwin remains the prime minister.

9 The General Conference on Communications and Transit produces conventions on the International Regime of Railways, the International Regime of Maritime Ports, the Transmission of Electric Power, and the Development of Hydroelectric Power.

10–20 The Council meets and is chiefly concerned with the Memel dispute.

11 The Council discusses the elimination of slavery.

12–13 The Conference of Ambassadors conveys to Italy and Greece the Commission of Inquiry reports on the Corfu affair that were made to the League.

13 The United States gives the League $75,000 to defray the costs of the inquiry into the traffic in women.

17 An agreement settles the dispute between Greece and Albania that began after Athens deported thousands of Albanian Moslems.

18 The Soviets agree to join League discussions on extending the Washington Conference naval principles.

20 The Council adopts a plan for the financial reconstruction of Hungary.

American banker Henry Morgenthau outlines a plan to resettle Greek refugees under League auspices.

27–30 The Conference for the Exchange of Health Officers hears physicians from five countries say that the American prohibition of alcohol has significantly improved the health of Americans.

1924

JANUARY

14 An American, Charles G. Dawes, becomes head of the committee of reparations experts.

American Charles G. Dawes was appointed head of the Reparations Commission on January 14, 1924.

16 A special Council session begins consideration of the Hungarian loan program, a League project condemned by Rumania.

21 Lenin dies. A succession struggle between Joseph Stalin and Leon Trotsky continues for almost four years.

22 Ramsay MacDonald becomes Britain's first Labour Party prime minister. He serves until November 4.

25 France and Czechoslovakia sign a mutual defense treaty.

27 Yugoslavia abandons its claims to Fiume in a treaty with Italy.

FEBRUARY

1 Britain extends diplomatic recognition to the USSR, a move that reflects the leftist policy of Prime Minister MacDonald.

3 Woodrow Wilson, an architect of the League, dies in Washington.

7 The Tangier Convention, between Britain, France, and Spain, provides for the permanent neutralization of the Tangier Zone of Africa.

9 The jurists studying the weaknesses of the Covenant in light of the Corfu incident refuse to recommend that all war be declared illegal.

15–25 The Naval Subcommittee of the Permanent Advisory Commission on Armaments meets. It hopes to extend the Washington Naval Treaty to additional countries but fails when Russia and Greece block the reductions.

18 The Council appoints the Memel Commission, led by an American, Norman H. Davis. On March 12, the Soviets protest any League action on Memel without Moscow's participation.

21 The League's Reparations Commission gives its final approval to the Hungarian loan. American W.G.P. Harding (no relation to the president) will administer the program.

24 Germany demands the return of its colonies, confiscated after the war, showing that even a moderate German government will not reconcile itself to the Treaty of Versailles.

MARCH

12 The Council finally accepts the Delimitation Commission's proposals in the Czech-Polish boundary dispute, subject to minor modifications.

13 The Council approves the report of the jurists who examined the League's competence in the Corfu dispute.

Answering complaints about restrictions on Austrian sovereignty, the Council informs Vienna that all the obligations of its reconstruction program must be met.

14 Both Lithuania and the Council accept a new draft convention making Memel subject to Lithuanian sovereignty. They request that Great Britain, Japan, Italy, and France also endorse it.

Two protocols for Hungarian reconstruction are signed in Geneva by Hungary and the Little Entente, clearing away the political obstacles to a League-sponsored loan.

15 The Council gives the Opium Committee authority to draft principles for upcoming drug conferences.

19 Turkish officials refuse to cooperate with the League in providing identity papers for Armenians still in Turkey. They claim that no Armenian refugees remain there.

21 The Parisian newspaper *Temps* proposes a French-English pledge to fight for the League in the event of a European political crisis.

23 Austrian opposition parties join the government to demand the end of League control over Austrian finances.

28 British officials ask the League to define its power to supervise the military clauses of the peace treaties. The request is viewed as a response to rumored military developments in Germany.

APRIL

6 The fascists, using violence, sweep the Italian elections.

9 The Dawes Plan for the financial rescue of Germany includes the restructuring of the German Reichsbank, the provision of foreign loans, and the reduction of reparations. Berlin approves the terms on April 16.

19 Ramsay MacDonald calls for German membership in the League.

MAY

1 The League begins supervising the Hungarian economy.

Greece becomes a republic after King George II is overthrown.

6 Czechoslovakia and Poland accept the final Council proposals on the Teschen boundary dispute.

8 The Memel convention is signed, giving future disagreements the status of international disputes and assigning the League specific responsibilities in handling them.

25 French socialist leader Edouard Herriot pledges that any government he leads would place the League at the center of its foreign policy.

26 A United States immigration act limits immigration from most countries and completely ends Japanese immigration. The Japanese unsuccessfully seek League relief for what they consider to be an affront.

JUNE

10 Mussolini's fascists murder socialist leader Giacomo Matteotti. The liberals and socialists protest by leaving the parliament, but this permits Mussolini to pack the legislature and consolidate his power.

11 **–17** The Council meets in Geneva and reviews the progress of the Austrian and Hungarian financial plans. It also passes a resolution asking members not to increase their military budgets pending the implementation of the general plan for arms reduction embodied in the Draft Treaty of Mutual Assistance.

11 Argentina pays its back dues and, on August 21, asks to return to Geneva.

Germany protests a Council discussion that appears to endorse a future French military occupation of the Saar.

14 Edouard Herriot becomes the French premier following the victory of a left-of-center coalition. He holds the post until April 10, 1925.

JULY

5 Responding to Dominion pressure, Britain announces that it will reject the Draft Treaty of Mutual Assistance.

15 Britain and Canada formally reject the Draft Treaty, ending all serious hope that it will become law.

Edouard Herriot became French premier on June 14, 1924.

16 **–August 16** The London Conference discusses and approves the Dawes Plan, which leads to stabilization of the European economy.

17 **–19** The Conference on Experts for the Exchange of Official Information discusses methods for facilitating intergovernmental communication.

26 The French Council on National Defense approves the Draft Treaty in spite of British opposition.

AUGUST

26 Ramsay MacDonald refuses to pledge that England will not exceed its present arms budgets.

29 **–October 3** The Council discusses the British-Turkish border quarrel over Mosul, a district in Iraq, and supervision of the armaments of the former Central Powers.

30 Eduard Beneš of Czechoslovakia presents a plan to the Disarmament Commission to control international arms traffic.

Ten nations were represented at the London Conference on reparations, held from July 16 to August 16, 1924. Among the delegates who discussed and approved the Dawes Plan were (front row, left to right) U.S. Ambassador Frank B. Kellogg, Belgium Premier M. Theunis, French Premier Edouard Herriot, British Prime Minister Ramsay MacDonald, Italian Minister of Finance de Stefani, and Japanese Ambassador Baron Senjuro Hayashi.

SEPTEMBER

1 –October 2 The Assembly convenes under Giuseppe Motta of Switzerland. It begins consideration of the Geneva Protocol for the Pacific Settlement of International Disputes.

4 A German Catholic convention opposes German membership in the League until the Vatican is admitted.

MacDonald opens the Assembly debate on security and arms by again calling for German admission to the League. France responds by calling for a Continental security plan.

The World Court says in an advisory opinion that the Conference of Ambassadors, in a four-year-old Albanian-Yugoslav border dispute, lost its authority to determine the frontier once it asked the League to consider the question. Of central importance in the dispute is Yugoslavia's claim to a monastery in St. Naoum that had earlier been placed under Albanian jurisdiction.

6 An Assembly resolution is passed that favors the inclusion of compulsory arbitration in all security plans.

9 The League begins planning for disarmament talks that include the United States.

Czechoslovakian President Eduard Beneš authored a plan to control international arms traffic.

10 An Assembly debate over security focuses on the Shotwell Plan, which defines an aggressor as any nation that refuses to submit a dispute to compulsory arbitration.

13 Beneš is asked to draft the Geneva Protocol using the Shotwell Plan as the centerpiece.

The Assembly discusses the French plan to amend Article 15.

16 Beneš presents his draft of the Geneva Protocol.

18 French Foreign Minister Aristide Briand charges that American abstention hurts the League.

19 Fridtjof Nansen travels to Berlin to discuss German entry into the League. On September 23, the German cabinet votes to request admission.

23 Reports circulate that American President Calvin Coolidge has abandoned his plans for a second disarmament meeting in Washington. The reports prove true, which leaves the League unchallenged in this area for the next three years.

The Assembly authorizes creation of the International Institute for Intellectual Cooperation, which will serve as the administrative arm of the League's Committee for Intellectual Cooperation.

25 The Assembly calls for Armenian relief efforts.

Republican campaign literature in the American presidential election quotes former Secretary of State Charles Evans Hughes as saying that the League is useless to the United States.

26 Amendments to articles 12, 13, and 15 go into effect, allowing for judicial procedures as an alternative to arbitration procedures.

27 The Albanians appeal to the League under Article 11, demanding that the Greeks evacuate fourteen villages in the Koritza Zone of Albania.

The Geneva Protocol excludes "domestic questions" as a subject for negotiation. Japan demands a debate over the meaning of the term "domestic questions" in light of the American claim that anti-Japanese immigration laws are solely a domestic question. Japan receives support from Greece and Belgium.

The Disarmament Commission schedules talks for June 1925, pending ratification of the Geneva Protocol.

28 The Council decides that communications relating to Memel should go directly to the governments represented on the Council.

29 The Dominican Republic becomes a League member.

The Bulgarians ask the League to appoint agents to supervise the treatment of the Greek minority in Bulgaria.

OCTOBER

1 The Geneva Protocol is submitted to the Assembly.

2 Forty-seven states in the Assembly approve the Geneva Protocol.

Belgium expresses its willingness to admit Germany to the League.

The Chinese delegate walks out of the Assembly when China is denied a seat on the Council.

The Democratic Party candidate for the American presidency, John W. Davis, calls for American entry into the League.

3 Greece tells the Assembly that it will evacuate the occupied villages in Albania's Koritza Zone.

Briand calls for German entry into the League.

27 **–31** An extraordinary Council session considers the dispute between Britain and Turkey over oil-rich Mosul.

28 The French government extends diplomatic recognition to the USSR.

29 The so-called Zinoviev letter urging British workers to start a revolution helps the British conservatives win a big victory in the general election.

30 Czechoslovakia becomes the first state to ratify the Geneva Protocol.

NOVEMBER

3 The Opium Conference convenes. On November 13, Britain and France propose the creation of state opium monopolies in the Far East as a means to control production.

4 Calvin Coolidge is elected president of the United States. Frank B. Kellogg, a conservative senator from Minnesota, becomes secretary of state, replacing the more internationally minded Charles Evans Hughes. Coolidge and Kellogg support American admission to the World Court but not to the League.

7 Stanley Baldwin again becomes prime minister as the British conservatives return to power. He holds the post until June 4, 1929.

11 A four-year frontier quarrel between Albania and Yugoslavia ends when Albania accepts Yugoslavian authority over the disputed monastery at St. Naoum.

15 The London newspaper *Observer* reports that the British government will assess its Dominion's reactions to the Geneva protocol before announcing its own position.

18 The last French troops leave the Ruhr.

19 British officials say they need time to study the Geneva Protocol, denying rumors that they intend to kill it.

DECEMBER

1 At the Opium Conference, Washington demands the creation of a central board of control.

8 The Council creates a Committee of Fifteen to study and codify international law.

9 The Council, fearing British opposition to the Geneva Protocol, postpones action on it until the end of March 1925.

To satisfy Upper Silesian claims, the Council approves the transfer of state insurance funds from Germany to Poland.

10 Lord Curzon refuses to discuss British policy toward the Protocol.

13 The Council accepts a French offer to locate the International Institute for Intellectual Cooperation in Paris.

20 The Albanians again appeal to the League, charging that Yugoslavia has been aiding bands of armed revolutionaries in their country.

22 German Foreign Minister Gustav Stresemann requests League membership but only if the League releases Germany from its obligations under Article 16.

The Mixed Commission on Turkish and Greek minorities affairs suspends its work to protest Turkey's imprisonment and planned expulsion of Greeks in Constantinople.

24 Costa Rica announces its intention to withdraw from the League for financial reasons. It resigns formally on January 22, 1925.

31 The Council settles the Greek-Turkish population-exchange issue by accepting Viscount Kikujiro Ishii's report.

1925

JANUARY

15 Hans Luther becomes the German chancellor, with Stresemann as his foreign minister.

16 The Soviets object to the compulsory-arbitration terms of the PCIJ statute. However, they do accept a League proposal to study the unification of tonnage for inland navigation.

20 The Allies transfer supervision of the German navy to the League.

The Second Opium Conference nearly collapses when the European countries, responding to the demands of their Asian dependencies, refuse to restrict the production of opium solely to medical and scientific use. As a result of this refusal, the Americans withdraw from the conference.

21 Albania becomes a republic.

Japan extends diplomatic recognition to the USSR.

27 The Second Opium Conference adopts a plan, originally proposed by the Americans, creating a central control board to coordinate antidrug measures. The board's decisions can be appealed to the League Council. On February 11, a convention is signed that incorporates this plan.

29 The League asks all nations, including nonmembers, to submit information on their passport and visa regulations in preparation for an upcoming conference.

Edouard Herriot restates his confidence in the League.

FEBRUARY

6 Three days after a subcommittee refuses to accept an American plan to limit the production of narcotics strictly to medicinal and scientific use, the United States withdraws from the Second Opium Conference.

9 The Germans propose a Rhineland guarantee treaty. The British appear receptive.

10 Reports surface that the Council will send the Geneva Protocol directly to the Assembly if Britain continues to delay ratification.

11 Greece protests to the Council that Turkey's expulsion of the Greek Orthodox Patriarch from Constantinople violates the minority provisions of the Treaty of Lausanne.

14 After hearing the Greek case against Turkey's expulsion of the Patriarch, the Council requests an advisory opinion from the PCIJ.

16 The Second Opium Conference accepts American and German participation in the selection of the Central Board of Control.

Over British objections, France seeks to check the private manufacture of arms at an upcoming meeting of the Committee on the Private Manufacture of Arms.

19 A major opium convention is signed as the Second Opium Conference concludes. Because of controversy, it does not come into force until September 25, 1928.

MARCH

1 The League's Health Organization opens the Eastern Epidemiological Intelligence Center in Singapore in an attempt to make the Health Organization truly international in scope.

3 By majority vote, the U.S. House of Representatives endorses entry into the World Court. Within twenty-four hours, President Calvin Coolidge, in his inaugural address, also advocates American membership.

7 British Foreign Minister Austen Chamberlain informs French Foreign Minister Aristide Briand that Britain will not ratify the Geneva Protocol. London formally rejects the Protocol on March 10, the same day that Briand defends the Protocol in one of the great speeches in the history of the League.

10 The Council rejects Stresemann's objections to the Article 16 obligations and tells him that German entry must be without qualification.

11 The Council accepts the World Court decision on the exchange of populations. It also discusses ways to protect private investment in a mandated territory.

14 The Council invites Germany to join the League. At the same time, it refers the security issue to the Assembly, seeking a revision of the rejected Protocol and thereby ending hopes that the Disarmament Commission will produce an acceptable arms-reduction agreement.

The Council asks for a PCIJ ruling on Turkey's expulsion of the Greek Orthodox Patriarch from Constantinople.

19–23 The Health Organization sponsors an International Conference on Sleeping Sickness, while its Malaria Committee plans an investigation of the Mediterranean region.

APRIL

2 The ILO censures child-labor conditions in the United States.

The Codification Conference meets to codify international law.

15 The Health Organization drafts a plan to standardize antitoxins and serums.

20 Moscow rejects participation in a Munitions Traffic Conference.

25 U.S. Secretary of State Frank Kellogg advocates World Court membership.

26 Field Marshal Paul von Hindenberg's election as president of Germany signals a revival of German nationalism.

Field Marshal Paul von Hindenberg was elected president of Germany on April 26, 1925.

MAY

1 A coal miners strike in Britain culminates in an unsuccessful general strike.

3 The Munitions Traffic Conference, the League's only notable success in the area of disarmament, opens with the Americans in attendance. Britain, with United States support, will introduce a resolution to ban gas warfare.

11 France agrees to negotiate a security pact involving the former Allies and Berlin in advance of Germany's League membership.

20 Germany protests to the League over alleged Polish expropriation of German-owned property in Upper Silesia.

27 As the opposition leader in Britain, Ramsay MacDonald denounces the idea of a four- or five-power security pact being a substitute for the Geneva Protocol.

30 The Economic Committee devises a strategy to eliminate trade barriers.

JUNE

5 The Munitions Traffic Conference agrees to draft a treaty banning gas warfare.

8 The Council cancels its request for a World Court advisory opinion in the Greek Orthodox Patriarch case after Greece and Turkey agree to settle the issue.

The Allies make German membership in the League a requirement for a mutual security pact.

The Munitions Traffic Conference includes bacteriological weapons in its poisonous-gas ban.

10–11 The Council rebukes Lithuania for mistreating its Polish minority. It also revises its procedures regarding Danzig so that the innumerable disputes in that city can be resolved at the local level rather than being referred to Geneva.

17 Fridtjof Nansen outlines a League plan to remove Armenian refugees from Greece.

18 The Geneva Protocol on Gas Warfare is signed a full six months before the first meeting of the Preparatory Commission for the World Disarmament Conference.

25 Greece and Turkey formally end their dispute over the expulsion of the Greek Orthodox Patriarch. Hours later, General Theodore Pangalos takes power in Athens following a coup d'etat.

JULY

9 The French government funds the International Institute for Intellectual Cooperation, to be housed in Paris. On July 29, the League's Committee for Intellectual Cooperation, the parent of the institute, inaugurates a campaign to eliminate errors from school textbooks.

AUGUST

3 The Greek foreign minister says that he may appeal to the League in protest over Bulgarian "terrorists."

4 American chemical producers denounce the protocol banning gas warfare.

12 Stresemann says that Germany must receive mandates when joining the League.

15 Britain charges that Turkey is violating the status-quo agreement concerning Mosul.

17 German nationalists demand Article 16 modifications before the Locarno security conference convenes.

Canada's foreign minister proposes that representatives from the British Dominions meet annually to coordinate their League policies.

19–21 A special Council meeting convenes to resolve the Mosul dispute. It refers the matter to the PCIJ. At British insistence, the Council calls another meeting on Mosul for August 23.

22 China refuses to join the Permanent Opium Board, established by the convention signed on February 19.

27 French troops complete their withdrawal from Ruhr cities.

SEPTEMBER

1–4 A Commission of Jurists meets in London to draft the security pact.

3–4 The Council hears arguments in the Mosul case and appoints a committee to investigate the dispute.

6 Reports circulate that London will propose the Rhineland Security Pact as a substitute for the Geneva Protocol.

7–26 The Assembly meets under Ruaol Danderand of Canada. It honors Mrs. Woodrow Wilson for her husband's support of the League.

10 The Council ends most of the restrictions on Austria's financial affairs, retaining only the measures that insure the loan repayment. The Austrians, however, demand an end to *all* controls.

25 The League's Humanitarian Committee approves the Nansen loan to aid Armenian refugees.

The Assembly reaffirms the link between security, arbitration, and disarmament, and asks the Council for a resolution to restrict the private manufacture of arms.

26 The Council authorizes the creation of the Preparatory Commission for the World Disarmament Conference. The commission begins its work on December 3 and continues meeting until the World Disarmament Conference convenes in February 1932.

28 German officials insist that League membership will not imply Germany's acceptance of the "war guilt" clause of the Treaty of Versailles.

OCTOBER

5–16 The Locarno conference refashions the diplomacy of Europe. Among its accomplishments are the Rhineland Security Pact, arbitration treaties, and the Franco-Polish and Franco-Czechoslovakian mutual assistance treaties.

6–9 At Locarno, Germany agrees to join the League and drops its demands concerning Article 16 and mandates.

14 President Paul von Hindenberg and the German cabinet approve League entry.

16 Briand, Chamberlain, and Stresemann initial the Rhineland Security Pact and the arbitration treaties.

19 Greek and Bulgarian troops exchange gunfire near Demir-Kapu.

21 Greece orders troops into Bulgarian territory.

22 Bulgaria appeals to the League under articles 10 and 11. The appeal arrives the following day.

London wires Paris and Rome in an effort to coordinate their appeals to Bulgaria and Greece. Briand instructs his officials to cooperate with the British.

23 Briand asks both sides of the Greco-Bulgarian dispute to withdraw and calls a special session of the Council for October 26. Chamberlain's decision to attend the session underscores Britain's concern.

24 The League position concerning the Greco-Bulgarian dispute is strengthened when Mussolini agrees to cooperate in a common front. Lord Cecil, in London, hints at using Article 16; while Athens, justifying its action as self-defense, nevertheless accepts the League's competence in the dispute.

25 Britain and France ask Bulgaria to withdraw its forces in order to give Greece no excuse to continue fighting.

26 The Council, with Briand as president, convenes under Article 11 and passes a resolution asking both Greece and Bulgaria to withdraw their troops. The resolution authorizes British, Italian, and French representatives to oversee the withdrawal.

27 Rumania and Turkey offer to mediate the Greco-Bulgarian dispute. Bulgaria rejects the offers while the issue remains before the League.

Vittorio Scialoja, Italy's representative to the League, raises a question concerning Article 16. Briand rejects the withdrawal of ambassadors from Athens as being "too feeble." And Chamberlain, in private, favors a naval demonstration if Article 16 is invoked.

28 The British Cabinet supports Chamberlain's contingency plan for a naval demonstration as long as Britain is joined by other countries. Amid rumors of Article 16 sanctions being invoked, Greece accepts the terms of the October 26 resolution.

29 The Council appoints the Rumbold Commission to investigate the Greco-Bulgarian dispute and then adjourns on October 30. The commission visits the Balkans from November 4 to December 1.

The Hungarian Parliament drops its plans to consider withdrawing from the League.

NOVEMBER

14 Washington sends arms statistics to Geneva, taking another step toward cooperation with the League.

20 The American Federation of Labor endorses the United States' entry into the World Court.

Albania protests to the League over an alleged plot by Greece to deport Albanian Moslems to Turkey.

21 In considering the Mosul dispute between Great Britain and Turkey, the PCIJ, in an advisory opinion, upholds the right of the League to adjust the disputed borders. The Court also upholds the Covenant's unanimity rule but says that the consent of the disputing parties is not necessary. Turkey rejects this finding on December 8 and refuses to accept further Council authority in the dispute, including the Council's decision on December 16, 1925, to place Mosul under a British mandate.

22 Stresemann puts the League on notice that Germany will press the minorities issue after its entry.

23 Soviet Deputy Foreign Minister Maxim Litvinov denies rumors that the USSR may join the League.

27 The Reichstag formally approves German entry into the League.

DECEMBER

1 The Locarno treaties are signed and, on December 12, deposited with the League.

Senator William Borah, the leading American critic of the League, announces that he would favor membership in a World Court that was completely divorced from the League.

4 The United States and the USSR both express a willingness to meet with the Preparatory Commission.

5 Hans Luther's cabinet falls in Germany.

6 Briand suggests that the Preparatory Commission discuss naval arms as well as land arms.

7 The Council defers a final decision in the Greco-Bulgarian dispute pending the Rumbold Commission's report. Greece eventually accepts the commission's military recommendations but objects to paying an indemnity to Bulgaria.

Lord Cecil opposes a French plan calling for League control of navies.

8 President Coolidge, in his State of the Union message, reiterates his support of PCIJ membership.

10 The League considers sending a dispute over Hungarian restrictions on Jews to the World Court.

12 Eduard Beneš drafts a working agenda for the Preparatory Commission.

14 Finding Greece responsible for the Greco-Bulgarian dispute, the Council requires Athens to indemnify Bulgaria for confiscated property and for material and moral damages.

16 The Council reaches a decision in the troublesome Mosul case, awarding Britain a twenty-five-year mandate over Mosul. When, in 1932, Britain and the League agree to grant independence to Iraq (until then also under a British mandate), the British mandate over Mosul automatically ends and Mosul becomes a province of Iraq.

19 The Soviets inform League officials that they will join the Preparatory Commission but will not go to Switzerland due to lingering hostilities from the Vorovsky affair.

23 The Coolidge administration, with the approval of Senator Borah, accepts the League's invitation to join the Preparatory Commission.

1926

JANUARY

4 The United States agrees to join the Preparatory Commission and will contribute $50,000 to its budget.

8 League officials estimate that the Preparatory Commission will meet for at least one year before scheduling the World Disarmament Conference. (It will actually meet for five years.)

9 The Soviets accept a League invitation to join discussions on inland waterways.

12 France, Italy, and Japan say that land and naval arms talks must be combined.

14 Stresemann, perhaps to appease the German right wing, says that Allied occupation troops in the Rhineland will delay Germany's appearance at the League.

15 **–25** Senate opponents of American entry into the World Court unsuccessfully filibuster to prevent ratification of the PCIJ Protocol. The State Department, meanwhile, agrees to register American treaties with the League.

16 The International Institute for Intellectual Cooperation begins operation.

23 The USSR informs Secretariat officials that no Soviets will participate in League work *in* Switzerland until the Swiss government accepts responsibility for the assassination of Mechislav Vorovsky in May 1923. However, the USSR says it will participate in League activity *outside* of Switzerland.

25 The Germans agree to join the Preparatory Commission.

27 The U.S. Senate ratifies the World Court Statute by a 76-to-17 vote. Ratification is accompanied by five resolutions, the fifth of which grants the United States a veto over the cases to be heard by the Court.

28 The French strongly protest any delay in calling a preliminary conference of the Preparatory Commission. On February 1, the preliminary conference is postponed over French objections.

30 The League invites Washington to participate in a conference on double taxation.

31 The Allies begin a staged withdrawal from the Rhineland, as specified in the Treaty of Versailles.

FEBRUARY

2 In an effort to encourage Soviet cooperation with the League, the Swiss government designates Soviet citizens as *persona grata.* The Soviets, however, remain unmoved.

10 Germany applies for League entry as a result of the Locarno understanding. Five days later, Drummond arrives in Berlin for procedural talks.

15 The State Department agrees to notify the League about all American international agreements.

Greece pays half of its indemnity to Bulgaria. It pays the other half on March 1, ending the Greco-Bulgarian dispute.

17 Responding to Soviet pressure, the League moves the arms talks away from Geneva. Switzerland objects.

18 **–19** As Germany prepares to join the League, Stresemann opposes any increase in the number of Council seats. He fears a dilution of German influence if the Council is enlarged.

The Council invites the United States to Geneva to discuss the American reservations to the PCIJ statute. On March 20, the Americans announce that they will reject the invitation.

25 Greece appeals to the League over its quarrel with Turkey regarding the Maritsa River frontier.

Spain insists on its right to a Council seat. Denied the seat, Spain later withdraws from the League.

26 Mussolini supports Poland's claim to a seat on the Council.

MARCH

2 France echoes Italy's support of a Council seat for Poland.

The Memel parliament asks the Council to review Memel's fiscal health. Lithuania objects when the Council appoints a committee to do so.

4 China applies for a permanent Council seat, while Brazil asks for the seat that had been reserved for the United States.

5 Sweden announces its opposition to expanding the Council, while offering to give its own seat to Poland.

6 Briand loses his post as French foreign minister, alarming League officials.

8–17 A special meeting of the Assembly, under Alfonso Costa of Portugal, focuses on the admission of Germany.

9 The Assembly postpones its plans to give Germany a Council seat after Spain, Brazil, China, Poland, and, later, Persia all demand permanent representation.

Turkey agrees to negotiate a solution to its latest border dispute with Greece.

11 A new French government returns Briand to Geneva.

Building on its decision of December 16, 1925, in the Mosul case, the Council formally resolves that the Turkish-Iraqi border should be set at the so-called Brussels line, which runs through Mosul. Mosul is placed under a British mandate scheduled to last for twenty-five years, although the British mandate over Mosul in fact ends when Iraq becomes independent in 1932.

12 The Council refuses to submit the United States' reservations to the World Court Statute to a group of jurists, thereby leaving the matter to the judgment of the countries that are Court members.

15 Lithuania announces that Memel has approved an agreement concerning financial questions.

16 The League postpones discussion of the Council-seat problem after Brazil refuses to accept a compromise involving the creation of semipermanent seats. The impasse also increases the bitterness of German nationalists.

17 Reports circulate that Italy, alone among the major League powers, has not expressed its regret at Germany's failure to secure a permanent Council seat.

20 The Council adopts the jurists' report on Memel, which says that Council authority over fiscal matters would not violate the key convention regarding that territory.

23 Although weakened by the dispute over Council seating, Baldwin and Chamberlain survive a no-confidence vote in Parliament.

26 Poland and Rumania sign a mutual security treaty.

APRIL

1 Washington officials are angered by a Secretariat letter calling on them to discuss their Court reservations at the next Assembly meeting.

13 The USSR rejects participation in the Preparatory Commission.

14 The Polish premier claims that his country will not disarm without security guarantees.

16 Because of Moscow's decision not to join the Preparatory Commission, the French government seeks to postpone the opening of the preliminary conference despite having earlier criticized those who counselled delay.

18 Beneš prepares a questionnaire on the effect a Soviet-German nonaggression pact would have on German entry into the League. Stresemann calls the questionnaire insulting.

19 Secretary of State Kellogg again rejects the League's invitation to discuss the American reservations to the World Court Statute.

24 Argentina agrees to send representatives both to the Preparatory Commission and to the Council Reorganization Committee, which was established to review the seating controversy.

Germany and the USSR sign a nonaggression pact, which reinforces their 1922 accord at Rapallo. Intended to reassure the Soviets after Locarno, it alarms the Western allies at the League.

MAY

3–12 A general strike is staged in Britain.

10 The Council Reorganization Committee hears Brazil reassert its demands for a permanent seat.

12 Marshal Jozef Pilsudski leads a military revolt in Poland. Although he rejects the office of president, he remains the de facto ruler.

13 China joins Brazil in demanding an expansion of the Council. Spain repeats its threat to withdraw if it is not granted a Council seat.

17 The Council Reorganization Committee provisionally accepts Lord Cecil's plan to increase the nonpermanent Council seats to nine.

The U.S. Surgeon General denounces the League's Health Committee for assuming the duties of the International Public Health Office, prolonging a controversy that has troubled the Health Committee from its very first days.

18–26 The Preparatory Commission for the World Disarmament Conference holds its first regular meeting.

20 The Americans propose a regional disarmament plan, since France will not disarm without security guarantees. Japan, however, calls for a separate naval pact with the United States and Great Britain.

22 French Premier Joseph Paul-Boncour proposes to strengthen the mutual-assistance clauses of the Covenant.

24 The drafting committee of the Preparatory Commission adopts a French proposal to send to the Council the question of mutual-security duties in cases of aggression.

JUNE

2 The Preparatory Commission's Military Subcommittee excludes trained reserves from the definition of "military effectives." This is a major victory for the advocates of conscription, led by the French.

4 The Military Subcommittee again sides with France when it defines the term "peacetime effectives" to include bases, ports of call, materiel, and livestock.

8 France recommends that the Preparatory Commission adjourn, but the United States and Britain oppose an early recess.

9 The Council declares that Austria has put its financial house in order. It also decides that a mandatory power is forbidden from recruiting natives for military service outside of the mandate territory.

10 Brazil announces its withdrawal from the League.

France and Rumania sign a friendship treaty.

The League grants Bulgaria a loan to resettle its refugees.

12 **–15** The Preparatory Commission discusses and rejects an American suggestion to reopen the question of including trained reserves in the definition of "military effectives."

16 Washington denies rumors that it encouraged Brazil to withdraw from the League.

17 The Permanent Mandates Commission approves the French administration of Syria.

The Spanish foreign minister calls the League "an organ of war." Spain's hostility to the League escalates in the wake of the Council-seat issue.

23 Spain suspends its League activity pending a Council resolution of the seat issue.

Swiss delegate Giuseppe Motta reveals an Italian threat to suspend participation in Geneva unless the Swiss curtail anti-fascist meetings there.

24 An Italian-League quarrel escalates amid rumors that Mussolini may try to block German entry into the organization.

27 The French threaten to withdraw from the discussions of the Military Subcommittee, which leads to a new formula for comparing naval strength. The criteria will include not just the tonnage of ships but also their age.

30 The Austrian Financial Commission ends its responsibilities, as does the commission to supervise the Hungarian economy. The League celebrates two of its major successes.

JULY

5 The Military Subcommittee accepts the French argument that land and naval strength cannot be divorced from each other.

15 The Briand Ministry falls as a result of the financial crisis. Briand, however, remains as foreign minister.

17 Senator Borah launches a national campaign against American membership on the World Court.

18 League officials denounce German demands for Alsace-Lorraine autonomy as "political."

20 The United States admits that only three nations have accepted the fifth Senate reservation to the World Court Statute.

23 The League's Financial Committee seeks £400,000 to aid Bulgarian refugees.

29 Germany announces that it will not attend the League Assembly unless it is assured of admission.

AUGUST

7 Spain and Italy sign a treaty of friendship.

9 The Military Subcommittee adopts the French argument about the interdependence of army, navy, and air forces. However, on August 19, France's call for an international body to supervise armaments is rejected by the United States, Britain, Italy, Spain, and Chile.

16 The Interparliamentary Union endorses German entry into the League.

17 Greece and Yugoslavia help to calm Balkan politics by signing a treaty of friendship.

19 **–21** Representatives from national information bureaus meet under League auspices.

20 Spain renews its fight for a permanent Council seat.

27 League officials announce a hands-off policy regarding the American reservations to the PCIJ statute.

Nicaragua protests to the League over Mexican aid to Nicaraguan rebels.

General Theodore Pangalos, the Greek dictator, is overthrown.

28 Nonmember Mexico tells the League it will ignore the Nicaraguan protest.

31 The American fifth reservation to the PCIJ statute is accepted by only seven nations, all of which are smaller powers.

SEPTEMBER

1 A Geneva conference convenes to discuss the American reservations to the PCIJ statute.

2 Canada, Sweden, and New Zealand attack the United States' fifth reservation. The big powers, perhaps viewing American entry into the Court as a step toward membership in the League, appear more conciliatory.

3 The Council Reorganization Committee proposes that Germany be given a permanent seat and that three additional nonpermanent seats be created. On September 4, the committee's report is accepted, and Spain announces that it will withdraw from the League.

7 The Spanish government ratifies the decision to withdraw.

The Military Subcommittee adopts the American criteria for limiting naval arms, which are based on a formula that involves tonnage, age, and gun caliber.

8 The Assembly, headed by Momchiho Nintchitch of Yugoslavia, admits Germany into the League by unanimous vote.

The following is the entry in the "Official Journal of the League of Nations" concerning one of the most divisive questions of the 1920s.

X. RESOLUTIONS ADOPTED WITHOUT REFERENCE TO A COMMITTEE.

ADMISSION OF GERMANY TO THE LEAGUE OF NATIONS: NOMINATION OF GERMANY AS A PERMANENT MEMBER OF THE COUNCIL: INCREASE IN THE NUMBER OF THE NON-PERMANENT MEMBERS OF THE COUNCIL.

I. The Assembly approves the report of the First Committee of the Special Assembly on the request of the German Government for admission to the League of Nations.

II. The Assembly approves the proposals put forward by the Council in its resolution of September 4th, 1926, regarding:

(a) The nomination of Germany as a Permanent Member of the Council;
(b) The increase in the number of non-permanent seats, which shall be brought up to nine.

[*Resolutions adopted on September 8th, 1926 (morning).*]

10 Stresemann and Briand deliver speeches to the League Assembly that are considered to be two of the most memorable in the organization's history; both men thrill their audience with visions of a peaceful future organized around Geneva and built upon a foundation of collective security and international cooperation.

11 Spain leaves the League.

16 **–20** The Council meets.

16 In a victory for Beneš and the Little Entente, Czechoslovakia and Rumania win nonpermanent seats on the Council. Other nonpermanent seats are held by China, Chile, Columbia, and the Netherlands.

Italy and Rumania sign a treaty of friendship, as Mussolini attempts to counter the June 10 Franco-Rumanian pact.

17 Meeting at Thoiry, France, Briand and Stresemann seek a comprehensive settlement of all the outstanding differences between their two countries.

20 French delegate Joseph Paul-Boncour's resolution to hasten the start of the World Disarmament Conference is approved by the Assembly's Third Committee.

22 **–27** The second meeting of the Preparatory Commission for the World Disarmament Conference is held.

24 After an eloquent plea by Lord Cecil, the Assembly adopts a resolution calling for a World Disarmament Conference to be held before September 1927.

25 The Assembly approves a comprehensive Slavery Convention in order to abolish the remnants of both the slave trade and slavery itself. It goes into effect on March 9, 1927.

OCTOBER

1 The United States, Japan, and Germany announce their opposition to budgetary criteria as a basis for disarmament.

2 Jozef Pilsudski becomes premier of Poland and consolidates a highly repressive regime.

3 **–6** The first Pan-European Congress meets in Vienna.

4 Although it left the League, Spain announces its intention to remain in the ILO.

6 The Mixed Committee, a new body reporting to the Preparatory Commission, proposes a convention to insure compliance with the poisonous-gas treaty of 1925.

9 The American delegation to the Preparatory Commission favors limiting ships by category, as was done at the Washington Conference.

18 A French proposal to apply Article 16 sanctions against a nation violating the poisonous-weapon ban is opposed by the United States, Great Britain, Japan, Italy, and Germany.

19 **–November 18** The Imperial Conference discusses and accepts the equality of all the British Dominions.

20 Seven nations tell the Preparatory Commission that they will not limit their trained reserves until they are guaranteed a system of real security.

23 Secretary of State Kellogg calls for ratification of the poisonous-gas convention of 1925.

27 The Mixed Committee reports on the economic aspects of disarmament. It also urges publicity to encourage nations to comply with their treaties.

30 The Germans are awarded the post of under secretary-general at the League. Drummond selects Albert Freiherr Dufour-Féronce to fill it.

NOVEMBER

13 Professor Gilbert Murray, a British internationalist and chairman of the Committee on Intellectual Cooperation, calls for Soviet entry into the League.

15 The Vatican denies that it will establish a bureau in Geneva.

19 Britain warns the Permanent Mandates Commission not to exceed its authority.

21 Guatemala joins the World Court.

25 The German Reichstag approves a resolution to have the PCIJ investigate the validity of the war-guilt clause of the Treaty of Versailles.

27 Italy and Albania sign the Treaty of Tirana; it legitimizes Mussolini's presence in Albania, a country in which Italy, Greece, and Yugoslavia all seek influence.

The World Court upholds the ILO's right to regulate the working conditions of employers as well as those of employees.

29 The Civil Subcommittee of the Preparatory Commission claims that economic and political categories cannot be separated when considering the future of disarmament.

DECEMBER

1 France proposes the establishment of a League radio station, which the Council approves on December 8.

3 South Africa and New Zealand join Britain in protesting a recommendation of the Permanent Mandates Commission to allow petitioners to appear in person. They also protest a recommendation to circulate a new questionnaire to mandate powers.

4 The Council adopts a report on Article 16 that recognizes the juridical basis for League action to prevent war.

5 Stresemann, Chamberlain, and Briand fail to agree on the final terms for transferring to the League the Allied military authority in Germany, handled since the war by the Inter-Allied Military Control Commission (IMCC).

7 The Council postpones consideration of Rhineland demilitarization until 1927.

8 The Council, uneasy with the slow pace of the Preparatory Commission, calls for an earlier date for a general disarmament conference.

9 Yugoslavia denies any intention to withdraw from the League as a result of the Treaty of Tirana.

The Council resolves to invite the United States and the USSR to discuss the private manufacture of arms.

12 The Allies agree to turn the IMCC's responsibilities over to the League in early 1927.

13 The Poles protest the scheduled end of the IMCC's role in Germany, while Stresemann, attempting to assuage their fears, says that the League could have prevented the Great War had it existed in 1914.

24 Drummond praises the recent American efforts to cooperate with the League.

1927

JANUARY

1 Costa Rica's departure from the League becomes official.

10 Rumania, objecting to arbitration in the dispute over the confiscation of Hungarian-owned land in Rumania, asks for Council consideration under Article 11.

17–21 The Conference of Health Experts, held in Paris, deals with child-welfare issues.

26 Drummond meets with Mussolini in Rome in order to facilitate Italian cooperation with the League.

31 The IMCC for Germany is abolished. Supervision of the military clauses of the Treaty of Versailles becomes the responsibility of the League.

FEBRUARY

1 The Opium Conference adopts a resolution calling for a global inquiry into opium use.

3 An attempt to overthrow the military dictatorship in Portugal fails.

9 Moscow refuses to join a League conference on refugee relief in Geneva because of the Vorovsky affair.

Great Britain's refusal to accept the United States' fifth World Court reservation ends all hopes of American entry. On February 18, France joins Great Britain in opposing the fifth reservation.

10 President Coolidge proposes the extension of the Washington Conference ratios to categories of smaller ships.

11 Persia notifies the League that it will limit its opium production to conform to the Opium Conference recommendations.

The Council agrees to call a conference of statisticians to create uniform economic figures.

18 The British make commercial concessions to China after facing a damaging boycott.

24 Drummond says that the Monroe Doctrine does not impede League activity in Latin America.

26 Washington accepts a League invitation to attend a conference on the private manufacture of arms.

MARCH

7 The Council, reflecting the influence of the Great Powers, rejects a Permanent Mandates Commission proposal to allow petitioners to appear in person.

The Council hears Hungary and Rumania debate the merits of using the Mixed Arbitral Commission in the land-claims controversy in Rumania.

12 The Council orders the removal of French troops from the Ruhr, replacing them with an international "railway defense force."

18 A Mixed Committee report on chemical warfare is rejected by the United States.

20 Yugoslavia's foreign minister invites the League to investigate charges that his nation is planning a war against Italy over Albania.

21 Mussolini denounces the League for its involvement in his quarrel with Yugoslavia.

26–28 The Preparatory Commission discusses and accepts Lord Cecil's contention that naval and air forces must be considered separately from land forces but rejects his plea to end conscription.

30–31 The Preparatory Commission accepts French proposals to permit the exchange of home and colonial troops and to limit the number of military officers on duty at any one time.

APRIL

1 The ILO approves two resolutions favoring the awarding of workers' compensation, one to accident victims and the other to victims of occupational diseases.

5 Italy and Hungary, both unfriendly to the League, sign a friendship treaty with each other.

6 Germany objects to a French plan limiting military budgets.

11 The Preparatory Commission's naval talks nearly collapse when Italy and Great Britain reject a French plan, authored by Joseph Paul-Boncour, to limit navies.

13 The United States joins Italy in opposing League control of international arms.

18 The Chinese nationalist movement splits into conservative and revolutionary wings.

22 Germany, fearful of French military reserves, announces that it will not accept any arms agreement that does not limit reserve strength.

25 Ignoring the Covenant, Italy claims that its citizens serving on the Secretariat are answerable directly to Rome.

25–30 The International Conference on Hydrophobia (Rabies) meets in Paris.

26 Cecil says that the prospects for disarmament are good in spite of the Preparatory Commission's deadlock.

MAY

4–23 The International Economic Conference, held in Geneva, hosts fifty nations, including the USSR, which returns to Switzerland for the first time since the assassination of Vorovsky. The United States also attends. The conference recognizes the coexistence of capitalist and communist economies, but it does little more than denounce trade barriers.

20–21 Charles Lindbergh completes the first solo transatlantic flight, improving American-French relations.

24 Germany notifies the Secretariat that it will bring to the Council the complaints of Germans in Memel, who live under Lithuanian rule.

26 The Russian-British commercial treaty is abrogated. On May 27, Britain breaks diplomatic relations with the USSR.

27 Czechoslovakia reelects President Tomáš Masaryk. Beneš remains as foreign minister.

JUNE

7–11 The Conference of Health Experts meets in Montevideo, Uruguay, to discuss ways to protect children.

Charles Lindbergh checks his plane, the Spirit of St. Louis, after completing his solo transatlantic flight to France on May 20, 1927. His trip improved American-French relations.

Tomáš Masaryk was reelected president of Czechoslovakia on May 27, 1927.

13 Austen Chamberlain proposes to limit Council meetings to three per year, a reform that is enacted at the end of the decade.

14 Stresemann says that if Germany is given a seat on the Permanent Mandates Commission, it will not demand the French evacuation of the Rhineland.

The Council approves an international loan to Estonia.

17 The Council promises to examine Nansen's plan to resettle Armenian refugees.

19 Bulgarian raiders move into Yugoslavia.

20 **–August 4** The Geneva Naval Conference, composed of Japan, Great Britain, and the United States, fails to extend the Washington Conference formula to categories of smaller ships.

JULY

4 China, protesting its "unequal" representation at the League, vows not to comply with any League actions unless given genuine equality. Three days later, the Chinese delegation leaves the Council.

30 Spanish Premier Miguel Primo de Rivera offers a plan for a new league.

AUGUST

8 The communists in China are purged by the nationalists under Chiang Kai-shek.

22 The Inter-Allied Military Control Commission announces that it will end its supervision of Hungarian military activity.

23 **–29** The third General Conference on Communications and Transit meets, as does the International Conference on Press Experts.

29 Lord Cecil resigns as Britain's delegate to the League.

30 The Interparliamentary Union says that the League should continue its efforts to codify international law.

SEPTEMBER

1 **–15** The Council discusses and grants Germany a seat on the Permanent Mandates Commission.

5 **–27** The Assembly meets under President Alberto Guani of Uruguay.

7 Poland submits a proposal to outlaw war. It also proposes that the League revive the Geneva Protocol.

8 The smaller powers in the Assembly protest the Council's policy of discussing important matters in secret.

10 John D. Rockefeller grants the League $2 million for construction of a library.

17 The Council fails to settle the Hungarian-Rumanian land-claims case after three days of negotiations. Hungary, therefore, demands that the case be submitted to the World Court.

Chiang Kai-shek led the Chinese nationalists in purging the communists in their country on August 8, 1927.

18 President Paul von Hindenberg repudiates Germany's responsibility for the war.

19 The Assembly's Disarmament Committee approves a Polish plan to outlaw war. It also approves a Nansen plan for the compulsory arbitration of international disputes and adopts a resolution calling for another conference on the private manufacture of arms.

21 Nansen's compulsory-arbitration plan is approved by the Judicial Committee of the Assembly.

23 Germany signs the compulsory-arbitration clause of the World Court protocol.

26 The Assembly adopts the Convention on the Execution of Foreign Arbitral Awards.

27 The Council deadlocks over the formation of the Disarmament, Security, and Arbitration Committee.

OCTOBER

10 Martial law is declared in Bulgaria to control the breakdown of order along the frontier.

15 Lithuania appeals to the Council under Article 11, claiming that Poland is threatening the peace.

17–25 International conferences are held for the Abolition of Import and Export Prohibitions and Restrictions, and on Epidemiological Intelligence.

NOVEMBER

8 A convention is signed to limit export and import restrictions.

11 France and Yugoslavia sign a treaty of understanding.

15 Canada gets a seat on the Council.

22 A new Italian-Albanian treaty once again extends Italian influence into Albanian affairs.

25 Germany and Russia reach a disarmament agreement in advance of the upcoming session of the Preparatory Commission.

30 The Preparatory Commission, opening its fourth session, hears Maxim Litvinov make a dramatic call for immediate and total disarmament, but the Western allies reject his proposal as a propaganda trick. The Preparatory Commission also creates the Committee on Arbitration and Security, chaired by Czechoslovakia's Eduard Beneš. Asked to join, the Americans refuse. This committee produces the General Act for the Pacific Settlement of International Disputes on September 28, 1928.

DECEMBER

2 At the Arbitration and Security Committee meeting, Germany says that the Covenant's Article 19 should be used to revise the Treaty of Versailles.

6 The Council endorses a conference to combat international counterfeiting.

7 The Council appoints a commission to investigate the Lithuanian-Polish border dispute.

10 Poland and Lithuania finally end their state of war, but quarreling between the two nations continues until the eve of World War II.

20 The USSR ratifies the 1925 Geneva poisonous-gas convention.

24 The Swiss government refuses to allow the League to establish a Soviet bureau in Geneva.

1928

JANUARY

1 Smuggled Italian arms destined for Hungary are discovered at the Austrian railroad station of Szent Gotthárd. The incident leads to a Council investigation of Hungary's efforts to violate the Treaty of Trianon.

18 The British Foreign Office endorses negotiating bilateral security pacts on the Locarno model rather than pursuing a general treaty to renounce war.

27 *The New York Times* reports that the United States contributes more money to the League than any country except Great Britain.

28 As president of the Conference of Ambassadors, Briand protests to the League about Bulgarian violations of the military clauses of the Treaty of Neuilly.

29 Germany and Lithuania sign a treaty on Memel that includes the compulsory arbitration of disputes. The treaty is later repudiated by Hitler.

FEBRUARY

1 The Little Entente asks the League to take action against Hungarian rearmament, which is in violation of the military restrictions of the Treaty of Trianon.

10 An Arbitration and Security Committee report favors regional pacts over general treaties.

20 The British recognize the independence of Transjordan, with some provisions for British financial control.

22 Several Latin American governments denounce the idea of regional pacts to ensure security.

Beneš proposes to include Hungary and Austria in the Little Entente.

23 After Nicolas Politis of Greece scolds the Council for inaction, the Council president calls on Hungary to halt arms smuggling.

MARCH

3 Mussolini ridicules the League in a Tyrol speech.

5 The Council creates a fund to facilitate cooperation among Latin American governments. It also accepts a Rockefeller Foundation grant to exchange information in the health area.

6 The Council votes to keep the League in Geneva rather than to move it to Vienna.

8–9 Resuming debate on the Hungarian-Rumanian land-claims issue, the Council adds two persons to the Mixed Arbitral Commission to hear arguments.

9 The Council asks Brazil and Spain to reconsider their withdrawals from the League. On March 20, Spain accepts, and it later receives a semipermanent seat on the Council. On April 9, Brazil refuses but calls itself "a devoted co-operator of the League"; its withdrawal becomes final on June 13.

23 The USSR submits a new disarmament plan to the Preparatory Commission, recognizing that Litvinov's call for immediate and total disarmament will not be taken seriously.

25 An architect who won the competition to design the League's new headquarters is arrested in Hungary for practicing without a diploma. The episode highlights Hungary's anti-League sentiments.

28 The U.S. Senate Foreign Relations Committee refuses to reconsider World Court entry.

APRIL

13 U.S. Secretary of State Kellogg proposes an antiwar pact to Britain, France, and Germany.

16 An ILO convention on the repatriation of seamen goes into effect.

At the Opium Conference, France, Japan, and Italy attack British shipments of drugs to the United States.

17 The Japanese charge that American Commodore Matthew Perry opened up Japan to the opium trade.

21 Briand sends Kellogg his own draft of an antiwar treaty.

MAY

3 The Chinese and Japanese clash in northern China, leading to Japanese control of some Chinese railways and an anti-Japanese boycott that lasts into 1929.

9 Albania appeals to the League under Article 11, protesting the treatment of Albanian and Moslem minorities in Greece.

20 The German elections show sharp gains for the socialists and losses for the nationalists.

30 The International Institute for the Unification of Private Law is inaugurated in Rome.

JUNE

4 Warsaw protests against the new Lithuanian constitution.

7 Albanian exiles appeal to the League against the tyranny of Albanian President Ahmed Bey Zogu.

8 The Council reaffirms that a settlement of the Hungarian-Rumanian land-claims case must rest on a decision of the Mixed Arbitral Commission.

The Opium Convention of 1925 receives enough signatures to become law. It goes into effect on September 25.

9 Claiming that Article 11 is reserved for only the most serious threats to the peace, the Council rules that Albania's appeal regarding Greece's treatment of minorities must be handled by the Minorities Section.

24 France devalues the franc by 75 percent.

JULY

13 **–15** Two ILO conventions on sickness insurance, one for industrial workers and one for agricultural workers, go into effect.

20 Hungary threatens to withdraw from the League if the Council refuses to reconsider the Hungarian-Rumanian land-claims dispute.

AUGUST

2 An Italo-Ethiopian treaty of friendship is signed. It is ignored by Mussolini in 1935.

15 Costa Rica asks the League to reinterpret the Monroe Doctrine if the League desires Costa Rica's re-entry.

27 The Kellogg-Briand Pact (Pact of Paris) is signed by fifteen nations that pledge the "renunciation of war as an instrument of national policy"; over fifty nations eventually sign. League officials see the pact as plugging a Covenant loophole that allows for legal war.

28 The Russians refuse to join the League's efforts to control the private manufacture of munitions.

31 The Council debates the Monroe Doctrine in secret session.

SEPTEMBER

1 The Council affirms its policy to open mandates for trade with, and investment from, all sources.

2 The Council accepts responsibility to look after "third parties" in Vilna.

3 **–26** The ninth session of the Assembly is chaired by Herluf Zahle of Denmark.

5 The International Educational Cinematographic Institute is inaugurated in Rome.

6 The Council appoints Austen Chamberlain as *rappateur* of the Hungarian-Rumanian land-claims case.

10 Former Secretary of State Charles Evans Hughes, who in 1921 barred Americans from nominating World Court judges, accepts an appointment as a judge on that court.

18 The Council urges free communication between Lithuania and Poland.

19 British Foreign Secretary Chamberlain succeeds in starting Hungarian-Rumanian discussions, which lead to a settlement of the land-claims controversy. The final terms include the liquidation of the reparations Hungary owes to other countries.

23 Italy and Greece sign a treaty of friendship.

24 The Assembly schedules an opium inquiry in the Far East, sets up an inquiry regarding alcohol abuse, and condemns bootlegging across international borders.

Costa Rica announces that it will return to the League.

25 The Assembly instructs the Council to study the PCIJ's authority to offer advisory opinions. It also recommends an early meeting of the major naval powers to extend the work of the Washington Conference of 1922.

American Secretary of State Frank B. Kellogg signs the Kellogg-Briand Pact in the Hall of Mirrors, Versailles, on August 31, 1928. This is the same room in which the Treaty of Versailles was signed in 1919.

26 The Assembly approves the General Act for the Pacific Settlement of International Disputes, which implements the Kellogg-Briand Pact. Signed by twenty-three states, it calls for arbitration, conciliation, and referral of disputes to the World Court.

27 The Council creates a Central Board to coordinate the attempts to limit opium production and traffic.

29 The United States rejects Anglo-French plans for a naval accord.

OCTOBER

1 The Soviets inaugurate their first Five Year Plan for industrialization.

2 Joseph Paul-Boncour revives his April 1927 naval-limitation proposals.

4 The Americans refuse to participate in selecting a Central Board for opium control despite their earlier support.

7–31 Numerous nonpolitical meetings are held, including the International Congress of the Popular Arts, the Technical Conference on Vaccination Against Tuberculosis, and the General Conference of Government Experts on Double Taxation and Tax Evasion.

23 The Economic Committee hears a call for a world entente on coal.

NOVEMBER

5 Herbert Hoover is elected president of the United States. Like his two Republican predecessors, he opposes American entry into the League yet favors participation in the World Court.

7 Poland and Lithuania sign a provisional agreement to facilitate minor frontier traffic.

15 Mussolini makes his Fascist Grand Council into a state mechanism to nominate candidates for high office and to coordinate governmental activities.

21 Drummond visits Poland, hoping to end the Vilna dispute.

28 Drummond arrives in Berlin for talks with Stresemann.

DECEMBER

6 Bolivia appeals to the League a day after Paraguayan troops attack a Bolivian outpost in the Gran Chaco, leading to a long-running dispute that drains League energies during the 1930s.

9–14 Stresemann, Chamberlain, and Briand meet in Lugano, Switzerland, to discuss European security.

10 The Council decides not to press the PCIJ for an opinion about what kind of Council vote—majority or unanimous—is needed to ask the Court to hear a dispute.

14 The Council appoints a Commission of Jurists to consider revising the PCIJ statute.

20 Great Britain and China sign a treaty after a bitter dispute concerning extraterritorial rights. With the treaty, London recognizes the Nanking government and its right to impose tariffs, and China abolishes import duties on many items.

1929

JANUARY

5 The Pan American Union sponsors the General Act of Inter-American Arbitration for the peaceful settlement of international disputes.

Yugoslavia becomes a dictatorship after its constitution is suspended.

7 American Elihu Root joins the jurists considering the World Court's response to the American fifth reservation.

15 The U.S. Senate ratifies the Kellogg-Briand Pact. Senator Daniel Reed of Missouri calls it "an international kiss."

19 Owen Young, president of General Electric, chairs a committee to review reparations in order to stabilize the German—and European—economy.

22 Britain, the Netherlands, and Japan shelve plans to limit the manufacture of narcotics.

30–31 The Opium Conference votes to name manufacturers who engage in the illicit drug trade. However, it rejects an American proposal to limit the manufacture of narcotics by a 7-to-4 vote.

FEBRUARY

6 Germany ratifies the Kellogg-Briand Pact.

9 The Litvinov Pact is signed, renouncing war among the Eastern European states.

11 Mussolini and the Pope sign the Lateran Accords; Italy recognizes Vatican City as sovereign, while the Pope finally recognizes Mussolini as Italy's head of state. The agreement increases Mussolini's prestige.

19 Secretary of State Kellogg sends notes to all the World Court members, inviting consideration of American membership.

21 Albert Thomas says that the League should emphasize the importance of racial equality as a way to combat the appeal of communism.

MARCH

4 Herbert Hoover is inaugurated as president of the United States.

5 Elihu Root submits a plan for American entry to the PCIJ that would allow the United States to veto Court consideration of any matter contrary to American interests.

6 Bulgaria signs a treaty of friendship with Turkey.

9 The Council adopts a British proposal for a new judicial system in Iraq.

10–19 A Commission of Jurists studies the Root plan for American entry to the World Court, focusing on the Monroe Doctrine and the need for unanimous consent to request a Court opinion.

12 Root offers a new formula for American Court entry that would give the United States equality with League members and the right to withdraw if the PCIJ considers a case over its objections.

17 The British refuse to approve the ILO's budget, claiming excessive expenditures.

Greece and Yugoslavia settle a dispute over a "free zone" straddling their common border, a zone over which both countries claimed rights. Ten days later, they sign a treaty of friendship.

18 The Commission of Jurists accepts Root's new draft formula relating to the American fifth reservation of 1926.

APRIL

9–20 The International Conference on the Suppression of Counterfeit Currency is held and results in an agreement signed by twenty-one nations. The USSR signs, but the United States refuses.

13 The Little Entente, Greece, and Poland oppose changes in League procedures to protect minorities.

16 Lithuania proposes a 10,000-ton limit for battleships at the sixth session of the Preparatory Commission.

22 The American delegate to the Preparatory Commission, Hugh Gibson, urges naval reduction, not simply limitation.

26 The United States announces that it will no longer count reserves among its military effectives. France supports the American position, while Germany protests.

Spain proposes the establishment of a League air force.

MAY

7–9 Bolivia protests to the League after a new clash is reported in the Chaco. At the same time, an Inter-American Commission of Inquiry discusses the dispute.

22 Bolivia charges Paraguay with a propaganda offensive as the chances for a Chaco settlement fade.

30 The Labour Party triumphs in the British elections.

JUNE

1 Bulgarian border raids on Yugoslavia sharply increase the hostility between the two states.

3 The Tacna-Arica controversy between Chile and Peru is settled when Peru receives Tacna and Chile gets Arica. Chile provides Bolivia with a rail outlet to the Pacific.

5 Ramsay MacDonald again takes office as prime minister in Great Britain. He serves until August 24, 1931.

7 The Young Plan, devised by General Electric President Owen Young, goes into effect. It spreads Germany's reparation payments over fifty years to reduce the immediate burden on the German economy.

10 Stresemann asks the Council to protect the citizenship of ethnic Germans in Poland. He also asks the Council to discuss a minority petition rather than refer it to the Minorities Section.

12 The Council approves Elihu Root's plan to permit the United States to withdraw a question from PCIJ consideration.

JULY

1 The Permanent Mandates Commission resolves to continue holding its discussions behind closed doors.

Bulgaria and Italy ask for action against high American tariffs by the League's Economics and Financial Section.

27 Poor health forces President Poincaré's resignation, leading to political instability in France.

AUGUST

6–31 The Hague Conference discusses the implementation of the Young Plan.

15 Germany ratifies the Opium Convention of 1925.

16 The General Act for the Pacific Settlement of International Disputes, intended to implement the Kellogg-Briand Pact, comes into force.

27 Anti-Jewish riots in Palestine prompt calls for Council aid to protect the Jews.

31 An arbitration treaty to settle the Chaco dispute is concluded by the Pan American Union, but neither Bolivia nor Paraguay ratifies it.

SEPTEMBER

2 Ramsay MacDonald announces that he favors cuts in all military areas, including naval and air forces.

2–25 The Assembly meets under Gustavo Guerrero of El Salvador, with all members but Argentina in attendance. Bolivia, Honduras, and Peru rejoin the sessions.

4–13 A conference of PCIJ members meets to revise the World Court Statute. It accepts Root's formula for American membership after receiving word that Henry L. Stimson, the new American secretary of state, favors it.

5 Briand proposes a European Federal Union, but it generates little enthusiasm at the Assembly.

6 At the Assembly, Britain proposes that financial aid be awarded to any country that is a victim of aggression.

The Council reduces its number of annual meetings from four to three.

Briand, calling the outlawry of war insufficient, asks that military force be used to back up the Kellogg-Briand Pact.

7 Greece proposes a treaty to link the Kellogg-Briand Pact with the Covenant in order to close the legal loopholes permitting war after Covenant procedures have been exhausted.

10 Peru introduces a resolution to draft a treaty linking the Covenant and the Kellogg-Briand Pact. The resolution is never approved, however.

11 China threatens to leave the League unless the Assembly forms a subcommittee to study extraterritoriality. On September 19, the Assembly agrees to create the subcommittee.

14 After the Assembly approves the PCIJ Protocol, which contains the Root formula, the American debate over World Court entry begins in earnest.

18 A resolution calling for a tariff holiday is introduced in the Economics and Financial Section.

19 The optional clause of the World Court Statute requiring compulsory jurisdiction of disputes is signed by India, France, Czechoslovakia, South Africa, New Zealand, Great Britain, and Peru.

The Soviet Union says it will reject League mediation following a clash with China in northern Manchuria.

26 After reaching a frontier agreement with Yugoslavia, Bulgaria ends the border raids.

OCTOBER

1 Britain resumes diplomatic relations with the Soviet Union.

3 The Kingdom of the Serbs, Croats, and Slovenes formally changes its name to Yugoslavia in order to reinforce national unity.

24–29 The stock market crashes in New York, creating worldwide financial instability.

NOVEMBER

6 Great Britain proposes to end its mandate over Iraq. The mandate ends in 1932.

8 A protocol to the 1927 Convention for the Abolition of Import and Export Prohibitions and Restrictions is proposed. It is designed to be implemented by a smaller number of states than was the failed 1927 Convention.

DECEMBER

5–20 The Third International Conference for the Abolition of Import and Export Prohibitions and Restrictions meets. It adopts the protocol to the 1927 Convention, which goes into force technically on January 1, 1930.

8 President Hoover authorizes American representative J. Pierrepont Moffat to sign the 1920 World Court Statute and the 1929 PCIJ Protocol containing the Root formula. Moffat signs them the next day.

11 Czechoslovakia and Poland refuse to sign the 1927 tariff convention.

13 The Council forms a committee to reconcile the Covenant and the Kellogg-Briand Pact.

The French government agrees to keep its trouble-plagued mandate over Syria.

20 Eighteen nations sign the protocol to the 1927 convention removing tariffs from over 200 commercial items, but the qualifications render the protocol meaningless.

22 A German referendum endorsing the Young Plan is a victory for internationalists and moderates.

Bibliography

The following English-language materials proved useful in writing this book. Most relate directly to the League, although many touch on the broader themes of interwar diplomacy. In light of the huge literature on the diplomacy of the 1919–1929 period, this bibliography does not pretend to be exhaustive.

Archival Materials

British Cabinet papers
British Foreign Office papers
Carnegie Endowment for International Peace papers
Documents on British foreign policy (published)
Cecil, Viscount Robert, papers
U.S. State Department archives
Documents on the foreign relations of the United States (published)
Hughes, Charles Evans, papers
International Labor Office archives
Kellogg, Frank B., papers
League of Nations archives
League of Nations Journal
League of Nations Association papers
Shotwell, James T., papers
World Peace Foundation papers

Memoirs, Books, and Articles

Adler, Selig. *The Isolationist Impulse: Its Twentieth Century Reaction.* New York: Abelard-Schuman, 1957. The standard work on American isolation, now somewhat outdated.

Alcock, Anthony. *The History of the International Labour Organisation.* New York: Octagon Books, 1971. The fullest account of the ILO's work, with special attention given to the organization's role in setting standards for its member states.

Ambrosius, Lloyd E. *Woodrow Wilson and the American Diplomatic Tradition.* Cambridge, Massachusetts: Cambridge University Press, 1987. A graceful study of Wilson's diplomacy. The author sees Wilson's league as an instrument to assert American control over international affairs without compromising the United States' independence.

Armstrong, David. *The Rise of the International Organisation: A Short History.* New York: St. Martin's Press, 1982. An unusually thoughtful history covering topics ranging from the League to regional organizations to "international regimes." The author views League success during the twenties as based more on illusion than reality.

Bailey, Thomas P. *Woodrow Wilson and the Great Betrayal.* New York: Macmillan Co., 1945. *Woodrow Wilson and the Lost Peace.* New York: Macmillan Co., 1944. These two books were among the first to challenge the conventional story that Wilson's opponents maliciously sabotaged the president's plans for the postwar era. Bailey notes Wilson's uncompromising stance as a major factor leading to the Senate's rejection of the Treaty of Versailles.

Barros, James. *The Aaland Islands Question: Its Settlement by the League of Nations.* New Haven, Connecticut, and London, England: Yale University Press, 1968. A detailed study of the League's first crisis. The author claims that power politics, not Covenant procedures, was the key to the League's successful resolution of a dispute that contained special circumstances unlikely to be repeated.

———. *The Corfu Crisis of 1923: Mussolini and the League of Nations.* Princeton, New Jersey: Princeton University Press, 1965. A detailed study of the League's first major failure in the collective-security area. The author argues that the League's inability to settle the dispute resulted from its dependence on Great Power agreement, as well as from the aggressive ambitions of Italy.

———. *The League of Nations and the Great Powers: The Greek-Bulgarian Incident, 1925.* Oxford, England: Clarendon Press, 1970. A brief but excellent study of one of the League's few successes in the area of collective security, based on archival research in London, Athens, Rome, and Geneva.

———. *Office Without Power: Secretary-General Sir Eric Drummond, 1919–1933.* Oxford, England: Clarendon Press, 1979. This thorough study of Drummond by the League's best historian argues that Drummond's success stemmed from the degree to which, contrary to popular belief, he was a highly political official with close ties to the British Foreign Office.

Bartlett, Ruhl J. *The League to Enforce Peace.* Chapel Hill: University of North Carolina Press, 1944. Still the standard work on the major American group favoring a league with force provisions.

Bassett, John Spenser. *The League of Nations: A Chapter in World Politics.* New York, London, and Toronto: Longmans, Green & Co., 1928. An optimistic history of the League by an

American internationalist who believed that when foreign ministers entered Geneva, they "drop for a time" their "nationalist feeling."

Bendiner, Elmer. *A Time for Angels: The Tragicomic History of the League of Nations.* New York: Alfred A. Knopf, 1975. Easily the most well-written history of the League, it recounts the League's triumphs and follies. Bendiner is especially critical of the conservatism of Secretary-General Eric Drummond, the disloyalty and dishonesty of Secretary-General Joseph Avenol, and the anticommunism that undermined collective security by isolating the Soviet Union. He argues that the League failed because "each nation remembered that its holy mission was to serve itself."

Bentwick, Norman. *The Mandates System.* London: Longmans, Green & Co., 1931. An early history of the mandates system, containing some good material on the system's origins.

Berdahl, Clarence A. *The Policy of the United States With Respect to the League of Nations.* Geneva, Switzerland: Librarie Kundig, 1932. A superficial survey of American contact with Geneva from an internationalist perspective.

Birn, Donald S. *The League of Nations Union, 1918–1945.* Oxford, England: Clarendon Press, 1981. This is a superb study of the most popular pro-League group in Great Britain. The League of Nations Union raised public expectations about League capabilities beyond what was reasonable, but the author blames the conservatives, not the League enthusiasts, for the ultimate failure of collective security because the conservatives feared using League machinery when necessary during the 1930s.

Blatt, Joel. "France and the Corfu-Fiume Crisis of 1923." *The Historian,* February 1988, pages 234–259. Blatt argues that Poincaré's support of Mussolini stemmed from both foreign policy and ideological considerations. The author claims that French conservatives, unlike the French left, saw the League not in idealistic terms but simply as an adjunct of French policy.

Brailsford, Henry Noel. *The League of Nations.* New York: Macmillan Co., 1917. One of the many wartime plans for a league, this one by an Englishman who favored force provisions.

Burton, Margaret. *The Assembly of the League of Nations.* Chicago: University of Chicago Press, 1941. Still the best study of its subject by a committed internationalist, it includes sections on the Assembly's origins and history. The book is organized topically rather than chronologically.

Butler, Sir Geoffrey. *A Handbook of the League of Nations.* London: Longmans, Green & Co., 1925. Seriously dated as a handbook.

Cecil, Viscount Robert. *A Great Experiment: An Autobiography.* New York: Oxford University Press, 1941. One of the few indispensable studies of the League, by the League's leading British advocate.

Clarke, John H. *America and World Peace.* New York: Henry Holt & Co., 1925. A series of lectures seeking to reverse the American rejection of the League by stressing that the organization was not a superstate. The author claims that the heart of the League was not its force provisions but rather "a pledge of national honor."

Claude, Inis L., Jr. *Power and International Relations.* New York: Random House, 1962. Claude, in his essay on the use of force to solve international problems, is especially skillful in defining the differences between the older balance-of-power system and the newer system of collective security.

———. *Swords Into Ploughshares: The Problems and Progress of International Organization.* New York: Alfred A. Knopf, 1956. A textbook treatment of international organization by one of its leading students, written from a "realist" perspective.

Conwell-Evans, T. P. *The League Council in Action.* London: Oxford University Press, 1929. An optimistic, even naive, view of the Council that sees that body as adaptable to "every kind of dispute." It downplays the use of the sanctions provisions.

Coyajee, Sir J. C. *India and the League of Nations.* Madras, India: Waltair, 1938. The author, having served with the Indian delegation to Geneva, offers a wildly pro-League account, with emphasis on the League's nonpolitical side.

Craig, Gordon A., and Felix Gilbert, eds. *The Diplomats: 1919–1939.* Princeton, New Jersey: Princeton University Press, 1953. A fine study of European and American diplomats, including essays about Sweden's Osten Unden; Czechoslovakia's Eduard Beneš, who served in Geneva during the 1920s; and Sir Eric Drummond, after he became Britain's ambassador to Italy.

Davis, Kathryn W. *The Soviets in Geneva: The USSR at the League of Nations, 1919–1933.* Chambery, France: Librarie Kundig, 1934. The author views Soviet relations with Geneva as going through four distinct phases. Soviet verbal hostility directed against the League often camouflaged a recognition that the League might indeed serve the USSR's interests.

Dell, Robert E. *The Geneva Racket, 1920–1929.* London: Robert Hale, 1941. A very cynical history of the League, it argues that the organization's original principles were betrayed when certain members converted it into a fraudulent instrument of Great Power politics.

Dexter, Byron. *The Years of Opportunity: The League of Nations, 1910–1926.* New York: Viking Press, 1967. A provocative account of the League's work stressing that without a core of military power, an international organization committed to peace will become an instrument of its most warlike member.

Dockrill, Michael L., and J. Douglas Goold. *Peace Without Compromise: Britain and the Peace Conferences, 1919–23.* Hampden, Connecticut: Archon Books, 1981. The authors argue that economic and social considerations played a distinctly subordinate role to the more traditional diplomatic and strategic factors in the thinking of British officials. The authors deemphasize the place of the League among Foreign Office officials.

Dubin, Martin David. "Transgovernmental Processes in the League of Nations." *International Organization* 37(1983): 469–493. This is a first-rate essay about the League's nonpolitical activity, using the methodology of social science to supplement the work of historical investigation. No one knows more about the League's Health Organization than does Dubin.

Duggan, Stephen P., ed. *The League of Nations: The Principle and the Practice.* London: George Allen & Unwin, 1919. Essays by American historians, diplomats, lawyers, and writers for a "guidebook" to show how the new League will solve problems in many areas of international life.

Dunne, Michael. *The United States and the World Court, 1920–1935.* New York: St. Martin's Press, 1988. Written by a British historian of internationalist sympathies, this work is the definitive account of the United States' unsuccessful attempt to join the Permanent Court of International Justice.

Egerton, George W. "Britain and the 'Great Betrayal': Anglo-American Relations and the Struggle for the United States Ratification of the Treaty of Versailles, 1919–1920." *The Historical Journal* 21 (1978): 885–911. An analysis of Lord Grey's unsuccessful mission to persuade President Woodrow Wilson to compromise during the treaty fight. The author places the blame squarely on Wilson for his rigid approach to the Covenant, claiming that Wilson's distrust of the British scuttled any real hope for an Anglo-American partnership.

———. *Great Britain and the Creation of the League of Nations: Strategy, Politics and International Organization, 1914–1919.* Chapel Hill: University of North Carolina Press, 1978. This book brilliantly combines the history of ideas and of politics. It shows how competing conceptions of a league clashed when British idealists supported Wilson to make the League a powerful agency, while the British government supported a more traditional approach that deprived the League of its enforcement machinery. The author also contributed an important essay to *The League of Nations in Retrospect,* by the United Nations Library.

Epstein, Jacob, compiler. *Ten Years' Life of the League of Nations.* London: May Fair Press, 1929. A semi-official summary of the League's work, containing many excellent illustrations.

Eyck, Erich. *The History of the Weimar Republic.* 3 vols. Cambridge, Massachusetts: Harvard University Press, 1962. The second volume contains the detailed story of Locarno and German membership in the League.

Ferrell, Robert H. *Peace in Their Time: The Origins of the Kellogg-Briand Pact.* New Haven, Connecticut: Yale University Press, 1952. The author traces the complicated arrangements whereby Secretary of State Frank Kellogg sidestepped attempts to tie the United States to the French security system by proposing a multilateral treaty.

Fink, Carole. *The Genoa Conference: European Diplomacy, 1921–1922.* Chapel Hill, North Carolina, and London, England: University of North Carolina Press, 1984. The most thorough study of the conference, based on extensive archival research, including the records of the major powers and of the League. Fink sees the Genoa Conference as a failed attempt to resurrect the diplomacy of an earlier age.

Fleming, Denna F. *The United States and the League of Nations, 1918–1920.* New York and London: G. P. Putnam's Sons, 1922. A polemical history of the Senate fight by a strong supporter of the League. The villain is Senator Henry Cabot Lodge.

———. *The United States and World Organization, 1920–1932.* New York: Columbia University Press, 1938. The author's account of the United States–League relationship is largely a story of frustration, betrayal, and ignorance. Although outdated in many respects, it contains some valuable material dealing with editorial opinion during the treaty fight and American contact with the League in nonpolitical areas.

Floto, Inga. *Colonel House in Paris: A Study of American Policy at the Paris Peace Conference, 1919.* Copenhagen: Universitets Forlaget Aarhaus, 1973. This Danish study suggests that House undermined Wilson at some critical points in the treaty negotiations. House was less loyal than he appeared.

Fosdick, Raymond B., ed. *Letters on the League of Nations.* Princeton, New Jersey: Princeton University Press, 1966. Sent or received by the League's first under secretary-general, the letters highlight the declining fortunes of the League in the United States and the dialogue among its supporters.

George, Alexander L., and Juliette L. George. *Woodrow Wilson and Colonel House: A Personality Study.* New York: Day, 1956. The authors utilize a psychohistorical approach (a "developmental study"), which is flattering neither to Wilson, who they see as subject to manipulation, nor to House, who needs Wilson to manipulate. Controversial and fascinating.

Grathwol, Robert. "Gustav Stresemann: Reflections on his Foreign Policy." *Journal of Modern History* 45 (1973): 52–70. The author claims that although Stresemann contemplated using force to expand Germany to the east, the German foreign minister feared it would lead to another Grand Alliance against Germany and therefore travelled the road to Locarno.

Greaves, H.R.G. *The League Committees and World Order.* London: Oxford University Press, 1931. A survey of the nonpolitical side of the League, stressing two tendencies—a movement toward autonomy from the Council by agencies like the ILO and Health Committee, and the task of putting League people in touch with groups outside the organization.

Harley, John Eugene. *The League and the New International Law.* New York: Oxford University Press, 1921. A short book that describes the Covenant as a new system of law rather than a system of ethics.

Harris, H. Wilson. *What the League Is.* London: George Allen & Unwin, 1925. A short and surprisingly helpful summary of the League's work that is not very judgmental.

Hill, Martin. *The Economic and Financial Organization of the League of Nations.* Washington, D.C.: Carnegie Endowment for International Peace, 1946. An excellent institutional history of the Economics and Financial Section that deemphasizes the role of individuals.

House, Edward Mandell, and Charles Seymour, eds. *What Really Happened at Paris.* New York: Charles Scribner's Sons, 1921. Essays by American experts at the Paris Peace Conference, including a succinct account by David Hunter Miller on drafting the Covenant.

Howard-Ellis, C. *The Origin, Structure, and Working of the League of Nations.* London: George Allen & Unwin, 1928. A big and optimistic book about the elimination of the "war mind" as a result of the League's commitment to international law.

Hudson, Manley O. *The Permanent Court of International Justice, 1920–1942.* New York: Macmillan Co., 1943. The standard work on the World Court, written by an American jurist who helped to draft its charter.

Jacobson, Jon. *Locarno Diplomacy: Germany and the West, 1925–1929.* Princeton, New Jersey: Princeton University Press, 1972. A scholarly study claiming that in spite of the mutual regard held by Briand, Stresemann, and Chamberlain, each man used

Locarno mainly to advance the specific interests of his country at the expense of the others. The author feels that the spirit of Locarno was more apparent than real.

———. "Strategies of French Foreign Policy After World War I." *Journal of Modern History* 55 (1983): 78–95. A skillful review that carefully analyzes how historians have treated Franco-German relations.

Johnsen, Julia E., compiler. *Reconstituting the League of Nations.* New York: H. W. Wilson Co., 1943. The book contains useful material, mostly articles that had previously appeared in journals and magazines, on the attempts to reform the League and on its nonpolitical activity.

Jones, Robert, and S. S. Sherman. *The League of Nations: Theory and Practice.* London: Sir Isaac Pitman and Sons, 1927. A partial League history, written from the perspective of Britain's League of Nations Union.

Jones, Samuel Shepard. *The Scandinavian States and the League of Nations.* Princeton, New Jersey: Princeton University Press, 1939. The author, a former director of the World Peace Foundation, argues that the Scandinavians, excluded from the process of peacemaking in Paris during 1919, re-entered the world of power politics to a limited degree as members of the League.

Kallen, Horace Meyer. *The League of Nations: Today and Tomorrow.* Boston: n.p., 1918. One of the early suggestions for a League charter, it contains provisions for military sanctions.

Keen, F. N., ed. *Towards International Justice.* New York: Harcourt, Brace and Co., n.d. (probably 1924). Ten essays written between 1915 and 1923 offering a range of British pro-League attitudes, with an emphasis on law as the key to order.

Keynes, John Maynard. *The Economic Consequences of the Peace.* New York: Harcourt, Brace, and Howe, 1920. One of the few books about the Paris Peace Conference that is still worth reading. A classic study of the reparations question.

Kimmich, Christoph M. *The Free City: Danzig and German Foreign Policy, 1919–1934.* New Haven, Connecticut: Yale University Press, 1968. A fine monograph that shows how the Germans sought to turn League machinery into a device to further the aims of their policy.

———. *Germany and the League of Nations.* Chicago and London: University of Chicago Press, 1976. The author traces the evolution of German policy toward the League from 1918, when Germany was perhaps the most enthusiastic supporter of a league, to 1933, when Hitler stood among the League's most public enemies. Kimmich believes that the Germans never really understood the League idea, using the organization mainly to weaken the Versailles settlement.

Knudsen, John I. *A History of the League of Nations.* Atlanta, Georgia: Turner E. Smith & Co., 1938. An early history of the League. Organized in a topical manner, it argues that public opinion is the key to preserving the peace.

Kolasa, Jan. *International Intellectual Cooperation: The League Experience and the Beginnings of UNESCO.* Warsaw, Poland: Polskej Akademii Nauk, 1962. The most informative work on this neglected part of the League's nonpolitical efforts.

Kuehl, Warren R. *Seeking World Order: The United States and International Order to 1920.* Nashville, Tennessee: Vanderbilt University Press, 1969. A detailed study of the American approach to the League emphasizing that Wilson's support for articles 10 and 16 conflicted with the judicial approach most congenial to his countrymen.

Lansing, Robert. *The Peace Negotiations: A Personal Narrative.* Boston and New York: Houghton Miflin Company, 1921. The memoir of the American Secretary of State, which does little to hide the author's frequent disagreements with President Wilson.

Latane, John H., ed. *Development of the League of Nations Idea.* New York: Macmillan Co., 1932. The documents and correspondence of Theodore Marburg, one of the American leaders in the pro-League movement during World War I. Contains the actual Senate reservations to the treaty, pro-League speeches, and many other documents.

League of Nations, ed. *Ten Years of World Co-Operation.* Geneva, Switzerland: Secretariat, 1930. A very comprehensive survey of League activity to 1930, written without much interpretative comment.

The League of Nations Starts: An Outline by Its Organizers. London: Macmillan and Co., 1920. Essays by pro-League politicians from many countries.

Leffler, Melvyn P. *The Elusive Quest: America's Pursuit of European Stability and French Security, 1919–1933.* Chapel Hill: University of North Carolina Press, 1979. A very impressive work. The author argues that American policymakers sincerely wanted both to protect France against Germany and to gain access to the German import market but feared that either might lead to unwanted complications abroad. In the final analysis, the Americans placed a priority on domestic, rather than foreign, policy.

Lodge, Henry Cabot. *The Senate and the League of Nations.* New York: Charles Scribner's Sons, 1925. Lodge's account of the treaty fight. This is a surprisingly thorough history, containing a valuable set of primary materials in the appendix—speeches, Congressional debates, and other documents.

Luard, Evan. *A History of the United Nations. Vol. 1: The Years of Western Domination, 1945–1955.* New York: St. Martin's Press, 1982. This history of the United Nations, written by a former British delegate to the organization, contains an excellent chapter entitled "The Lessons of the League." According to Luard, the League did not possess sufficient clear-cut obligations in the event of a breach of the peace; the Covenant could not require military cooperation; and the legal procedures of the Covenant did not measure up to the political challenges.

McClure, Wallace. *World Prosperity as Sought Through the Economic Work of the League of Nations.* New York: Macmillan Co., 1933. With an introduction by Sir Arthur Salter, this is a very comprehensive work, ranging in topics from the organizational details of economic activity to the economic jurisprudence of the World Court. It remains an essential digest for anyone studying this subject.

Madariaga, Salvador de. *Morning Without Noon: Memoirs.* Farnborough, Hampshire, England: Saxon House, 1973. A witty, perceptive, and occasionally irreverent account of the League by a Spanish delegate and head of the Secretariat's Disarmament

Section. Better on the 1930s than on the 1920s.

Mangone, Gerard J. *A Short History of International Organization.* New York: McGraw-Hill, 1954. Surveying international organization back to the ancient period, this book includes one rather ordinary chapter about the League.

Manning, C.A.W. *The Policies of the British Dominions in the League of Nations.* London: Oxford University Press, 1932. A cynical interpretation of the cooperation given to the League by Britain and the Dominions (only Canada, the author believes, lived up to its commitments).

Marburg, Theodore, ed. *Draft Convention for the League of Nations.* New York: Macmillan Co., 1918. Includes comments by the editor, a leading internationalist.

Margalith, Aaron M. *The International Mandates.* Baltimore, Maryland: Johns Hopkins Press, 1930. The fullest study of the early mandates work of the League, stressing the limited power of the Permanent Mandates Commission.

Margueritte, Victor. *The League Fiasco, 1920–1936.* London: William Hodge & Co., 1936. A survey of League political activity, which the author claims was leading to the "idiotic suicide of the White Races." The author bemoans the weakness of the League.

Margulies, Herbert F. *The Mild Reservationists and the League of Nations Controversy in the Senate.* Columbia, Missouri, and London, England: University of Missouri Press, 1989. Focusing on ten senators, Margulies argues that the mild reservationists did more for ratification than did Wilson but that they were ultimately unsuccessful because of partisan forces over which they had only limited control.

Marks, Sally. *The Illusion of Peace: International Relations in Europe, 1918–1933.* New York: St. Martin's Press, 1976. A well-written survey arguing that policymakers outside Germany deluded themselves into thinking the League and the agreements of the postwar years were a solid foundation for cooperation when, in fact, nationalistic rivalries lurked just under the surface.

Marquand, David. *Ramsay MacDonald.* London: Jonathan Cape, 1977. A sympathetic but critical biography of the Labour Party leader, which covers in great detail his League policy during the twenties.

Matsushita, Masatoshi. *Japan and the League of Nations.* New York: Columbia University Press, 1929. A book of limited value arguing that Japan could contribute much to a genuinely universal league, in contrast to a "local" (European) league.

Mayer, Arno J. *Politics and Diplomacy of Peacemaking: Containment and Counterrevolution at Versailles, 1918–1919.* New York: Alfred A. Knopf, 1967. A massive study of the Paris Peace Conference written from a leftist perspective that views Wilson as proposing that the League secure a liberal international order to counter the threat of revolutionary communism.

Miller, David Hunter. *The Drafting of the Covenant.* 2 vols. New York and London: G. P. Putnam's Sons, 1928. This classic memoir provides one of the most valuable records of the American contribution to the Covenant. Miller was part of the group advising President Wilson in Paris, and he included in this work the key drafts of the Covenant by both Americans and others.

———. *The Geneva Protocol.* New York: Macmillan Co., 1925. Containing a very valuable appendix, this short book argues that the Protocol would greatly strengthen the international system and that its arbitration clauses are more important than its sanctions clauses.

Minor, Raleigh C. *A Republic of Nations: A Study of the Organization of a Federal League of Nations.* New York: Oxford University Press, 1918. The author outlines plans for a judicial league.

Mitrany, David. *The Problem of International Sanctions.* London: Oxford University Press, 1925. Mitrany, one of the most important writers on international organization, stresses the centrality of sanctions to the League, while calling for an obligatory system more modest than that which existed in 1925.

Morley, Felix. *The Society of Nations: Its Organization and Constitutional Development.* Washington, D.C.: Brookings Institution, 1932. The author was director of the Geneva office of the League of Nations Association. This impressive study of the League uncovers some serious operational shortcomings.

Morrow, Dwight W., ed. *The Society of Free States.* New York and London: Harper and Brothers, 1919. A series of articles ranging widely over the issue of international organization, from Czar Alexander's 1777 plan of confederation to the clash between order and freedom in the 1919 American draft covenant.

Myers, Denys P. *Handbook of the League of Nations Since 1920.* Boston: World Peace Foundation, 1920. A handbook touching on hundreds of topics, from the composition of the League Council to League-sponsored conventions on rabies.

Neufang, Oscar. *The United States of the World.* New York and London: G. P. Putnam's Sons, 1930. A comparison of the Covenant and the American Constitution, written to explain why the United States remained apart from the world organization.

Nicolson, Harold, *Peacemaking 1919.* New York: Grosset and Dunlap, 1965. A combination essay and diary of the Paris Peace Conference, written by a British participant who became one of the League's champions in the Foreign Office. Filled with insight.

Noel-Baker, P. J. *The Geneva Protocol for the Pacific Settlement of International Disputes.* London: P. S. King and Son, 1925. A lengthy defense of the Geneva Protocol that advocates compromise to secure British support.

———. *The League of Nations at Work.* London: Nisbet & Co., 1926. Written by one of Britain's leading proponents of the League, this book offers a "plain sketch" of the organization. Useful for a study of Noel-Baker more than for a study of the League.

Northedge, F. S. *The League of Nations: Its Life and Times, 1920–1946.* New York: Holmes and Meier, 1986. Although the author did not use the League archives, he has written an insightful and thought-provoking history of the League's political activity. He tends, at times, to overstate the English influence and concludes that although the sad failure of the League stemmed from many factors, including the lack of universality, the chief problem was Article 10's impracticality, for it aimed to freeze the political and territorial status quo.

———. *The Troubled Giant: Britain Among the Great Powers, 1916–1939.* London: University of London, 1966. An exhaustive study of Britain's policy that sacrifices analysis for narrative. It painfully notes the mistakes that led to World War II.

Ostrower, Gary B. *Collective Insecurity: The United States and the League of Nations During the Early Thirties.* Lewisburg, Pennsylvania: Bucknell University Press, 1979. Contains two chapters dealing with the American approach to Geneva before the Manchurian crisis.

Paish, Sir George, ed. *The Nations and the League.* London: T. Fisher Unwin, 1920. An anthology of ten pro-League essays by men as prominent as Léon Bourgeois of France, Nicholas Murray Butler of the United States, and Fridtjof Nansen of Norway.

Percy, Eustace. *The Responsibilities of the League.* London: Hodder and Stroughton, n.d. (probably 1919). This pro-League essay seeks to analyze the British and Commonwealth roles within the new organization, while rejecting the idea that the enforcement provisions of the Covenant are central to its work.

Phelan, E. J. *Yes and Albert Thomas.* London: Columbia University Press, 1936. A friendly account of Thomas at the International Labour Organisation by one of his chief deputies.

Phelps, Edith M., ed. *Selected Articles on the League of Nations.* New York: H. W. Wilson Co., 1918. Pro-League material from a very wide variety of sources.

Pollock, Sir Frederick. *The League of Nations.* London: Stevens and Sons, 1922. A practical but very outdated exposition of the Covenant.

Quigley, Harold S. *From Versailles to Locarno: A Sketch of the Recent Development of International Organization.* Minneapolis: University of Minnesota Press, 1927. A short overview of the League, most valuable for its appendix, which contains the texts of the Draft Treaty of Mutual Assistance, the Geneva Protocol, and the Locarno Treaties.

Ranshofen-Wertheimer, Egon F. *The International Secretariat: A Great Experiment in International Administration.* Washington, D.C.: Carnegie Endowment for International Peace, 1945. The author, a League official for ten years, has written the definitive study of the Secretariat. An indispensable work for those studying League machinery.

Rappard. William E. *The Geneva Experiment.* London: Oxford University Press, 1931. This book stresses the conflict between national sovereignty and international solidarity as exemplified by the League. Rappard, a Swiss scholar and former head of the League's Permanent Mandates Commission, argues that war remains inevitable unless states cede more of their sovereignty to the League, which he calls not a superstate but a "humble clearing house of international relations."

———. *International Relations as Viewed From Geneva.* New Haven, Connecticut: Yale University Press, 1925. Rappard argues that the absence of the United States left Geneva trying to assert Anglo-Saxon ideals of justice without sufficient power to make them effective. A "League to Enforce Peace" was turned into an ineffective "League to Outlaw War."

Riches, Cromwell A. *The Unanimity Rule and the League of Nations.* Baltimore, Maryland: Johns Hopkins Press, 1933. A superb analysis of the veto, which according to the author constituted a serious impediment to the political work of the League.

Rovine, Arthur. *The First Fifty Years: The Secretary-General in World Politics, 1920–1970.* Leiden, Netherlands: A. W. Sijthoff, 1970. A thorough study of the office and of the men appointed to it, although this work does not measure up to that of Barros in dealing with Sir Eric Drummond.

Salter, Sir Arthur. *Memoirs of a Public Servant.* London: Faber and Faber, 1961. An autobiographical work containing wise observations by the chief of the Secretariat's Economics and Financial Section.

Schiffer, Walter P. *The Legal Community of Mankind: A Critical Analysis of the Modern Concept of World Organization.* New York: Columbia University Press, 1954. More a historical and philosophical commentary than a strictly legal work, analyzing the key legal concepts behind the League and the United Nations.

Schuker, Stephen A. *The End of French Predominance in Europe: The Financial Crisis of 1924 and the Adoption of the Dawes Plan.* Chapel Hill: University of North Carolina Press, 1976. This book argues that the financial crisis following the Ruhr occupation ended France's dominance in European diplomacy, making France more dependent on both Britain and the League for defense against Germany.

Schulte Norholt, Jan Willem. *Woodrow Wilson: A Life for World Peace.* Berkeley, California: University of California Press, 1991. This is old-time biography at its best. The author views Wilson as a tragic hero because, for all his noble intentions, the president deeply misunderstood the nature of the world he sought to change.

Schwabe, Klaus. *Woodrow Wilson, Revolutionary Germany, and Peacemaking, 1918–1919: Missionary Diplomacy and the Realities of Power.* Chapel Hill, North Carolina, and London, England: University of North Carolina Press, 1985. A major study of Wilson's diplomacy, written by a leading German diplomatic historian who, contrary to Arno Mayer, downplays the importance of ideology in the formulation of Wilson's policies.

Scott, George. *The Rise and Fall of the League of Nations.* London: Hutchinson Publishing Group, Ltd., 1973. A well-written and comprehensive history of the League that relies heavily on British Cabinet papers opened in the early 1970s. Like F. S. Northedge, the author exaggerates the importance of Britain in the League.

Shotwell, James T. *On the Rym of the Abyss.* New York: Macmillan Co., 1936. Written during the Ethiopian crisis, this is mainly an essay about the importance of American cooperation in organized efforts to keep the peace. The author suggests that regional organization may be more useful than the League's collective-security mechanism.

Shotwell, James T., ed. *The Origins of the International Labor Organization.* 2 vols. New York: Columbia University Press, 1934. The first volume is a traditional history of the organization by one of the United States' leading internationalists. The second contains many valuable documents.

Shotwell, James, and Marina Salvin. *Lessons on Security and Disarmament From the History of the League of Nations.* New York: Kings Crown Press, 1949. A short series of chapters attempting to prove that the League produced helpful precedents for the United Nations. It includes excellent summaries of important problems and the texts of key documents.

Smith, Gene. *When the Cheering Stopped.* New York: Morrow, 1964.

A well-written and colorful account of Woodrow Wilson's 1919 welcome by Europe, his work at the Paris Peace Conference, and his subsequent fight for treaty ratification.

Stevenson, D. *French War Aims Against Germany, 1914–1919.* Oxford, England: Clarendon Press, 1982. An excellent survey of the subject, containing one of the few accounts of French plans for the League of Nations. The author sees Georges Clemenceau as hoping to use the League as an extension of the wartime alliance.

Stone, Ralph. *The Irreconcilables: The Fight Against the League of Nations.* Lexington: University of Kentucky Press, 1970. A perceptive study of the treaty fight that views League opponents in the U.S. Senate as human beings and not caricatures. It contains excellent short analyses of each of the sixteen "irreconcilable" senators.

Stresemann, Gustav. *Diaries, Letters and Papers.* 3 vols. Edited by Eric Sutton. New York: Macmillan Co., 1935. The first volume contains primary material relating to Locarno and to Germany's membership in the League.

Stromberg, Roland N. *Collective Security and American Foreign Policy: From the League of Nations to NATO.* New York: Frederick A. Praeger, 1963. An intellectual survey of American thinking about collective security, written from a "realist" perspective.

Sweetser, Arthur. *The League of Nations at Work.* New York: Macmillan Co., 1920. A League primer for Americans, authored by the second highest official in the Secretariat's Press and Information Section.

Temperley, A. C. *The Whispering Gallery of Europe.* London: Collins Publishers, 1938. This classic account of the League's disarmament work, authored by a leading member of Britain's disarmament delegation, offers a critical but sympathetic perspective, along with colorful personal portraits.

Temperley, H.W.V. *A History of the Peace Conference of Paris.* 6 vols. London: Frowde and Hodder and Stoughton, 1920. The most comprehensive account of the conference, written by a member of the British delegation from a decidedly British point of view.

Tillman, Seth P. *Anglo-American Relations at the Paris Peace Conference of 1919.* Princeton, New Jersey: Princeton University Press, 1961. A thorough study of American and British diplomacy at the conference that illuminates European attitudes as well. The author sees a fundamental community of interest between Britain and the United States often ignored in the formulation of specific policies. He argues that the most "enlightened" elements of the treaty (including the League) came from London and Washington.

Tractenberg, Marc. *Reparations in World Politics: France and European Economic Diplomacy, 1916–1923.* New York: Columbia University Press, 1980. A model of careful research, this book argues persuasively that France was less punitive toward Germany at the Peace Conference than was previously believed.

United Nations Library. *The League of Nations in Retrospect: Proceedings of the Symposium.* Edited by Zara Steiner. Berlin: Walter de Gruyter, 1983. This is the most valuable single source for the study of the League. It contains twenty-four essays in English and French by the leading contemporary historians of the organization. For the 1920s, the essays on the following topics are of special importance: the League as an institution (Jean Siotis), Drummond (James Barros), Great Britain (George Egerton), Germany (Christoph Kimmich), the United States (Gary Ostrower), disarmament (Maurice Vaisse), colonialism (Yves Collart), technical assistance (Alexander Menzies), refugees (Atle Grahl-Madsen), and minorities (Richard Veatch).

Veatch, Richard. *Canada and the League of Nations.* Toronto, Canada, and Buffalo, New York: University of Toronto Press, 1975. This is the most comprehensive treatment of the Canadian relationship with Geneva, showing how Ottawa used the League to establish its independence from Great Britain in the area of foreign policy, while displaying indifference bordering on hostility to the collective-security sections of the Covenant.

Verma, D. N. *India and the League of Nations.* Patna, India: Bharati Bhawan, 1968. A much superior account than that of Coyajee, it argues that India's participation in League political activity was "counterfeit" in that it merely mirrored British positions.

Walp, Paul K. *Constitutional Development of the League of Nations.* Lexington: University of Kentucky Press, 1931. A Ph.D dissertation, this is a mostly uncritical study of the Assembly-Council relationship.

Walters, F. P. *A History of the League of Nations.* 2 vols. London, New York, and Toronto: Oxford University Press, 1952. This is the most complete history of the League, although it is outdated in some respects. The author, a former deputy-general of the organization, understandably writes with a pro-League bias and tends to see League failures as more the result of men than of underlying economic or political forces. The book emphasizes narrative history rather than analysis.

Wambaugh, Sarah. *The Saar Plebiscite With a Collection of Official Documents.* Cambridge, Massachusetts: Harvard University Press, 1940. A study of this diplomatic thicket by a former League official, with a focus on the 1935 vote.

Webster, C. K. *The League of Nations in Theory and Practice.* London: George Allen & Unwin, 1933. An early history of the League that treats the 1920s as an "experimental stage" and argues that education will be the key to the League's success.

Wells, H. G. *The Idea of a League of Nations.* Boston: Atlantic Monthly Press, 1919. Sees the League as a necessary starting point—but only a starting point—to keep the peace.

White, Stephen. *The Origins of Détente: The Genoa Conference and Soviet-Western Relations, 1921–1922.* Cambridge, Massachusetts: Cambridge University Press, 1985. Discusses how the conference, which attempted to establish a collaborative basis for diplomacy between East and West, failed because the forces opposing collaboration were greater than those favoring it. The author recognizes that the League played a very small role at the conference.

Widenor, William C. *Henry Cabot Lodge and the Search for an American Foreign Policy.* Berkeley, California: University of California Press, 1980. In this fine book, Widenor disputes the work of those who claim that Lodge was motivated mainly by his quest for personal or political advantage; rather, he sees Lodge as a serious student of international affairs who fundamentally rejected Wilson's conception of the League.

Williams, Bruce. *State Security and the League of Nations.* Baltimore, Maryland: Johns Hopkins Press, 1927. Focusing on the major security treaties, from the Draft Treaty of Mutual Assistance to Locarno, the author claims that neither the United States nor Great Britain appeared willing to embrace genuine international jurisdiction in order to keep the peace.

Williams, William A. "The Legend of American Isolationism in the 1920's." *Science and Society* 18 (Winter 1954): 1–20. The author argues that the demands of business made the United States highly active in the foreign field and that League nonmembership must not obscure American involvement abroad.

Wilson, Florence, ed. *The Origins of the League of Nations Covenant: Documentary History of the Drafting.* London: Hogarth Press, 1928. Contains the key drafts of the Covenant.

Wilson, George Grafton. *The First Year of the League of Nations.* Boston: Little Brown and Co., 1921. A sketchy account about establishing the League's machinery.

Winkler, Henry R. *The League of Nations Movement in Great Britain, 1914–1919.* New Brunswick, New Jersey: Rutgers University Press, 1952. The author traces the growing British support for the League, outlining the numerous schemes for a new league, while finding the conservatives and liberals (in contrast to the labourites) generally unwilling to challenge the framework of sovereignty.

Wolfers, Arnold. *Britain and France Between Two Wars.* New Haven, Connecticut: Yale University Press, 1940. This work remains among the major studies of interwar European diplomacy and reflects the disillusionment with the League after the start of World War II.

Woolf, Leonard. *International Government.* New York: Brentano's, 1916. Woolf saw international organizations as an important step on the road to genuine world government.

World Organization: A Balance Sheet of the First Great Experiment. Washington, D.C.: American Council on Public Affairs, 1942. A series of essays by American and European internationalists that focuses on most of the critical issues facing the League during its twenty-year history.

Wright, Quincy. *Mandates Under the League of Nations.* Chicago: University of Chicago Press, 1930. A massive work that examines the development and structure of the mandate system, placing it into the general framework of international law.

Yearwood, Peter J. " 'Consistency With Honor': Great Britain, the League of Nations, and the Corfu Crisis of 1923." *Journal of Contemporary History* 21 (October 1986): 559–580. The author questions the conventional view that the League failed in the Corfu crisis and argues that the League's main British champions, Lord Cecil and Harold Nicolson, fully supported London's policy to have the Council of Ambassadors, not the League, work out a settlement.

Zilliacus, Konni [Roth Williams]. *The League of Nations Today: Its Growth, Record and Relation to British Foreign Policy.* London: George Allen & Unwin, 1923. An essay trying to prove that British and League aims were fully compatible, by one of England's most energetic League supporters.

Zimmern, Alfred. *The League of Nations and the Rule of Law, 1918–1935.* London: Macmillan and Co., 1936. A pro-League history containing extensive background material and a fine chapter on the drafting of the Covenant but not much narrative history of the 1920s.

About the Author

Gary B. Ostrower has taught American history at Alfred University since 1969. The New York City native received his undergraduate degree from Alfred, and his master's and doctoral degrees from the University of Rochester. He has received three Excellence in Teaching awards from Alfred and has been a visiting lecturer at the University of Pennsylvania.

Dr. Ostrower is currently president of the Society for the Study of Internationalism. His first book on the League was *Collective Insecurity: The United States and the League of Nations*. He has published many articles and reviews on the subject of international organization, and is currently writing a history of the United States and the United Nations.

Dr. Ostrower enjoys skiing, jogging, tennis, and golf. He and his wife, Judith Samber, have two children, Sarah and Peter. They live in Alfred, New York.

Index